NEW BOY

LIFE AND DEATH

AT THE WORLD HEADQUARTERS

OF THE JEHOVAH'S WITNESSES

Keith Casarona

Copyright © 2019 Keith Casarona, Sedona, AZ 86336

All rights reserved. No part of this book may be reproduced in any form or by any electronic or mechanical means, including information storage and retrieval systems, without permission in writing from the author, except for the inclusion of brief quotations in a review.

ISBN: 9781090984159

© The Oregonian. All rights reserved. Reprinted with permission.

This book is dedicated to my Jehovah's Witness friend Gayle.

This book is also dedicated to James Olson and Robert Stillman and the millions of other people who have been victims of religious abuse. This book is dedicated to the thousands of people who have lost their parents, children and family members by way of the cruel practice of shunning. This book is for the thousands of suicide victims, people who could not live with the guilt and shame that the Jehovah's Witnesses thought system created for them. This book condemns this religion and all others religions that have been instrumental in the death, suicide and insanity of millions of people around the world.

The people and events in this book are real. Their real names have been used. I do not judge or condemned any person in this book, only the religious thought system that created them.

I want to thank Naomi Rose and Erika Finch my editors who skillfully brought this book together.

Special thanks to Randell Watters (also an ex-Bethelite) and his amazing website freeminds.org.

I also want to thank Simon who has created the Jehovah-Witness.com website and the hundreds of people there that helped gather much of the important information that is in this book. This book could never have happened without their help.

The use of copyrighted material in this book falls within the Fair use Provisions and particularly as pertains to criticism and parody.

—KC

I have very deeply looked into the endless destruction and genocide that religious ideologies and dogma have inflicted upon human beings. I have seen how damaged human souls are, how deeply depressive, meaningless, and prone to exploitation are the lives that many live. Religious dogma is at the root of this epidemic meaninglessness. Behind that is the thirst and cry for love. —Mark Seelig

Chapter One
The Pledge of Allegiance

It is estimated that over 1,300 people have jumped off the Brooklyn Bridge since it was built in 1883. Now with the increased size of New York City's population and with the amount of stress in the world, it is now estimated that two people a month make the same plunge. In the four years that I lived in the Brooklyn Heights area (which is close to the Brooklyn Bridge), I knew of three people who killed themselves by either jumping out of or off of buildings. James Olson was one of them. They say he jumped, but he was really pushed. Some of the people who killed him are dead now.

Just a few feet away from the Brooklyn Bridge, there is a huge, six-building complex. This prime piece of Brooklyn real estate has amazing views of lower Manhattan. The oldest building there was built in 1926 and is located at 117 Adams Street. Over many years, the factory complex soon expanded with five more buildings. One of these buildings was a thirty-story residence. This is so workers can live just a few yards away from where they worked. This factory complex stretched from the base of the Brooklyn Bridge to base of the Manhattan Bridge. Each of these enormous structures occupied a full New York City block. Some of these massive buildings were connected by sky bridges so men and materials could move from one department to the next with greater ease.

This complex was the largest printing facility in the world at the time. There was no factory that matched this factory's total monthly production of books and magazines. Every month, millions of books and magazines were printed in dozens of different languages and then shipped out to more than two-hundred countries all over the world by way of trucks, trains and New York City's harbors.

Besides its size, this was no ordinary printing facility. Some of the many things that made this factory unique was the fact that all of these workers were volunteers from all over the world and most of the workers there were between the ages of nineteen and twenty-four. Another thing that made this factory unusual was the fact that everyone working there from the head of the factory complex, Max Larson, to the young boy that cleaned the toilets, James Olson, received the same pay every day. That's right, in the 1970s they were paid just 73 cents a day! That didn't go very far in New York City even back then. Plus, there was only one way you could work in this factory. You had to be a member of their club. This is a very exclusive club. In fact, there is only one person for every one thousand people in the world that were in this club. The name of the club is the Jehovah's Witnesses.

Over the years, tens of thousands of people have come from all over the world to take a tour of this unusual factory complex. Some days the tour groups were continuous as hundreds of people toured the complex from the early morning until the closing bell rang at 5:40 p.m.

There were many people who took these tours and would leave this factory shaking their heads in disbelief. Many of the jobs that were preformed seemed insane to normal outsiders, no matter what the pay might have been.

On top of the Adam Street building were letters three feet tall, which commanded the people who were passing by to, "READ GOD'S WORD THE HOLY BIBLE DAILY." This statement wasn't entirely true, however. Of course, they wanted you read the Bible, because, they were producing Bibles inside the factory. However, they really didn't want you to read just any old Bible. They weren't too keen on you reading the King James Version or the American Standard Version or any of the other 1,753 versions of the Bible that are available. The Bible they wanted you to read was the Bible version they were producing in their own factory. This was, of course, The New World Translation of the Holy Scriptures. This green Bible is the only one that uses the name Jehovah throughout.

There, in the heart of the factory, were forty rotary printing presses churning out Bibles and hundreds of other hardbound books. These books were not made like books in other binderies around the world. For instance, many bindery lines in the factory consisted of only three to four machines. All of the other bindery lines on the planet at that time had five machines. But the "Brothers," in their infinite wisdom, figured out that they could save themselves tens of thousands of dollars by not buying one or two of the machines to complete the assembly line.

How could they possibly do this? The manufacturer of the machines who had been setting up book bindery lines for many years wanted to know. Easy, the Brothers said: *Instead of buying your machines that would take one book out of the rounder and place it into the back liner, we will instead insert a human being to do the same job.* Yes, they could save themselves a ton of money by paying someone only 73 cents a day to do the same job as the machine. The factory representative of the bindery machines couldn't help but laugh and told them they wouldn't be able to find anyone stupid enough to do that kind of insane work.

How could you find someone to stand in the same spot for hours every day and do the same repetitive motion fifteen-thousand times each and every day for months on end? The factory representative said that even if you paid them one hundred times that daily wage, no sane person would ever do that kind of work.

He was wrong of course; they had hundreds of volunteers who were anxiously waiting the opportunity to do just that. People willing to do anything to serve their god even if it cost them their own sanity.

He was right in the sense that no sane person would want that kind of job. He forgot about the religious zealots of the world, of which there was no short supply in the Jehovah's Witnesses.

One of the books produced there was *The Truth That Leads to Eternal Life* which was a Bible study textbook published in 1968. The *1975 Guinness Book of Records* included this book in its list of highest printings. According to the Watch Tower Society, by May 1987, the publication had reached 106,486,735 copies in 116 languages. This was just one of the hundreds of books they produced in the New York factory.

Jehovah Witnesses could sell the hardbound book *The Truth That Leads to Eternal Life* from door-to-door for only 25 cents. But they don't like using the word "sell." Instead, the Jehovah Witnesses would ask for a 25-cent contribution. How could this hardbound book be made and sold for only 25 cents and still make a profit?

The answer would be found at the world headquarters of the Jehovah's Witnesses.

The Watchtower Bible and Tract Society listed the book value of its assets as $1,451,217,000 on its 2015 IRS Form 990-T. So, selling millions of *The Truth That Leads to Eternal Life* books for only 25 cents and paying their workers only 73 cents a day does add up to some serious money made over the years!

Fast forward to 1972, when I too was one of those religious zealots.

The day came when the Brothers showed me that spot in between the two bindery machines. This was the same spot where hundreds of other Brothers had stood before me. I too, would become the missing machine that connected the other two machines. That one-foot-by-one-foot piece of real estate was located between machines called the rounder and the back liner. That was the spot where a single hour turned into eternity for many of us who stood there. This would soon be my new home for many months.

I stood there in the same spot, eight hours and forty minutes a day. My job was to take a book out of the rounder, and shove it into the back liner. When one book came out of the rounder, I would turn it upside down and put it into the back liner. Another book came out of the rounder and went into the back liner. More books out of the rounder and into the back liner. I took thousands of books out of the rounder and placed them into the back liner every day.

John Chapman once said, "The present in New York is so powerful that the past is lost." For many of us working on the bindery lines, there was no past or future. There was only that one moment, the moment when the one book was pushed out of one machine and into our waiting hands, only to be put into another machine. That one moment that took place 15,000 times each and every day.

This produced thousands of hours of boredom to look forward to. Plenty of time to think. What did we think about? After many months of standing there you had time to think about just about everything. On one of those days that felt like eternity, my thoughts drifted back to a day in my third-grade class at La Fetra Elementary school in Glendora, California.

The 9 a.m. bell rings. It's Tuesday morning in Mrs. Mallet's class. She is an attractive forty-year-old woman with thick black glasses and short black hair. She purses her dark red lips together and turns and faces her class. As if she were a Marine Corp drill instructor, she announces, "All rise." The eight and nine year olds scramble out of their seats and stand at attention next to their desks. All eyes are on the American flag hanging in the corner next to the blackboard. The children all know what is next. It's time for the *Pledge of Allegiance*. The children have one hand by their sides and one hand on their hearts.

With a stern look, she starts the sacred oath. "I pledge allegiance to the flag of the United States of…" The whole class chimes in. All the children except for one. An eight-year-old boy stands next to his desk. He has both his arms by his side and says nothing. He has a slight frown on his face as the rest of the kids go through the motions of saluting their flag. The pledge is over and all the children sit back down at their desks. Mrs. Mallet turns from facing the flag. "Class, before we start today, we will be having Susan's birthday party. Who would like to help with the cake and ice cream?" The kids raise their hands with great excitement. The boy who would not take part in the *Pledge of Allegiance* ceremony squirms in his seat and says nothing. Mrs. Mallet has a big smile on her face as she looks the boy's way. "So, would you like to be excused from the birthday party today?"

The boy nods his head, as if to say yes. He stands up from his chair. Mrs. Mallet says, "Then you may leave and sit in the hallway until we are done. I will come and get you when the fun is over."

Mrs. Mallet really doesn't like this boy. She doesn't like his whack job of a mother or their stupid religion either. Her husband fought in the war and got half his leg blown off on Iwo Jima so people like this kid and his mother could enjoy their religious freedom in this country. How dare he stand there and not respect the flag that gave them that freedom!

The boy stands up from his desk and heads towards the door. He turns to look at the birthday cake on the teacher's desk. He then turns to see many of the kids in the classroom with their eyes on him as he walks out the door. He walks a few steps and sits down on the concrete walkway next to the classroom door. After a minute, he can hear the noise of the birthday party going on inside the classroom and finally the happy-birthday song for Susan. The boy has tears in his eyes. Twenty minutes later, Mrs. Mallet opens the door and steps in the hallway.

"We're done now, you may come back in." The boy stands up and the students watch him as he walks back into the classroom. Kids are walking up to a wastepaper basket and throwing their used paper plates away. He looks over to where the birthday cake was and sees a pile of crumbs. Susan is licking a spoon covered with pink frosting. She looks at the boy and sticks her tongue out at him. He sheepishly returns to his seat.

Alright kids, everyone get back to your seats. Today we are going to talk about the greatest man in American history, George Washington. We're going to talk about how the

United States of America is the greatest country in the world, too."

The boy looks up at the clock on the wall: two hours before recess. The bell finally rings and the kids jump out of their seats to get their lunch boxes.

The boy sits at the end of the cafeteria table by himself and eats his baloney sandwich. Sometimes kids will sit with him but mostly he sits alone. He thinks about what his mother told him: *It's always better to be lonely than be in bad company.*

A few minutes later, he is in the schoolyard, watching two boys playing tether ball. Susan and another girl walk up to him. "So why wouldn't you come to my birthday party, Keith? You're weird!"

"I'm not weird, it's my religion," Keith fires back.

Susan smiles. "Oh really? Then your religion is weird."

"It's not weird."

"Well, I think your religion is stupid and you are stupid too."

Keith turns and walks away toward the playground. The girls follow him, and walk a few feet behind. "Keith's religion is stupid," they chant. "Keith's religion is stupid!" Keith thinks of the pictures he saw in his mother's new book and thinks to himself, *Someday they will be sorry they ever said that!*

Chapter 2
The Journey Begins

My story doesn't really begin with me in elementary school but begins with my parents and my grandparents. Like all families, our ancestors' decisions have helped create the backdrop of our lives and our stories. Yes, all of us are still dealing with the decisions some of our family members have made for us. Many of these decisions were made years before you and I were ever born. Many of these decisions were made by people we have never even met. These people died long before we ever came on the scene. These decisions concerning where they choose to live may have affected the place you now live. The religions your relatives believed in could have been passed down to them by their parents. These people, in turn, would try to pass their thought systems down to their children. This would possibly effect many future generations in one way or another. What kind of education, morals and even the sexual peculiarities your ancestors had, may be things you are still having to deal with today. These,and other things, all affect our upbringing and thus our lives. Many of our decisions we make later in our lives would be a direct result of the programming we were given as a young child.

There are many different roads a person can take and each crossroad brings on all new possibilities.

My first possible crossroad happened to me when I was only a couple of days old. I was still in the hospital with my mother. Somehow there was a mix up. Another woman was taking me home by mistake. As I was leaving with her, I started crying. My mother heard this cry and told the nurses that the baby who was crying was hers. Much to everyone's surprise, she was right. Who knows, I could have ending being raised by a good Catholic family and not by the Jehovah's Witnesses at all. In which case, this book would have never even been written.

There is no need to go back generations of my family – to all those wonderful and strange people who helped shape the attitudes and behaviors of my two parents, Norma and Marty – to set the groundwork for this strange story. Like most people, my parents have proved to be the key players.

My mother was a Kansas farm girl of Czechoslovakian and German ancestry. My father was a New York City Italian. Needless to say, these two people had little in common. They were brought together by way of World War II. If it weren't for the war, they probably would have never even met. Besides killing a lot of people, war brings a lot of people together. In their case, it was love at first sight.

My mother never talked much to us kids about her years growing up in Kansas during the Great Depression and there was a good reason for that.

One of her few childhood memories she relayed to me was about a hot summer day in Kansas. She and her family were driving down a dusty dirt road going to church. All of the windows were rolled down and dust was pouring into their 1931 Ford. Her father, who loved chewing tobacco, decided to spit a big wad of it out of the open window. The wind caught the black juice and propelled it back into the back seat of their car and all over my mother and her white dress.

My grandfather was a gambler and the town bootlegger. He owned a pool hall. I think of him as kind of like the character Ryan O'Neal played in the movie Paper Moon. He spent a lot of time out of town "on business." He didn't do much to take care of his wife and kids.

On the night of February 12, 1934, my grandfather was on one of his long road trips. My grandmother, Mabel, was alone with their four small children. She was only twenty-eight years old and pregnant with their fifth child. With no money, no food and no hope, she took matters into her own hands. I have no idea what was going through her mind that cold Kansas winter night. The night she bled to death after her failed abortion attempt with a coat hanger.

After her death, my mother and her brothers and sister were shipped off to different relatives. My mother was only eight years old when she went to stay with her grandfather on her father's side. He loved Norma. A lot. How many people get a free farm worker and sex slave dropped into their laps?

We didn't find out what happened to Mom until many years after her death. In fact, I was the one who brought it up to my father. I told him I thought Mom had been sexually abused as a child. He didn't want to believe it at first.

There were some strange things about Mom, I told him. Like when he would come home from work and wanted a kiss from her. If we kids were around, she would push him away. Dad told me he hardly ever saw her nude – the lights were always out. She was very sly. Needless to say, the sex was terrible, he told me. Years later, my father had the story confirmed about her grandfather from another family member. It put a lot of the pieces of the puzzle together.

My father, who had sex with many women before he met my mother, loved the fact that Mom was a "good girl." Mom told him there would be no sex before marriage. This was the type of girl you should marry, my dad thought to himself. He soon found out there would be little or no sex after marriage, too.

Anyway, my mom made her escape from Kansas when she was just 17. In 1943, she moved to Southern California. Her relatives were sad to see her go. She moved in with an aunt and got work immediately. The war was going strong and California was booming in the 1940s. I'm sure she felt like her life could finally begin.

My dad, on the other hand, had grown up in the Bronx in a close-knit Italian family. Sunday dinners with all of the relatives were always fun. They would start around 3 p.m. after Mass, and there was always lots of good food and conversations. The grandfathers were nice to their grandkids unlike my mother's side of the family. I think my dad enjoyed his childhood. He always had a twinkle in his eye when he talked about growing up during the Great Depression. He was the oldest male of four children. As the first-born male in an Italian family, he was spoiled rotten.

Women run the show in most Italian families. Many of the men love it that way. They end up marrying someone who starts out being their lover and moves into the role of their mother. This is what happened with my father. My folks had a total parent/child relationship. My mom became the mother/parent to her brothers and sister when her mother died. She was in mother mode when she met my father. My father, on the other hand, was the kid who never grew up. You can see these kinds of relationships in many marriages.

The story of how my dad and mom first met went something like this:

They were both at a USO club in Santa Monica, California, in 1943. Big band music was playing. My dad was looking pretty good in his corporal uniform. He said Mom was the prettiest girl at the dance. He gathered up his courage and walked up to my mother. She was only seventeen and sitting alone at a small table. She had a yellow rose pinned to her white dress.

"So... tell me, why is the prettiest girl at this dance sitting here all alone, with no one to dance with? Is your dance card full?" My dad asked.

"No, my dance card is not full, Corporal. Maybe I'm more woman than most men can handle."

"Wow that sounds dangerous."

"Very dangerous!"

"Okay…how about a test drive? How about a dance? I'm Marty Casarona."

"Alright, Marty, you look brave enough. I'm Norma Johansen."

"Oh…a German. I'm a lucky guy!"

"And you're an Italian. This could mean trouble."

My dad took my mom by the hand to the dance floor, and they began to dance. After about one minute, he smiled. "This isn't so bad."

Mom said nothing and just smiled back. Before she knew it, my dad's hand started to move down her back. His hand ended up touching the top of her butt. Mom pulled away from him and slapped his face as hard as she could. Mom was upset and left the dance floor. She went back to take her chair. Dad was dazed, standing there alone with his face beet red. People around the dance floor started to laugh. With tears in his eyes, he walked back over to mom and got down on his knees. Mom looked in the other direction.

"Please...please I'm so sorry," he said with remorse.

She turned and looked at Dad and just smiled. It was love at first sight for sure.

They got married in Jackson, Mississippi, in 1944 and just like the song says, "They got married in a fever." My dad was going to be shipped overseas. He wanted to make sure no one would snap up my mother while he was away. Plus, since there was a possibility of being killed fighting the Japanese, he begged my mom to tie the knot. He thought if he was going to die, he might as well have sex with my mom first. Since she was one of the few women who turned down my father's advances, it would be one more notch on the belt.

This reminds me of the only "sex talk" my dad ever gave me. I was sixteen and walking down the hall. My father was shaving in the bathroom.

"Keith, come here for a minute." My dad never took his eyes off the mirror. "Your mother wanted me to talk to you about…. uh…you know…sex." "Oh," was my only response.

"I'm sure you know how it all works. So, I have only two things to say to you. Be careful. The last thing you want is to get some young stupid girl knocked up…right?"

"Uh…that's right, Dad."

"Okay. The other thing I want to tell you, is to always go after the good-looking girls. They are just as lonely as the ugly ones! Got it?" "Yeah…sure, Dad."

"Make me proud son."

My dad was a New York City hustler for sure. His grand adventure began when he got shipped overseas. He spent two-and-a-half years in Honolulu, having the time of his life. He would have tears in his eyes years later when he would tell everyone he ever met that those two years were the best years of his life.

He told me many times, with a gleam in his eye, "You could have been half Japanese!" I didn't really know what he meant by that. Before he died in 2012, he told me about his secret love affair with a young Japanese girl on Oahu.

My dad told me that Hawaii was a paradise back in the war years. There was just one problem: no women. Well, there were women, but there wasn't enough of them. There were tens of thousands of young service men who longed for a woman's companionship on the island. It was the law of supply and demand, and demand was high. It was so high that there were literally lines in front of whorehouses in downtown Honolulu. My dad hated lines and sloppy seconds, let alone sloppy three-hundred-and-fifteens.

He was always looking for short cuts in his life. Ways to "beat the house," as he would say. Nothing gave my father more satisfaction than beating the system, any system, which is why my father didn't make a very good Jehovah's

Witnesses. Whereas the Jehovah's Witnesses are all about following rules, my dad was all about bending them, if not completely breaking them. Some of the rules he never really liked were the "no smoking" and "no sex outside of marriage rule." He wasn't keen on the "no gambling" and "no lying and no stealing" ones, either.

My father, even though he was married, had a real problem in Hawaii. How was he going to get laid? More importantly, how was he going to get laid and not pay for it?

One Saturday, he and a couple of friends, decided to explore the island of Oahu. They took their jeep and drove it to the north end of the island. They found small villages nestled in the jungle paradise. To their surprise, they also found a lot of Japanese-Americans living there. They stopped at a shack that looked like some kind of restaurant and ordered a couple of beers. The old man who served them was pleasant enough. They couldn't help but notice a couple of good-looking Asian girls working in the back.

My dad had to ask, "You folks Chinese?"

"No, my friend, we're of Japanese ancestry."

"Really? We thought they shipped all you Japs…I mean, you folks, to camps."

"No…many but not all. We are good Americans. In fact, my son is serving with the 442 Regiment in Italy. Have you boys seen combat yet?"

"No. We are with a headquarters' unit and will probably never leave Hawaii."

"Well, my son has. He has killed lots of Germans and Italians!"

"Hey, Pops, I'm Italian!"

"Really? Did they ship off any of your family to the camps like they did ours?"

"No, they didn't."

The old man just stood there and shook his head.

Even my Dad could see the irony in it. "I know it's pretty messed up."

"Yes, it is son. In fact, my family can't even go down to Honolulu without the servicemen there giving them some kind of beating."

"How do you get your supplies then?"

"With great difficulty."

Dad got a strange look on his face. There was an angle here for sure.

The old man started to smile. "I must admit we don't see too many of you guys up on this end of the island, which is fine by us."

Dad smiled. "Really…what is your name?"

"Mutsuhiro."

"Well, Mutsuhiro, that is about to change."

My dad was a staff sergeant and had this great job in the motor pool. How did he get this job? He lied. He said he was an ace mechanic before the war. He knew very little about how motor vehicles worked at all. He literally did nothing all day long. If a vehicle needed repair, he would just delegate it to someone else, or red tag it. If it were red tagged, they would just load it up on a barge, take it out past the reef and push it into the blue Pacific Ocean. Funny how all these folks back home were saving cooking grease and trying to scrape together ten dollars to buy a war bond, and my father had no problem destroying a whole jeep because it had a cracked windshield.

However, if you needed a jeep, Dad was your man. He would trade jeeps and other vehicles for favors. Sometimes he lent out all the jeeps. For example, if an officer asked for a jeep to go to town on a date, sometimes he might get an eight-ton truck instead. He loved giving the officers grief and doing deals on the side: It was a double bonus. My dad hated any kind of authority.

During the war, gas was selling for 15 cents per gallon and was highly rationed. However, on the black market you could sell it for almost two bucks a gallon. Dad told me how he would steal gas from the Navy. The motor pool would send their five-thousand-gallon tanker truck to the shipyard. My dad got the idea to strap on twenty-five-gallon jerry cans to the side of the truck. The Navy hated to fill those small cans, but they did anyway.

Dad's commanding officer would get the receipt for 5,100 gallons of gasoline and call in my father.

"What the hell is this, Sergeant? Our truck only holds 5,000 gallons."

"You know those Navy guys. They are all screwed up." Yep, my dad had an answer for everything.

One of my father's greatest coups was sugar for sex. If there was anything harder to get than gas during the war, it was sugar. One of my dad's friends was Walter, the mess hall sergeant. He told Walter about all the lovely, horny Asian women that lived on the north end of the island. It wasn't long before two jeeps that were loaded down with 50-pound bags of sugar, coffee and gas were heading north to do some trading with some of his new Japanese-American friends.

After a couple of months of this, my dad and his friends were treated like kings. Not only did the villagers get some sugar in their coffee, they were treated like real people.

Yes, in the end, the girls were waiting there with open arms – and open legs too.

So, I guess I could have been half-Japanese. Maybe there is a half-brother or sister of mine somewhere in Hawaii who looks half-Italian too. Who knows?

However, there was a part of my father that was Japanese, even though both his parents were full-blooded Italian emigrants. How could this be?

All Dad's dental work was done for free in the Army. The Army used silver for dentistry. Dad needed some crowns implanted, but he wanted gold crowns instead of silver. It was going to cost him a small fortune using the Army's gold.

"No problem." His dentist told him. "You can get all the gold you need for under a hundred bucks."

"How?"

"Easy, the first Marine division is in town. They got the gold you are looking for." "The Marines have gold?"

"Yes, they do. It is Jap gold, son!"

"Jap gold?"

"The Marines do some dentistry work on our Jap friends. After they kill them, they collect their gold fillings from their teeth."

"Oh."

"If that bothers you, you can always pay full price." So, guess where his gold crowns came from?

There was another story he loved to relate. I must have heard it a hundred times. It was the chocolate-for-whiskey story.

One day, my father was chomping down on a Hershey chocolate bar. There were two more on his desk, all of which he had stolen out of the C-ration kits. A young officer from Alabama strolled into the motor pool to get a jeep.

"What's that you eating there, Sergeant?"

"A chocolate bar."

"Well, I really like chocolate, and it's hard to get it around here."

"It sure is, but whiskey is even harder to get."

Whiskey was rationed and hard to come by. The officers were entitled to one-fifth of Three Feathers Whiskey per month. There was plenty of beer for everyone, but not much hard liquor was available.

"I don't drink," the officer said.

My dad got that look in his eye. There was a deal in the making here. "I'd be happy to give you ten Hershey chocolate bars for your bottle of whiskey."

"Really? You could do that?"

"Sure. It'll be tough, but I could make that happen." It wasn't that tough. My dad had access to hundreds of boxes of C-rations where he could steal all of the chocolate bars he wanted.

So, this went on for many months. They traded chocolate bars for whiskey. Dad had a waiting list for the booze. He would get as much as $80 a bottle. This was my father's finest moment: screw the establishment and make money, too. What could be better?

Things do change. The battalion went on a forty-mile hike one day. Everyone stopped for lunch. The young lieutenant who had struck the deal with my dad sat down on a rock and opened up his C-rations. Much to his surprise, he looked down at his Hershey chocolate bar and realized it was the same kind that my father was selling him.

The next day, the lieutenant called my father in for a talk. All hell broke loose.

"So, Sergeant Casarona, what do you do with the whiskey I've been giving you?"

"Selling it mostly."

"How much a bottle?"

"About $40 a bottle."

"Ok…. Our deal is still on but I want $30 a bottle on top of the chocolate."

"Yes, sir!"

Dad was still coming out on top.

Yes, my father was having the time of his life in Hawaii. Wheeling and dealing and making new friends. Then the worst possible thing happened. The war ended. The party was over. He told me on VJ Day you could hear a pin drop in the barracks. There was no celebration. Their two-year vacation in Hawaii would soon be over. It would be back to the real world before they knew it. All the kids out of the pool.

I always wondered how he ended it with his Japanese girlfriend. I remembered seeing her picture in his Army photo album once. My father had a big dilemma; he already was going to have a hard time explaining his new German-Protestant wife to his Italian-Catholic family in the Bronx. So, I don't think his Japanese-Buddhist girlfriend ever had a chance. Yep, my dad had one too many women in his life. Because of that choice, I ended up half German rather than half Japanese.

Dad's family never did like my mother and her strange religion anyway. In their minds, my dad was supposed to have come home to the Bronx and marry a nice Italian-Catholic girl. Marty was always the rebel, one of the few things I learned to like about him in my later years.

My mother died in 1983. In 1991 my 69 year old Father married Marina, a twenty five year old woman from Costa Rica. In 1993 early one morning I called my Father up. A sleepy Marina answered the phone. "Hello." A little surprised I asked. "Is my Father there?" She handed the phone to my Dad. I wasn't surprised my father was still sexually active. "Hey Dad." With no joy in his voice, he announced. "I need to tell you something...I got married."

Marina always wanted to own a dress shop. So of course he bought her one. What did my high school dropout Father and she know about the apparel business? I don't know. They both learned a lot about that kind of business after he lost hundreds of thousands of dollars trying to make it work for her.

The marriage ended shortly after she went back to Costa Rica and came back pregnant. She told my Father she had been artificially inseminated. My Father believed her for about a year. One day he found a picture of her with their baby and the guy who had volunteered to artificially inseminate her.

He always loved Asian women though. When Dad died in 2012, his girlfriend, (or who knows maybe it was his wife) was 40 years younger than him. She was from Thailand.

He told me he had the best sex of his life with her. It was all about the sex for him and all about the money for her. When he died, he left her everything. Judging from how often he told me they had sex – and what his net worth was at the time of his death – I figured it cost him about

$880 every time they had sex. I hope it was the best sex he ever got, because he could have gotten a Las Vegas hooker for the same money. Yes, she had him wrapped around her little finger, as did my mother and his second wife Marina.

Dad sent me his will in 2007. It outlined how he basically gave everything to his girlfriend. It didn't bother me that I wasn't mentioned, but he made no provisions for his grandchildren. I was very upset about this and called him up.

"Dad, I don't care about me, but nothing for your grandkids?"

"Relax, I got you guys covered," he said.

"Really? What are you talking about?"

"I'm making you the executor to my will. This is your ace in the hole."

"What are you talking about?"

"It's simple. This is how it will work. Once I'm dead, you, as the executor of the will, can contest it."

"What?"

"After I'm dead, I don't give a shit about her. You can contest the will and get all the money back."

I try to live my life very Zen. However, I can't recall a time when I have been so angry. I totally lost it.

"Are you out of your mind?" I yelled. "The last thing I want to do after you're dead is get a lawyer and spend thousands of dollars trying to clean up the mess you've created." "But Keith, you have the ace in the hole."

Needless to say, when my father did pass away in 2012, I didn't get a lawyer to straighten out the mess he had the joy of creating.

Dad was totally uxorious when it came to the women in his life!

Chapter 3

The Door-to-Door Salesmen

Southern California wasn't Hawaii after the war, but it sure was close. The weather was great, there were plenty of jobs, and the smog hadn't infiltrated yet. My dad did what thousands of servicemen did after the war -they came back home to their girlfriends or wives and started new lives.

My folks bought a 1,100-square-foot, three-bedroom, one-bath home in Azusa, California, on the G.I. bill. My father soon started working as a lather again. It was the same job he worked when he dropped out of high school at 16 in 1938. Yes, his freewheeling days were over. He was a family man with bills to pay.

I was born in 1949, and my sister was born in 1952. I enjoyed two Christmases before the two Jehovah's Witnesses showed up at our door. My sister never did have a Christmas to celebrate. Not that she cared.

You don't see them much anymore, but back in the 1950s, people bought all kinds of things from door-to-door salesmen. It was a time when milkmen would still deliver milk right to the house. I can remember the milk bottles with the cream floating on the top next to our kitchen door. There was the Helms Bakery truck on our street with fresh bread delivered right to our neighborhood. Of course, we also had the Good Humor Ice Cream trucks with the music announcing to every kid in the area that it was time to find their mother for some loose change.

My mother bought all kinds of things from door-to-door salesmen. The stainless-steel cookware was nice. She also bought us the 1956 World Book Encyclopedia. It was something every kid needed at the time. I was only seven, but I loved looking at all the interesting pictures. Just a few years later, of course, much of the information was out dated and not of much value. (Just like life, valuable information one minute is of little use the next.) We bought many items from the famous Fuller Brush salesman. My mom almost bought me an accordion once from a fast-talking salesman. I'm glad she passed on that one. There is only one thing worse than learning to play the accordion and that's being forced to listen to someone who is learning to play the accordion.

My mother never received permission from my father for anything she bought. And boy, was he pissed when he got the bill for three-hundred-and-nineteen dollars for the stainless-steel cookware. It was a lot of money for my poor old dad to pay back in 1955. I bet the encyclopedias were hundreds of dollars too.

My father told me once that one of the biggest mistakes he ever made was turning over the household finances to my mom. He tried to get the control back years later, but my mom wouldn't have it. Just like in his Italian family, the woman ran the whole show. He would come home every week and hand his paycheck to her.

In 1952, my mother bought something really strange from a door-to-door sales person. No one was expecting it, for sure. It was a religion. This turned out to be very expensive: The cost turned out to be hundreds of thousands of dollars over the many decades that followed. The cost for this religion mentally and emotionally, who can say? Even though she has been dead for more than thirty years, the debt she incurred is something that her children, grandchildren and her great-grandchildren are still paying for till this very day. Yep, the gift that keeps on giving.

One warm Saturday morning in Azusa, two sweet little old ladies were knocking on the doors of houses in our neighborhood. They looked pretty innocent. These two little old ladies were looking for new club members.

And they had quite a story to tell my mother. It was a story that made her quake with fear, a story that confirmed my mother's worst fears. The ladies pulled out their Bibles and showed her scripture after scripture that said Satan, the devil, was in charge of everything here on Earth. He was in control of all the governments, churches and businesses.

They showed her just how bad people really are. They read to her Second Timothy, chapter three, where it says, "But know this, that in the last days grievous times shall come. For men shall be lovers of self, lovers of money, boastful, haughty, revilers, disobedient to parents, unthankful, unholy, without natural affection, implacable, slanderers, without self-control, fierce, no lovers of good, traitors, headstrong, puffed up, lovers of pleasure rather than lovers of God; holding a form of godliness, but having denied the power therefore. From these also turn away."

My poor mom. She looked like someone had just shot her dog. She knew in her heart they were right about how bad people really are. She had felt this way for many years. Yes, the world was a terrible place. She knew how bad people really were ever since her drunken seventy-year-old grandfather came into her bedroom late one night and sexually abused her when she was eight years old.

The old ladies could see it in her face. They had truly found one of "God's sheep." They got a gleam in their eyes. It was time for the close. It was time to give her the good news. What was the good news, after scaring the shit out of my poor mom? The good news they had for her is that god was really pissed too. So pissed that very soon he would be coming down here with his son and kicking some serious ass. How much ass would be kicked? Billions of people would soon be dead. However, there was more good news: She and just a few others could be saved. Yes, she could save herself and her family too, if she joined god's only true people and did what was required of her. She needed to spread the word about the coming destruction of the vast majority of mankind. Time was running out back in 1952. It was time to spread the good news! They sold my mother two magazines for ten cents and left. They would be coming back to study the Bible with her every week at no charge, just because they were nice. The bill, of course, came much later.

Anyway, they started off studying the Bible with her. To do this, they needed the help from numerous "Bible study aids." Of course, the only Bible study aids that were approved by god were the ones that were produced by the Watchtower Bible and Tract Society. The most popular one at that time was the *Let God Be True* book. Bible study aids are needed because the Bible needs deciphering. The little old ladies informed my mother that the Bible can be very vague in places, so the aids can help you and point you in the right direction.

I found out years later that there are more than 20,000 different Christian sects in the world. I wonder if they have "Bible study aids," too. Aids to point you in the 20,000 different directions you can go in trying to figure out the mind of god and what the Bible is really trying to say. Wow! 20,000 different Christian concepts of what god is trying to tell us. The funny thing is, the vast majority of these people all feel they have the only truth that god is trying to convey.

Years later, I thought how truly blessed I was. Was it fate or chance that I was practically born into the Jehovah's Witnesses? The Jehovah's Witnesses believe in neither of those two ideas. Yet lucky me, I get dropped into the only true Christian faith out of 20,000 others! What are the odds of that?

The Bible study aids the two women showed my mother would help explain why god got so pissed off in the first place. It seemed that in the beginning of Creation with

Adam and Eve, Satan challenged god to a contest. He said that, given enough time, he could turn everyone on the planet against him.

Satan won the first round of this contest with Jehovah, when he turned the first two perfect people, Adam and Eve, away from god. God wanted a rematch. Satan said, sure. Bring it on. For about six thousand years, Jehovah and Satan have been fighting over who could get the most followers. Now the time was almost up. Very soon, the ladies told my mother, the very great day of god the almighty was coming. The great war of Armageddon.

The war between god and man. The funny thing about this war is that god is supposed to be killing billions of men, women and children because they chose Satan instead of him. It turns out that there is only about one Jehovah's Witness to every thousand people on the planet. So, a lot of these people that He will be wiping out have never even met a Jehovah's Witness or know who Jehovah is at all.

Most of the people are not going to make it, just like in the time of Noah. God's answer to this huge loss in the popular vote is to kill off all those who vote against him.

If you read the Bible, this has been going on since the beginning of time. Have you ever wondered why there are no Amalekites, Perizzites, Hivites and Jebusites today? If you believe the Biblical accounts of history in the Old Testament are accurate, it may be because god commanded the Israelites to slaughter those groups – men, women, children, infants and even their animals. Maybe god has some anger issues?

When you think of genocide, who do you think of? Yep, the guy from World War II. The most hated man to ever live. Hitler may have killed millions of Jews and other peoples but he did leave their farm animals alone. Even though Hitler didn't believe in Jehovah, he and Jehovah had something in common. They both believed genocide is a good idea.

The Jehovah's Witnesses are still waiting for Armageddon. This will be the granddaddy of all massacres/genocides on the planet. I say "massacre" and not "war" because no one can fight against a god. It will just be god wiping out most of mankind. It sounds like one hell of a massacre to me.

So, what will happen to Satan after this war is over? He's killed or even tortured, right? Nope. God gives him mercy. Yes, billions of his followers get death, and Satan gets a long prison sentence. That's right. God has a better idea. He is going to put Satan in prison for one thousand years. God likes to test his people, and Satan is good at this. Because numbers-wise, he has won all of the competitions. So, after one thousand years, god is going to let him out of jail. He needs to test all his perfect people one last time. If you choose correctly, you get everlasting life with the rest of god's people. If you choose incorrectly, you get squashed like a cockroach. This seems like a no brainer. But according to the Bible, a big percentage of the people would rather die than live with god's people for eternity.

Let's look at the scoreboard and god's track record so far, according to what the Bible says happened and will happen in the future.

Adam and Eve: Satan gained two people, God gained zero.

Noah and the flood: God could save only eight people out of thousands or maybe even millions of people.

The Great War of Armageddon: God's people number only about eight million. Satan's people number around eight billion. It looks like god can save only one person out of one thousand.

What happens after the Great War and at the end of the thousand years of peace? We don't know. But the Bible says a "great crowd" would go Satan's way. So, looking at the numbers, it looks like Satan has three or four victories and god has zero or maybe one.

Back to my mother's indoctrination and why she thought this was a wonderful idea. It was a year of hard studying for my mother as she tried to get this all straight. Navigating the mind of god is not easy stuff.

After a few weeks of studying the Bible with her new friends, it was time to meet the rest of the congregation. I don't remember the first meeting we went to. I was too young. But I heard about it years later. Everyone "love bombed" my mother. What is love bombing? It goes like this: You go to the meeting place of the Jehovah's Witnesses, which is called the Kingdom Hall. You will be introduced to many different smiling faces. They will then love you to death. The "love bomb." "Norma, this is Brother Jones."

"Norma, we are so happy you are here."

"I love your baby, Norma. Just call me Sister White."

You get the idea. Everyone loves you. We are all brothers and sisters in god's big happy family.

My mother had finally found a home. A real home with people who really seemed to like her. After years of being an outsider and with no real family around – at least family she liked – she finally got her adopted family.

Mom never asked my baby sister and me if we wanted to join her new club. She, of course, didn't consult my father, either. How many people on this planet are in religions their parents choose for them? I would guess the vast majority.

They say everything in life is timing. It's so true. Timing is everything! Ask any salesman.

There is a story about a man who lives in New York City. He is of average age and build, nothing special to look at. He spends all day walking up and down Madison Avenue. He walks up to 150 to 200 women a day. He looks them straight in the eye and asks them, "Do you want to fuck?" And yes, his face gets slapped often. He gets cursed at.

There are a lot of upset women out there after that rude question. He also has sex with two or three of these women a day who liked his question and thought it was a good idea. He said in an interview, "Some of these women were really gorgeous too." He also said, "It's all about timing and persistence. It's a numbers game."

What is the purpose of this story? I guess to illustrate the concept that no matter how wacky or strange an idea can be, if you talk to enough people, there are always a few whack jobs out there that think it's a great idea!

Of course, that is why there are telemarketers. If no one bought the strange stuff these guys were selling, there would be no telemarketers.

So I guess, the Jehovah's Witnesses' story of the coming great destruction of the vast majority of mankind is music to a few people's ears.

With millions of Jehovah's Witnesses knocking on doors everyday they are bound to find some new recruits. In fact according to the society's own statistics for just the year of 2017, it took an average of 13,880 hours of field service/door-to-door activity to create just ONE new convert! That means it would take one Jehovah's Witness 1,735 days (or 4.7 years) at 8 hours a day of door knocking to find just one new member. It looks like the guy who is getting total strangers to have sex with him is doing better than the Jehovah's Witnesses are in recruiting new members.

The Jehovah's Witnesses hold large biyearly meetings called circuit assemblies. At these assemblies they will share wonderful stories about people who were getting ready to commit suicide. They were tired and done with life. However, before they killed themselves, many would beg for god's guidance or a sign of some kind from heaven. A few minutes later, Jehovah's Witnesses would knock on their door with their "good news." Naturally, the people who were going to commit suicide would think it was god coming to rescue them. Thousands of people a day think about killing themselves. How many of those people are thinking about killing themselves on Saturday or Sunday mornings? This is the most likely time that a Jehovah's Witness will be knocking on their door.

Sorry. I can't kill myself right now. God is knocking on the front door.

Timing is everything.

Chapter 4
The Pecking Order

My mom was looking for a new family, and she finally got it. My mother loved what the two little old ladies were selling. She got a god, a religion, new friends and most of all, hope. Yes, the timing was perfect for her.

Part of becoming a Jehovah's Witness was finding out how evil the holidays are. The little old ladies told my mom that it seems Satan and his pagan friends were behind the whole holiday thing: Christmas, Easter, Halloween, birthdays, Valentine's Day and Independence Day. Anything that had any fun involved was something the devil probably started. Since the world was so bad, it was important to stay away from any of its influences. It's really a closed society. Unless they are Jehovah's Witnesses, friends outside the faith are highly discouraged. To marry a nonbeliever is even worse.

My mom loved her new religion. She brought us kids up to love it too, and we did. By the time I was in my teens, I was a full-blown, self-righteous Jehovah's Witness. My father never did fully embrace it. He told me years later that the day he was baptized, he knew it was the biggest mistake of his life. That didn't stop him from doing it. He would always say, "Just give in for the sake of peace." So, he was baptized to please my mother. It worked for a while.

Being baptized means you agree to all the Jehovah's Witness rules. As you know, my father wasn't big on rules, but he went along with them "for the sake of peace" in the family.

For many years, we were a classic Jehovah's Witness family. We would go to the Kingdom Hall three times a week. We attended the meetings for two hours on Thursdays when they had the Ministry School and Service Meetings. You'd find us there for two hours and fifteen minutes on Sundays when they had the Public Talk and The Watchtower Study. We also went to a private home on Tuesday nights for what is called the Book Study. We would meet at the Kingdom Halls and private homes on Saturday mornings to organize our Field Service or Field activity. Yes, four days out of every seven, we were involved with some kind of church activity. As my mother would say, "An empty mind is the devil's workshop." The church leaders knew it was important to keep you busy and keep your mind full of church stuff. Smart guys, those church leaders.

Field Service is the door-to-door activity where Jehovah's Witnesses try to sell their thought system to other people. That is what the two little old ladies were doing when they found my mom. Of course, some call it something different. Some call it "spreading the good news." What is the good news? Just like the little old ladies explained to my mom, the good news is, warning people of the coming destruction of the current system of things. After this destruction, god would bring his government to the Earth and make it a paradise. The ones who survive this war would live in peace with perfect bodies and will never get old or die.

Spreading this "good news" was the most important thing a person could do as a Jehovah's Witness. The concept was that we were saving people's lives. Just like in the time of Noah, people needed to repent and take advantage of the opportunity for salvation by joining god's only true religion on Earth.

Men, women and children all go from door-to-door, spreading the message. The minimum requirement was ten hours a month. Each person who did this was called a "Publisher."

The Jehovah's Witnesses said that we were all the same in god's eyes. That everyone was equal. To prove this, they call everyone "brother" and "sister." Sadly, this really isn't the case. There were those in every Kingdom Hall who were definitely considered more "spiritual" than others. That being said, this is a partial list of their rankings as a Jehovah's Witness in all the congregations around the world. This rank made a difference in how people treated and respected you. These are some of the rankings as of 2001. They have changed very little over the years.

Unbaptized, Irregular Publisher: Someone who is going out in field service inconsistently and is not baptized yet. This rank is okay if you are a child, not if you are an adult.

Inactive Publisher: Someone who is baptized and who has not gone out in field service for more than six months.

This person is weak spiritually and should be avoided.

Irregular Publisher: Someone who is baptized who might miss a full month of field service every now and then. This person is also weak spiritually, but not as bad as an inactive publisher.

Regular Publisher: Someone who never misses a month in field service. This person is in "good standing."

Axillary Pioneer: Someone who is putting in a minimum of 60 hours a month in field service (the hours now have been lowered to 50). This is a super-charged publisher and is admired by others.

Pioneer: A person who puts in a minimum of 100 hours a month in field service (the hours have now been lowered to 70). Except for being an Elder, this is the highest rank in the congregation.

Special Pioneer: Someone who puts in a minimum of 150 hours a month in field service (the hours have now been lowered to 130). There are very few of these around now, if any.

Ministerial Servant: Males who want to be promoted to the rank of Elder someday must first be a Ministerial Servant. The Ministerial Servant does all the jobs in the Kingdom Hall that the Elders don't have time to do, or want to do. After many years of this activity, the Elders can then decide if a Ministerial Servant can join their club.

Book Study Overseer: This position was held by a Ministerial Servant or Elder.

Elders: The most respected position a male can have in the congregation. In a congregation of one-hundred, there are anywhere from three to ten (or more) of these guys. Women can never hold this position.

The Anointed Ones: Men or women who are part of the select group called the 144,000 or "Little Flock." These people have a heavenly hope and plan to rule as kings and priests with Christ in Heaven. Surprisingly, even though they will be kings in Heaven, these people (unless they are also Elders) have virtually no power or authority in the congregation while they are still alive.

Elder's Wife: This position technically holds no power (if you believe men never listen to their wives). But, many times the Elders find out from their wives what is really happening in the congregation.

So, as you can see, there was a definite pecking order in the congregation. Though Jehovah's Witnesses say they are all equal in god's eyes, they definitely didn't look at each other in that same way. It's a male-dominated religion with women and children coming in second and third.

Just a side note. If you go to any Kingdom Hall around the world, you will notice a couple of things. Right off the bat you will notice that there will always be way more women in attendance than men. Why is this? Because there are a lot of unbelieving mates/spouses and most of these unbelieving mates happen to be male. So my family, with my unbelieving father and believing mother was more the norm and not the exception to the rule. Though the men run the religion, women make up the vast majority of its followers.

Women can be Publishers, Axillary Pioneers and Pioneers. Women are not allowed to be Ministerial Servants or Elders. In fact, an Elder in the Kingdom Hall could be removed as such if his wife was not submissive enough to him or to any other males in the Kingdom Hall.

In a congregation, you'd have ten or more different rankings of less than 150 people. Most everyone knows their ranking and the rankings of those around them. If you don't know their rank, many will bring it up to you when you first meet. "Yes, I'm a Pioneer!" or "I'm serving as an Elder."

There are other rankings outside the local congregation.

City Overseer: He (males only) is in charge of the whole city. These are cities with many congregations in them.

Circuit Overseer: He (males only) is in charge of 12 to 15 different congregations or one circuit.

District Overseer: He (males only) is charge of 12 to 15 circuits. This position has been done away with.

Zone Overseer: He (males only) is in charge of a whole country.

Gilead Student: A missionary assigned to a foreign country. These can be male or female.

Bethelite: A worker at one of the branches or the world headquarters. These can be male or female. At Bethel there are too many rankings to even mention here. Service department, writing department, kitchen, laundry, toilet cleaners and so on.

The 144,000 or "Little Flock" or Anointed Ones: As mentioned above this is a select group of people who believe they will go to Heaven to reign as kings and priest with Christ. The older ones in this group are generally respected. The younger anointed ones, not so much. The judgment here is that god would only choose "older and wiser" ones before he would pick a young person, with little or no track record. This group has no power unless they are in the select group of anointed ones known as "The Governing Body" (males only) in which case they have all the power. There are now only eight of these guys at Bethel who run the whole organization. They are appointed to do this by the Holy Spirit, which really means by god himself. Though they say they are just imperfect men (false modesty), their word is law.

The Jehovah's Witnesses purposely keep their congregations small, usually 100 to 140 people. That way, they can keep better tabs on you and better tabs on each other. Big brother is always watching. The Elder's job is to keep the congregation clean and free from any wrong doing. Someone can be "marked" as "bad association" thus adding one more category to their long list of spiritual levels.

If you missed more than a couple of meetings or too much field service, you might get a phone call or a visit from someone making sure you were okay and not spiritually sick.

Besides the five meetings a week the Jehovah's Witnesses would meet many days during the week to engage in the "door-to-door activity." These people would meet at the local Kingdom Hall or in private homes. There they would be broken down into smaller groups called "car groups." These groups consisted of four to eight people. Your "car group" was the best place to find out what was really going on in the Kingdom Hall. Part of the fun in going out in the field service is catching up on all the gossip. Even though this is discouraged, it has always been done. There is lots of information exchanged on the activities of our fellow Brothers and Sisters.

Whether you are god's chosen people or not, people just feel better knowing they are doing better than others. It's like saying, "See god, what a good person I am." Plus, it's really fun to have some piece of information that others don't have, some little piece of dirt. It's just human nature. Though most of it is harmless, a lot of it can be real nasty stuff. Yes, the Brothers and Sisters know way too much about their fellow Brothers and Sisters. It was one big happy family as long as you know the pecking order.

I saw a bumper sticker on a car many years ago. It said, "Please god protect me from your people."

Chapter 5

The Little Girl and Her Dog

The funny thing is, no matter how strange your life, it's easy to get used to it. My life seemed normal back then. Life in the 1950s was simple. As a kid, it was school, meetings at the Kingdom Hall and field service.

One of the most fun things to do happened twice a year. It was called a Circuit Assembly. All of the congregations in a circuit would meet for a four-day assembly. Because of the financial hardship on everyone, they were shortened to three days. Now they are only two days and some are only one day. The Jehovah's Witnesses would rent a building somewhere central in the area where eight hundred to one thousand people would show up. Sometimes we would travel to different cities and get a hotel or motel there. Now, most all the witnesses don't have to rent buildings in different towns. They have built Assembly Halls. These large buildings, owned by the Society, are set up perfectly to handle their assemblies. Even though they have been paid off for many years, the Brothers and Sisters are still encouraged to contribute thousands of dollars for their use.

The meetings were pretty much the same as the ones in the Kingdom Hall. There were talks about how to be more effective in the Field Service and how to get more converts. The Ministry School helped everyone to be better public speakers. It's not unusual to see a child of ten years old or less standing before a thousand people and giving a five-minute Bible sermon. There were talks about the evils of materialism and the sin of immorality. There were always talks about the "Last Days" and how we are so close to god's day of vengeance. There were people sharing experiences about how they found "The Truth." They call their faith The Truth. So, you are either in The Truth or out of The Truth.

There were also talks about being "A Pioneer." A fulltime minister for the Lord. This was something all young adults were encouraged to do. "Yes, it is time to serve the Lord. The end is coming very soon." In the late 1960s, the Society started talking about 1975 being the end. The Witnesses have predicted the end of the world as we know it many times over the years. This date was pushed almost as has much as the year 1914 had been pushed many years before.

The assemblies provide what the Witnesses call "spiritual food" to the Brothers and Sisters. They also provide an opportunity to meet other Witnesses from other parts of the state. Everyone is dressed up in his or her finest attire. It's also an opportunity to meet available (Jehovah's Witnesses only) members of the opposite sex.

Another thing the Witnesses had besides the Circuit assemblies are the larger District and International assemblies.

In 1958, my whole family went to The Divine Will International Convention in New York City at Yankee Stadium. This convention topped them all — the biggest convention of all time for the Witnesses. New York City has never had a convention like this one, before or since. Most of the Witnesses in the United States and thousands of Witnesses from 122 countries flocked to New York City.

This was an eight-day assembly. We sat in the sun for hours on end, listening to talk after talk. Most of us were dressed up in white shirts and ties. Some of the Brothers never took off their dress coats. They told us that we needed to make a favorable impression on all of the outsiders. Yes, we were all good Witnesses and would do anything to get more spiritual food, including sweating our asses off.

The assembly started every day at 9:15 a.m. and lasted until 9:00 p.m. It could last even longer if Brother Knorr, the president of the Society at the time, decided to give one of his famous concluding prayers. Over 200,000 people stood there after twelve exhausting hours with crying babies. We were all praying too! We were praying for him to finally say the word "amen" so we could all get out of there and get on those hot subway trains for our commute back to our hotels or camp grounds. Some people didn't get back to their accommodations until 11:00 or 12:00 at night. Many of the poorer Brothers had to go all the way to New Jersey to their tents in campgrounds. Then it was up at 6:00 a.m. to do it all again. For Knorr and his crew, it was a 20-minute limo ride back to their luxury accommodations at Bethel.

The last day of the assembly was Sunday, August 3rd. There were so many people there that they let us sit on the playing field. There we were, sitting in the middle of center field of Yankee Stadium, listening to Brother Knorr tell us how Jehovah would make the Earth into one big paradise one day soon. The final attendance ended up being over 200,000 at Yankee Stadium and over 50,000 at the nearby Polo Grounds. That was almost sixty years ago, and Yankee Stadium has never broken that attendance record. Yes, Knorr gave the mother of all prayers at the end. It was almost like he didn't want to let us go. No one has ever broken his record for the longest prayer ever given at Yankee Stadium: more than thirty minutes long.

The conventions were where the Witness organization would release their new publications. These books would be bought to be read and studied at the congregation book study. Eventually, they would be taken from door-to-door to be placed in the hands of those who wanted to receive the "good news" for a small donation. The books were never sold, that could be illegal in some cities because of the Green River Ordinance.

A *Green River Ordinance* is a common United States city *ordinance* prohibiting door-to-door solicitation. Under such an *ordinance*, it is illegal for any business to sell their items door-to-door without express prior permission from the household. This law protects residents from unwanted peddlers and salespersons, by prohibiting door-to-door solicitations without prior consent. *Green River ordinance* takes its name from the city Green River in Wyoming. Green River was the first city to enact this *law* in 1931.

To get around this law the Jehovah's Witnesses would ask people to make a small contribution or donation to help "defray" the printing cost. A lot of the time, the Witnesses would buy their literature at the Kingdom Hall and just give it away to people they met. So the society got paid for their literature whether we did or not.

The Society would release two to three new books every year. They have written hundreds of these Bible study aids over the years. The Witnesses could hardly wait to get these new books. They desperately wanted to get the "new truths" or, as the Society calls it, the "new light," from their Bible study aids. These books would then be placed in the Kingdom Hall libraries to be used as reference materials. However, recently many of these older publications from the 1940s through the 1990s are now disappearing out of the local Kingdom Hall's libraries all around the world. Why are these books disappearing? These old publications that contained so much wonderful "new light" are being tossed out because the information in them have turn out to be false and inaccurate and downright incriminating. It seems the wonderful "spiritual food" we got back than has turned out to be a big embarrassment to the now leaders of the organization. George Orwell said it perfectly in 1984. "The past erased. The erasure was forgotten, the lie became the truth."

Anyway, every week we would meet in a private home for a one-hour meeting called, you guessed it, "The Book Study." These books would be studied line-by-line, paragraph-by-paragraph. We would study only ten to fifteen paragraphs a week, looking for hidden treasures in every word. Sometimes, it would take many years to get through the larger books.

I'll never forget one of the books that we acquired back in 1958 at the New York Divine Will convention. It was titled *From Paradise Lost to Paradise Regained*. There were drawings in it depicting Armageddon. The book contained pictures of buildings falling down on people as they ran around in terror. One picture had the Earth opening up and people falling into this large chasm. It showed a dog and a little girl trying to hold her doll as they fell into the open abyss. Thank god we couldn't see the little girl's face. I was only nine years old, but I thought Jehovah was not messing around if he was going to kill little girls along with their pet dogs.

I found out years later that my god Jehovah had a long history of killing lots of men, women and children over the years. I needed to get with the program or god could be throwing me down that hole with my dog.

There was no time to waste back in the 1960s and early 1970s. No time to think about jobs. College educations were not just frowned on, they were highly discouraged. Very few Jehovah's Witnesses were going to college back then. If you did go to college to seek a higher education, you were considered to be a spiritually weak person. It was never said to your face, but the message was loud and clear from their platforms at the Kingdom Halls and assemblies. You'd be talked about behind your back, or in the car groups that went out in the Field Service.

There was much talk of staying single and not getting married at all. It was no time to settle down and start a family. The Society knew if you got married, the odds of staying in the ministry full time were very low. So not only were less people getting married but many who were married decided to forgo having children for a while. They would wait until The Great Tribulation was over. Then it would be safe to start their families.

Brother Knorr made it a law that no children were allowed at Bethel. That meant that thousands of married couples that had served at the Bethel headquarters of Jehovah's Witnesses around the world would give up having any families while they were there. This meant that many who have served there for thirty, forty and even fifty years gave up having a family for this privilege. There were a lot of very bitter couples back there after 1975. People who had believed "the end" was coming any day. The only thing that ended was their possibility of having any children.

There was a scripture that was quoted a lot back then: "And woe unto them that are with child, and to them that give suck in those days! … For then shall be great tribulation, such as was not since the beginning of the world to this time, no, nor ever shall be."

You can see that back then, if you had children, you could be considered a very selfish and inconsiderate person.

Many times, the older Sisters in the Kingdom Hall would bring this scripture up to the younger Sisters who were thinking about having children.

Chapter 6

What Flag Would Jesus Salute?

My mother and leaders of the Jehovah's Witnesses organization told me that the end was coming very soon. I was encouraged by my mother and many others in the congregation to be baptized. I was baptized on January 7, 1967, and began full-time ministry as a Pioneer in May of 1968.

In fact, my Mother told me when I was younger that I would never even get out of high school before the end would come. She was wrong about that. I did graduate high school in 1967. Even her grandkids graduated high school. Soon her great grandkids will be finishing high school also. Yet even to this day, fifty years later, Jehovah's Witness parents are telling their children that the end is near and that they too, will probably never finish high school. The beat goes on.

I was pretty much a loner in high school. Most of the Jehovah's Witnesses didn't want to hang around me (Chapter Seven will explain why), and "worldly friends" that were non-Jehovah's Witnesses were not allowed. Anything outside the Jehovah's Witnesses was considered "worldly." This referred to people of this world and not of god. Satan was in control of this world, so we had to stay free from anything he was controlling especially his people. What did this include? School sports, school clubs and school dances where they played the devil's music.

It was written in Luke (and Witnesses love to quote), "I have written to you, fathers, because you know him who is from the beginning. I have written to you, young men, because you are strong, and the word of God abides in you, and you have overcome the evil one. Do not love the world or anything in the world. If anyone loves the world, the love of the Father is not in him. For all that is in the world—the desires of the flesh, the desires of the eyes, and the pride of life—is not from the Father but from the world."

High school wasn't very enjoyable. As a good Jehovah's Witness, all school functions like school dances and sports events were considered off limits. All "worldly" associations after school were strictly frowned upon.

By the time 1966 and 1967 rolled around, the Vietnam War was going strong. I went from the kid that no one really noticed or cared about to one of the most hated kids in my high school. The reason being, nationalism was at fever pitch.

Jehovah's Witnesses are neutral when it comes to all politics. If forced to join a military service, they will choose to be a conscientious objector instead and go to prison.

My classmates were now hostile towards me. They didn't like it when I didn't salute the flag. When I didn't stand up for the National Anthem, people would come up to me and start yelling. I was spit on and slapped. People would ask me why I wouldn't salute the flag. I would say, "What flag would Jesus salute if he was here on Earth? All of them? None of them? Or just the American flag?" I would still get slapped. People are not really interested in logical questions like that.

Or students would say, "So, you won't fight for your country?"

"No," I'd reply.

"Well," they'd say. "What would happen if everyone thought the same way as you do?"

"I guess if everyone thought the way I do, there would be no more wars!"

They would look at me with a blank look on their faces for a second, then fire back. "No! I mean if everyone in THIS country wasn't willing to go to war."

People love to believe in the "us or them" concept, whether in politics or religion. What did more than sixty-thousand Americans and more than one-million Vietnamese die for anyway? After all those people killed each other, Vietnam still became a communistic country. Yet I was the weird guy in school because I didn't want to go to war.

I had a friend in high school named Clark. He had been raised as a Jehovah's Witness also. By the time he had graduated, he had left the Jehovah's Witnesses. He joined the army and went to Vietnam. In 1987, I found him in California and called him up. He said he went to Vietnam and had "no regrets." I said, "I didn't go to Vietnam, and I have no regrets, either."

No, I didn't go to Vietnam, like so many of my classmates did. I didn't believe in war back then. I still don't believe in war now. I believe the Jehovah's Witnesses got this one right. Yes, Jehovah's Witnesses are pacifist, yet sadly the god they are worshipping is not.

Interesting that no one in my graduating class died in Vietnam, but five guys who went over there returned and killed themselves. So, unlike my friend Clark, I guess some of my classmates had some regrets.

Chapter 7
Easy to Join, Tough to Leave

Jehovah's Witnesses claim to love everybody. But there are some people the Witnesses actually do hate. The people they hate the most are former Jehovah's Witnesses. If you join them and are baptized, you better stay in their faith. Your baptism is for life, with no parole. Just like in the Mafia: Once you are in, there is no changing your mind later on.

There are three basic ways people become Jehovah's Witnesses.

The first way is very rare. It's called "informal witnessing." A Witness will meet a person not in the Field Service and strike up a conversation. It could be a schoolmate or workmate. I say mate and not friend because friendships outside of their organization are highly discouraged. People may say, "I have a friend who is a Jehovah's Witness." But really, how much of a friend is he to you? Did he ever invite you over for dinner? Probably not. If, indeed, you did have a Jehovah Witness friend and you did lots of things together, the Witness was either doing it on the sly, or was someone not in good standing in the Jehovah's Witness organization. Anyway, with informal witnessing, the conversation will start with the Witnesses asking you some questions about how you feel about the current system of things. They are hoping you might be looking for a change or, better yet, maybe even god's intervention. From there, they will then introduce you to some of their literature, thus hoping to start a home Bible study with you, which of course will hopefully lead to your baptism.

The second way is through field service (door-to-door activity) in which Witnesses go to every house in a neighborhood or "territory." If no one is home, the Witnesses will mark a slip with a "NH" (for Not at Home) next to that address. They will keep calling back at that same house for up to three times. They will make many visits trying to talk to everyone in that neighborhood/territory. After a few months, they will turn the territory back in to the "territory overseer," they will then "check out" a new/different territory and start the process all over again. Some territories in remote areas might not be canvassed for many years. Some territories could be worked every two to three weeks. The Witnesses will knock on your door, looking for, as they call it, "sheep-like ones" or "people receptive to the good news." They will leave their literature hoping you will read it. They will call back every week afterwards until you tell them not to come back anymore, or you tell them you want a home Bible study.

From the early years of the church through the 1980s, people mostly joined the religion by way of its door-to-door or field service activity. This old method of creating Jehovah's Witnesses has now slowed to just a trickle. If you look into their "Year Books" that has all the gains and loss statistics for all the different countries worldwide it becomes clearly evident that whatever growth is happening is coming in mostly from the third world countries. The poor countries of the world where the concept of an abundance of everything in a paradise Earth, living in perfect health, sounds pretty darn good.

The third way is sex /reproduction. Even though the society has tried its best to discourage its members from marriage over the years (like right before 1975) still Jehovah's Witnesses continue to marry and have sex. This is how the vast majority of Jehovah's Witnesses are now created.

What has changed over the years? Two things: 1. Millions of Jehovah's Witnesses are having sex with millions of other Jehovah's Witnesses 2. People are now more educated. Thanks to the internet, people can really research religions before they join them. Not too many people nowadays are looking for a religion that got started in the 1870s by a bunch of Germans from Pennsylvania. A religion that doesn't believe in any holidays or blood transfusions, is sexually restrictive and has been preaching the coming of the end of the world as we know it, for over a hundred years. This type of religion just doesn't seem very attractive to people nowadays.

These are the ways Jehovah's Witnesses are created. After you learn the facts about their religion, they will want you to join their church by being baptized to show the world your dedication to your new god, Jehovah. By the way, the Witnesses don't like people to call their church a "church."

They feel that their organization is superior to the rest of the organizations that call themselves churches. They want to be in a whole new different classification. However, the definition of church is this: A particular Christian organization, typically one with its own clergy, buildings, and distinctive doctrines. So, welcome to their church.

The Witnesses preach against child baptism. They say they want the person to make a fully conscious decision to join their faith. How could a baby know what religion they want to join? This is a very good point. However, it is not unusual for Jehovah's Witness parents to encourage their eight or nine-year-old children to be baptized. I guess infants don't know what they are doing when it comes to serious decisions, but eight and nine year olds do. I was baptized at seventeen. This was unusual for someone who was almost born into the faith. No words were directly spoken about it of course, but there were a lot of what-are-you-waiting-for remarks. The average age of children who were raised in the faith being baptized when I was growing up was twelve to thirteen. Things haven't changed much over the years and these are the same ages children are getting baptized even to this day.

For many years, if you wanted to be baptized, you would just get in line and get dunked. Nowadays, they will set you down and ask you more than a hundred questions. These questions are to make sure that you are in agreement with the Societies' policies and that you are loyal to their organization and Governing body. The Governing body is a group of eight men who run the whole show.

There is one very important question they should ask you before you are baptized, but for some odd reason they don't. That question should be: "Are you aware that if you join this religion by being baptized, if you ever change your mind at any time in the future and decide to leave it, you will be shunned? This means your friends, parents, children and relatives will have nothing to do with you for the rest of your life."

So, what is this shunning all about? This is the biggest tool The Watchtower and Tract Society possesses to control its members.

One dictionary says shunning is to persistently avoid, ignore, or reject (someone or something) through antipathy or caution. To avoid, evade, steer clear of, keep one's distance from, have nothing to do with.

Yep, shunning is a pretty powerful tool. How many people out there could handle being shunned by all of their family members? Yet, if you ever decide to leave this religion, that is what could be in store for you.

Maybe it doesn't matter if they ask this question because most eight and nine year olds would probably tell them yes anyway.

Wouldn't it be funny if they said no? "Mom, Dad, I changed my mind! I'm not getting baptized. Since there is a strong possibility I might decide to be a homosexual twenty years from now, I've decided not to get baptized after all. This way we can still be friends and you won't have to shun me!"

This really isn't that funny because if thousands of kids could see their lives down the road many years later, they would certainly have never allowed themselves to be baptized in the first place. Sometimes joining the club is the worst thing you can do.

If you are unrepentant and get dis-fellowshipped and thus shunned, that's one thing. If you are dis-fellowshipped but are repentant and want back into their organization, this is a whole different ball game. You must endure a brutal reinstatement process. Since they love you so much, they will let you come back to their meetings. You can sit in the back of the Kingdom Hall with your eyes looking down, feeling the shame of your transgression. No, they don't put a large scarlet letter on your clothes, but they might as well for how they treat you. No one can talk to you. You will get a lot of stares. This will happen for months or sometimes even years. You will be treated this way until the Elders decide you have paid the price for your sins. They must determine if you are truly repentant or just trying to put on an act of looking repentant. The more times you are dis-fellowshipped, the longer they will make you wait to get back in again. Or if they just don't like you for some reason, you will have to wait longer, too. Every group of Elders is different. In one congregation, you could be back in "good standing" and reinstated in just a few months for having sex before marriage; in another congregation, it could take a few years for the same offense. In some congregations, you might not get dis-fellowshipped at all for the same offense. If you are friends with some of the higher-ups or children of some of the Elders, you might get some special consideration. Yes, you might just get "reproved" (this is a reprimand that may or may not be announced to the whole congregation) with no dis-fellowshipping at all. In fifty years as a member, I saw this happen dozens of times.

I know it sounds strange, but for some odd reason, many unbaptized people are treated better then baptized people in the organization. For example, a Jehovah's Witnesses family could have two children. Let's say the children are twins. One child is baptized and one is not. They both end up doing an activity that is not approved of by the Witnesses. If the baptized one is dis-fellowshipped, he will be shunned for sure. However, the unbaptized one can't be dis-fellowshipped because he never made a commitment by being baptized. So, he might not be completely shunned. In this case, by making the decision as a child to be baptized, you are at a greater disadvantage than your unbaptized sibling. This brings us to our next question.

So, you must be baptized first in order to be shunned by Jehovah's Witnesses later? Well, not necessarily. You can still be shunned if you are not baptized. You might be "marked." This is usually done unofficially. The Elders or an Elder or just a group of Brothers and Sisters talk among themselves and determine which individuals in the Kingdom Hall should be considered "bad associations." You might not even know that you are marked. Most of the time, this is done unofficially. Sometimes it is done officially. NOTE: I don't think this is true any longer. Usually a "marking talk" is given without any persons name being attached. In this case, the Elder will make an announcement to the whole congregation that certain people are considered to be bad associations. So, you might not even know that you are on their shit list. One way you will know is that people will start acting very differently around you. Yes, the unofficial shun.

I know all of this is very confusing.

This happened to me in high school. I was shunned. Did I do something inappropriate? Nope, I was the perfect Jehovah's Witness child. I was guilty by association. Who did I have contact with that were considered bad associations? My parents. Yep, good old Mom and Dad. This interesting story will be told in the next chapter.

So back to the many ways you can be shunned.

There are only four ways of leaving the Jehovah's Witnesses. So, there are four ways that could lead to shunning. I say "could" because options three and four have some loopholes.

You are "dis-fellowshipped." You commit some kind of sin in the eyes of the Witnesses. For example, you commit "immorality," meaning you have sex before you are married or you are married and have sex with someone besides your spouse. There are other sins you could commit, but these are by far the most popular. Once a sin has been committed, you meet with three Elders in the local congregation. If they feel you are not repentant enough for your sins, they will expel you from the congregation. Sometimes, even if you are repentant enough, they will still expel you anyway. They will do this to make an example of you to others, or because they just don't like you. It's a good old boy country club, and sometimes favoritism comes into play. You could be dis-fellowshipped in one Kingdom Hall and just get a slap on the wrist in another for the same offense.

The second way to leave is you "disassociate" yourself. You send a letter to the local congregation and resign your membership.

Note: If either No. 1 or No. 2 above occurs, you will be definitely be shunned. You can never again have ANY contact with any of your Jehovah's Witness friends or family. You are dead to them.

In recent years, a new way to leave the Witnesses has become popular. It's called "fading." This is a tricky one. People who don't want to make a complete break from the Witnesses like this option, usually because the thought of not ever talking with their parents, spouses, children, siblings and loved ones is more than they can bear. It works just like it sounds. You move away from them slowly. Many times, this requires an actual move to a new town or state. You might even tell your family and friends that you are still an active Witness, but in reality, you have moved on to a new life. Others have called this a "double life."

This phrase has been coined to describe mostly teenagers and young adults who have two different lives. These are kids who are trying to keep their parents happy and will pretend to be a good Witness by going to the meetings and out in field service. However, on the weekends, they will party down and act like worldly people. Whether you are a double lifer or a fader, the results can be disastrous if caught. You could end up in the "back room" with the three Elders. This rarely goes well.

The fourth and final option is death. Many who couldn't face options No. 1, 2 or 3 have chosen this one. Yes, you can break free with suicide. There was a time when I even considered this option myself. I have known at least a dozen people who have exercised this option. I guess on some unconscious level I have personally contributed (by way of apathy) to at least two people choosing this way out. But just because you died or killed yourself doesn't mean you can escape shunning. Yes, even dead people can be shunned. Many Witnesses have boycotted their family member's funerals because they were not in good standing in the organization when they died. Sadly, for many, there is no forgiveness even after you're dead. My mother wouldn't let my father go to his own father's funeral because it was inside a Catholic church.

So yes, you can be shunned as a dead person.

Yet the Witnesses think of themselves as an organization of love.

Chapter 8

A Monkey on a String

My mother never really had much respect for my father. According to her, my Father was weak and "not a good spiritual head of the family." She probably knew that deep down inside, he wasn't buying the program. Whenever there was a problem in the family, my Father just continued his "just go along for the sake of peace" program.

Years later, I really disliked him. Not because he wasn't a Jehovah's Witness anymore, but because he knew it was all bullshit for years and never said a word to us kids about it. Yes, his just-give-in-for-the-sake-of-peace attitude affected my kids, their kids and me. He told me years later that I would have never listened to him anyway, and he was probably right. However, at least he could say he tried to warn us. No, he was more worried about his relationship with my mother than his relationship with us Children. He had turned over the raising of us kids to my mother. He was MIA. We were on our own.

My mother never really liked my father, even up to the very end of her life. All those years of him kissing her ass got him nothing.

In 1959, when I was ten, my mother took my sister and me to Hawaii for the summer. I found out years later that she never told my father before she left. He came home from work one day and we were gone. She did this three or four times while we were growing up. She would just take off and not tell my father where she was going. However, she would always return home before school started. I'm not quite sure what this was all about. Maybe she found out about one of his many infidelities. Maybe it was putting him on notice to shape up. I really don't know the reason for the separations, but when we came back, he appreciated her more than ever.

Maybe she was like her grandfather (not the one who sexual abused her) and just had a wandering soul. He would take off for months during the Great Depression and never tell anyone. Not even his wife. Sometimes he just wouldn't come home from work. Instead, he would hop a freight train out of town. One day, on one of his rare visits back home, the noon whistle blew. He came home for lunch, as was the custom in many small Midwest towns back then. He told his wife, "I'm not working for those guys anymore after today. They're all a bunch of idiots." After his lunch, he went back to work digging a well. But my great-grandfather didn't come home that evening and he didn't hop a freight train out of town either. That afternoon, he was at the bottom of a twenty-foot well. He was digging out the muck and smoking a cigarette. There was a small gas pump running on the top of the hole that was pumping out the water that was seeping in. One of the guys he was working for did turn out to be an idiot because he accidently kicked a can full of gasoline into the hole. No more freight trains for gramps. He was burned to a crisp as he was trying to claw his way out of the hole. His wandering days were over.

My mother had strange relationships with all the men in her life, including me. Before the events in 1961 described below, she loved my father in some strange way. She really thought her new religion would get my father back on the right path, back on the straight and narrow. Yet every congregation seemed to have its problems and my father was quick to point those problems out to my mother.

Finally, in 1960, they decided to go on a grand adventure and move to Long Island, New York. There they thought they would find a new life. My father was going to start a pizza-by-the-slice business with my uncle. We started attending the Babylon New York Kingdom Hall. The pizza business never happened, we all headed back to Southern California in 1961.

You know what they say: "Wherever you go, that's where you'll be." The same problems my parents had in California with each other turned out to be the same problems they had in New York.

My parents started attending the Glendora Congregation in 1961. My mother had a strange feeling about the congregation. There was something going on there that just didn't feel right. There was a huge exodus of people leaving this congregation's Kingdom Hall, too. So, my parents (probably mostly my mom) decided to go to the Azusa Kingdom Hall instead. The ironic thing is, we lived only about a hundred yards from the Azusa congregation's territory line. As it turned out that hundred yards would change our family's life forever.

Mom requested her Publisher record cards to turn in to her new Kingdom Hall. In those days, you had to go to the Bible study overseer to get your record cards. These cards reported all your Field Service activity and any other information a new congregation might need to know about you. They like to keep close tabs on everyone.

They don't give these cards to the Publishers themselves any more. Now, they mail them to your new congregation. The reason is that people would get their cards and throw them away and stop being Jehovah's Witnesses. The Society wants to know if you quit nowadays. Why is that? The only reason I can think of is so they can punish you. They want to be able tell everyone that a certain Brother or Sister is no longer a Jehovah's Witness. That way, they can make sure everyone knows when you leave. No fading allowed. Let the shunning begin!

Something strange happened when Mom requested the cards. Instead of Mom getting the cards, the Brothers in charge said they wanted to meet with my parents. Back in the 1960s, there were three Brothers in charge of the congregation: the overseer, the assistant overseer and the theocratic ministry overseer or the Bible study overseer.

At the meeting, the three Brothers requested my parents stay in the Glendora congregation. In essence, they needed to stop the exodus out of the Glendora Kingdom Hall. Since my family was well known in the hall, they chose to make an example of us. There really was no rule about going to a congregation outside your territory, so my parents held their ground.

My parents ended up writing a letter to the Brooklyn Bethel, the headquarters of the organization, to complain about these overseers. My parents didn't know it at the time, but the letter that they wrote was not confidential. The headquarters forwards all letters to your overseers or Elders. So, these overseers got really mad. There were more meetings and more yelling. At one point, they called my father "a monkey on a string." I'm not sure what that means. Whatever it meant, my dad didn't like it and let them have it. I heard there was a lot of yelling and name calling that went on in those meetings.

All my parents wanted to do was go to a different Kingdom Hall. It ended up with my mother being publicly reproved and my father dis-fellowshipped for "slander and rebelliousness against the organization." They said they would have dis-fellowshipped my mother, too, but she had a bad heart and the shock might kill her. They were right, it would have killed her.

For many years, when you got dis-fellowshipped or publicly reproved, the presiding overseer would announce your expulsion/reproof, and they would announce the sin you committed to justify this action to the whole congregation.

"Brother Jones has been dis-fellowshipped for immorality!"

"Sister Smith has been publicly reproved for gossiping and drunkenness."

The Society stopped doing that years ago. Why? Because they thought it was a cruel and unloving thing to do? No. I'm sure they would still love to do it that way. They stopped announcing the nature of the sin because they were being sued for defamation of character and losing these court cases.

 I'm guessing my father could have done some activity that might have deserved this kind of punishment. So maybe on some level he did get justice. On the other hand, my mother was the perfect Jehovah's Witness follower and what they did to her stabbed her through the heart.

This treatment by the Witnesses totally destroyed our family. My father blamed my mother and her religion for his public humiliation. My mother was in total shock and disbelief that there could be such an injustice in Jehovah's loving organization.

My father ran a crew of about thirty men on a construction site. One day he overheard one of his men tell another: "You know Marty got kicked out of his church. What kind of terrible thing do you do to get kicked out of a church? Have sex with farm animals?" My father had a lot of pride, so this cut him to the core.

My father stopped going to most of the meetings. He didn't need any more humiliation. My mother was a diehard. She was never going to give up. She was more diligent than ever. Our whole family was of course shunned. So, we got the looks at the Kingdom Hall and the whispering behind our backs. She never flinched.

We ended up going to the Azusa congregation anyway. Why not? We had paid the price for wanting to go there already. Six months of faithful meeting attendance in her new congregation and her public reproof was lifted. My mother was in good standing again. True, she was forgiven, but do you think people in a small congregation really forget stuff like that?

My parents went to the circuit overseer to straighten this problem out. He was on his last trip through his circuit and didn't want to get involved. The next circuit overseer wasn't much better. Since these three Brothers were appointed by the Society and thus were considered appointed by god himself, they were untouchable.

Since my father was still dis-fellowshipped, in 1964, my parents flew back New York City to the world headquarters of the Jehovah's Witnesses. My parents wanted to plead their case to the big boys. They talked to Harley Miller in the service department. After hearing their story, he set up a special committee to retry their case. Finally, after three years, the matter was reopened. My parents were not just reinstated they were exonerated. It didn't matter anymore for my father. He would never be an active Jehovah's Witness again. He would lead my mother on by going to the meetings now and then and, of course, the Memorial/Passover every year. He was done. He would never let them hurt him that way ever again. He told me years later, "If that is what they call love, I'll go somewhere else." I thought my father was stupid and foolish back then, and I didn't believe him. Later, I saw at Bethel how right he was.

What happened to the three overseers who did this to my parents? Nothing happened to them. Oh, guess what? They all left the religion years later also.

According to the Society, all Elders and servants are appointed directly by god's Holy Spirit. So, I guess it was god who made the real mistake here, not these guys. Of course, whenever things like this happen in the organization, the Witnesses will be the first to tell you "we are all imperfect." Yet, why are you telling your people that god appoints your leaders? Just another Catch 22 in action.

Bottom line: Even though our family did nothing wrong, we were all still shunned by the Witnesses. So, shunning is not just reserved for wrongdoers. Anyone in good standing or not can experience this unique Jehovah's Witnesses' punishment.

There was one family that didn't shun me. Dale Young was basically my only childhood friend growing up. Both his brother Mitchell and his sister were very nice to me and my family.

Dale's sister was a courageous soul because she organized a couple of gatherings/parties for us young kids in the congregation. We set around and drank punch and ate potato chips. We even danced (slow dances only) no rock 'n roll of course and definitely no "twisting the night away." As the Jehovah's Witnesses kids of today know the devil's music will not be tolerated in anyway. Looking back at those gatherings, they were so benign and placid as to be laughable. So, of course, the Brothers had to talk to her father about them. The wild parties had to stop immediately. Everyone out of the pool!

Being a Jehovah's Witness kid wasn't easy. It was common to hear, "when in doubt, the answer is no!"

The few parties she gave was the extent of my social life growing up. Because of the disgrace of my parents, I was excluded from the majority of all other Witness gatherings.

I was shunned by the Jehovah's Witnesses and disliked by my schoolmates. A rock and a hard place.

However my path was clear back then, I was determined to show them all. I would become a super Jehovah's Witness. I would pioneer and go to Bethel. The word Bethel in the Bible means "The house of god." This was the world headquarters of the Watchtower Bible and Tract Society. To serve at the world headquarters was the ultimate privilege of service for young men my age in the organization.

I would show them all. Yes, I would make my god and family proud of me one day.

Chapter 9

Only About 90 Months Left

In March 1968, the Kingdom Ministry declared: "Just think Brothers, there are only about ninety months left before 6,000 years of man's existence on earth is complete." This date worked out to be October 1975.

Even though this was over fifty years ago, the Kingdom Ministry went on to state, "The majority of people living today will probably be alive when Armageddon breaks out, and there is *no* resurrection hope for those who are destroyed then. So now more than ever, it is vital not to ignore that spirit of wanting to do more."

The Society says they never pushed that date. What would *you* call it?

College for me could never be a consideration. There was no time for a worldly education with 1975 being just around the corner. After I graduated high school, I got a job at Taco Bell. I made $1.25 an hour, and I got my tacos at half price.

In May 1968, just two months after the Kingdom Ministry declaration, I moved to Kansas. There was no time to waste. I would be like so many other Jehovah's Witnesses and "move to where the need is greater." This was a phrase that was used a lot back in the 1960s and 1970s. It meant that people who were bored, tired or just super zealous would contact the Society to find out where there was a need for more Brothers and their families. These were places where the ratio of Witnesses to normal people was well above the national average. These places were usually rural communities in the Midwest or Deep South. The Society would send you a list of congregations. If you answered the call, you would quit your job, sell your house and move to the other end of the country to help out a "weak" congregation.

This was used as a status symbol many times. Brothers and Sisters would be quick to point out how they gave up good jobs or business opportunities for the sake of putting the "kingdom interest" first. They would point out how they sold off everything and moved to an area that needed help. As if to say, "Look at us. We are so spiritual that we are willing to give up our comfortable lives and move to Timbuktu to serve the Lord."

A person couldn't help but notice that many times these families were not necessarily stronger and didn't become pillars in their new congregations. Instead, like most people, they brought their problems with them.

In 1968, I saw the movie *Doctor Zhivago*. There is a famous line about Pasha as he is running down the battlefield with shells exploding everywhere. "Happy men don't usually volunteer." I had no idea what that meant at the time.

Years later, I found out exactly what it meant.

Some made a life in their new locales, while others headed back home after a few years. Many never did fit in and felt out of place. Plus, many of the locals didn't like these strange newcomers with their uppity we-are-here-to-help-you-hicks-out attitudes. Many of the locals didn't like the idea that they needed to be helped out in the first place.

In Kansas, most of the Witness pioneers were from the Pacific Northwest or California.

Some of these Brothers had a little money saved up after they sold everything off. Others, like myself, had to find employment working for minimum wage. They soon found out there was a reason many of these remote and rural areas didn't have a lot of Jehovah's Witnesses in them. There was little or no work. The attitude was: No worries. Armageddon is coming soon, and we'll make do. Besides, Jehovah will provide for us since we are putting him first in our lives. We are willing to sacrifice our time and comforts for happier times in the near future, when the new system will be here.

From the 1880s until this day, the Society has talked about the sins of materialism. There have been many articles in their publications about the evils of collecting material things. The scriptures have said, "Store up your treasures in Heaven not here on Earth." The Witnesses have driven this point home at their conventions. They will tell you that the love of money is the root of all evil. Yes, Jesus loved the poor and as the scriptures say, "It's easier for a camel to get through the eye of a needle than for a rich man to enter the kingdom of God." So, making lots of money was definitely frowned upon.

Thus, many of the Witnesses would wear their poverty like cloaks of honor. They didn't pursue worldly educations or good jobs, and they didn't like the Brothers and Sisters that did.

Sometimes they would make snide comments to others who had more than them. "Hey, Brother, nice new car!" This was not a compliment. This really meant, "Looks like you're doing too much overtime at work." Some would fire back, "Well, Jehovah has blessed me."

"Oh really? So, Jehovah is blessing you and cursing me because I'm poor?"

We finally got new light on the matter. They told us at a Circuit Assembly not to say, "Jehovah is blessing me" anymore when it came to money. They didn't want the poorer Brothers to think they weren't being blessed, too.

There have been many celebrities and sports stars that gave up good careers in "the world" to serve the lord. Many of the Witnesses didn't like Michael Jackson or Prince, who were raised as Jehovah's Witness. The Society loved the money they gave them, but they never approved of their lifestyle. The ones that did give everything up were touted as heroes and examples to the rest of us.

I have heard that the there was a brief window of time where the Society relaxed the rules on higher education. It only lasted a few years. Now young Jehovah's Witnesses are very much discouraged from pursuing higher education.

In my generation, this was not the case. Just another thing on which the Society has back peddled on.

Around 1995, when I was still a Jehovah's Witness, something strange happened. I was a real estate agent in Portland, Oregon. I met a real estate investor from California. He had made a fortune in the real estate market in the San Francisco Bay Area in the 1960s and 1970s. One day we were both in my car looking for his next investment property. I was very intrigued about his career in real estate. "Steve, what was your most interesting real estate deal?"

He got a slight smile on his face. "Do you mean strange or where I made the most money?"

"I don't know," I said. "How about strangest."

"Well, in 1973 I bought this guy's house in San Jose. What was strange was he wanted to sell his house to me, but he didn't want to move. He and his wife wanted to rent the house from me."

"Why would he do that?" I asked.

"Well," he said, "it turned out he was in some crazy religion that believed the world was going to end in 1975! Can you believe that shit?"

"Ah…yes…I guess I can. Was he a Jehovah's Witness?" I asked. "I think he was. Why?"

I just had to say it. "Because I'm a Jehovah's Witness too." He grew silent.

"So how did it turn out with you and this guy?" I asked.

"Not good," he said. "When the end of the world didn't come in 1975, real estate in the Bay Area started to go through the roof. I had to keep raising the rent on him. Finally, he had to move out five years later because he couldn't afford to live in his own house anymore. I sold the house four years after that and made over $300,000 on the deal. He was a real idiot for sure." Steve couldn't help but rub it in about how stupid this guy was. I wondered to myself how many other Witnesses had done something similar.

This was just one guy out of thousands of people who bought into the 1975 prediction. To people outside the Jehovah's Witnesses, we must have looked like total nut jobs.

After the bubble burst in 1975, and god failed to make his presence known yet one more time, Jehovah's Witnesses relocating all over the country pretty much slowed to a trickle.

Somehow, moving to Farmerville, Louisiana, Salina, Kansas, or Narragansett, Rhode Island, didn't seem like such a great idea anymore. I had moved to all three of these locations.

No one, including the Watchtower Bible and Tract Society, really knew when Armageddon was going to happen now, so for most of the Jehovah's Witnesses it was time to stay put.

Chapter 10

Kansas and The Beach Boys

After high school in 1968, my mother and I decided that the best thing for me was to move back to Salina, Kansas. The "need was great" there, and the Witnesses needed pioneers. My mother told me not to tell my father about these plans. She said he wouldn't understand, so she would break the news to him herself. That was fine with me. I didn't really care for my father at that time. The reason being was that he wasn't taking the spiritual lead in our family anymore. Dad had bailed out of the program, and I hated him for that. My mother also did a good job in driving a wedge between him and me. She would consistently tell me what a disappointment he was. Maybe she was afraid I would pick up some of his bad habits. Just another classic case how this religion can split up families.

My dad told me years later that my mother never did tell him I was moving out. He came home from work one day and asked her where I was. With a blank look on her face, she told him that I had moved to Kansas to pioneer. He wept. I never even said goodbye to him. I have no idea what sick pleasure my mother got out of doing that.

I was eighteen, and I was on a grand adventure, moving 1,500 miles away. I packed up my 1956 Ford and headed south two miles to Foothill Boulevard, which was the old Route 66. I turned left and just kept going right out of Los Angeles. Though I have visited the Los Angeles area many times over the years, I really never thought of that area as home. It was a strange world I grew up in, with no friends outside the faith and few friends in the faith. I really never did fit in back then. There was a huge sense of freedom yet sadness, too, when I left. On some level, I don't think I really ever had a childhood. I was taught to be strong and independent; to act like an adult from an early age. My religion and my mother told me the only approval I needed was Jehovah's. That was how I lived my life. So, with my Bible in my hand, I went to Kansas to save the world. The problem was, I couldn't even save myself.

Wherever you go, that's where you will be.

One of the first things I saw once as I crossed the border into Kansas was a bumper sticker that said, "Suicide is redundant if you live in Kansas."

I got to Salina at about 1:30 in the morning. I ended up spending my first night in Salina, Kansas, in jail. It was too late to get a motel. I really didn't want to spend the money anyway for just a few hours of sleep. So, I drove to a city park and tried to sleep in my car. At about 5:30 in the morning, a cop knocked on my window with his flashlight. After talking to him for a few minutes, he was convinced that I was a runaway and a draft dodger. So down to the police station we went. I convinced the cop to wait a few hours before we started calling everyone to prove my story was true. I never told any of the local Brothers I was moving there. I'm sure the congregation overseer Merle Freeman was quite surprised to get a call from the police asking if he knew me. Merle came down to the police station. After the police heard his story and mine, they let me go. Merle had a strange look on his face as he shook my hand on the sidewalk and welcomed me to Kansas. I worried that it was only my first day there, and I was already getting a bad reputation with the local Witnesses.

The congregation in Salina included about eighty Publishers. It was a mix of farmers and city folks. There were three to four families who had moved in from other states to help out. I was the only Pioneer there at the time.

I rented a room in some old lady's basement for $45 a month. I got a job at a hamburger joint called Sandy's. It was just like McDonalds only with a different name. Yes, Jehovah did indeed take care of me, I thought. I was now making $1.40 an hour. I made $30 to $35 a week, plus I didn't have to worry about food because I could buy hamburgers for only 15 cents each.

I was completely devastated when I was fired from Sandy's on Easter Sunday in 1969 because I wouldn't pass out chocolate Easter eggs. I was working on the French fryer when the assistant manager Hank told me to take the window so Billy could go on break. I told him, "Fine but I will not be passing out any Easter eggs." Hank told me I would pass them out or find another job. I took off my apron and left. As a good Jehovah's Witness, I would have nothing to do with any worldly holidays, especially Easter.

The funny thing is, my roommate and Pioneer partner, Roy Baty, got fired too. He wasn't even working the window. Sandy's manager, Gary Kerscher, had to go into work, in spite of his holiday, because without me, the restaurant was shorthanded. Gary's face was beet red, and he was mad as hell when he walked through the door. He looked right at Roy, who was working the grill, and said, "Do you believe the same way Keith does?" Roy said, "Yes, I do." Gary said, "Then get the hell out of here!"

Back in the 1960s, you could still fire people because of their religious beliefs.

I tell people to this day that I thank god I was fired from Sandy's or I would still be working there to this day.

Many of the Pioneers I pioneered with were janitors. This way they could work at night and knock on doors during the day, plus you could make more than minimum wage. In Kansas, over 90 percent of all the Pioneers were from somewhere else. There were even some "special" Pioneers serving there. They would put in 150 hours of Field Service per month. They were directly assigned to be there by the Society. They were paid $100 a month if they made their time quota. As a regular Pioneer, we were required to put in 100 hours a month of Field Service. There was no financial assistance for us. We were on our own.

My Pioneer partner Roy Baty was from Southern California, also. He showed up in Salina in the fall of 1968. He was quite a sight in his 1958 Dodge pickup with his German shepherd tagging along. He, too, had come to serve "where the need was greater." He told me years later he really didn't want to pioneer. He did it so he could get a 4-D classification so he wouldn't have to go into the Army and end up in Vietnam. We became good friends there in Kansas and were Bethel roommates. He followed me to Louisiana where he worked for me in Trim Line. He later moved to Oregon. He was in my wedding, and I was his best man in his wedding. Still, he has not talked to me in over 18 years because I'm no longer a Jehovah's Witness. He told me he wouldn't talk to me because I had "burnt that bridge." Yes, I guess he is right. I have burned that bridge.

July 12, 1968, was a strange night for me. The Beach Boys had a concert that night at the Memorial Hall in Salina. The concert was one block away from my apartment. As I was lying on my bed in my basement apartment, I could hear them sing every song with the roar of the crowds in the background. I had grown up in Southern California and now it seemed Southern California had followed me here. I lay there thinking about all the fun things I never did, the high school dances and games I never went to. How I missed my high school class graduation and the all-night trip to Disneyland. I had no class pictures and no class ring. I never dated a girl or even kissed one. I felt very alone that night in that dark basement, but nothing would shake my faith. I knew that I had given up all these things so I could serve my god, Jehovah.

I think back to that night now and wonder what would have happened if I got out of my bed and went to the concert. Just one of the many missed opportunities because of my Jehovah's Witness belief system.

It seems I had grown up in Southern California in the 1960s and missed the whole experience of living in that magical time period.

Chapter 11
"Have Sword will Travel"

Roy Baty and Tom Ottowell were my first roommates in Kansas. Roy and I moved into Tom's duplex. That turned out to be a total disaster. Roy put his dog in the basement. We came home from Field Service one day to find Roy's dog had completely destroyed everything Tom had stored down there. Plus, Roy hadn't been down there in a couple of days so there was dog shit everywhere. We told Roy that either he or his dog had to go. We all ended up renting a one-bedroom duplex on Crawford Street. The rent was only $90 a month. Tom got the upstairs bedroom and Roy and I shared the basement area without the dog.

Tom was a diabetic and a strange duck. He was studying to become a Jehovah's Witness. He had a college education and was a draftsman and engineer for Beech Air Craft. You couldn't ask for two people so totally different from each other than Tom and Roy. Roy was a five-foot, three-inch redhead who was literally bouncing off the walls with nervous energy. At Bethel, he would get the nickname "The Banty Rooster." Tom stood at six-foot, four-inches and walked around like a ghost. Tom loved to walk around the house munching on a bag of Doritos. He would walk into a room, look around and just say, "Hmm." Years later, I found out his wife would call him "the professor." All I have to say about that is, "Hmm."

I spent most of my time with Roy since we not only worked together at Sandy's but pioneered together too. To be honest, Roy was a strange duck, too. He was raised as a Jehovah's Witnesses also. His mother was one of the "Anointed Ones."

The Anointed Ones are a very small group of Jehovah's Witnesses that plan to go to heaven and not live forever in a paradise Earth like the rest of us. They believe, according to Revelation, that this number would be only 144,000. Back in the Sixties, there were just a few thousand Anointed Ones out of millions of Witnesses. Even though the Society says the number of Anointed Ones should be dwindling down, the opposite is true. Almost 50 years later and their numbers are about the same. Just one of many strange things the Society can't really explain.

One time when Roy's mother was staying with us, I heard her say, "Please god, take me out of here. I'm sick of this place." I don't think she was talking about our house in Kansas. I think she mean the planet Earth. Maybe she was tired of this place and wanted to go home. She didn't seem to be a very happy person, just like my mother. Roy's father reminded me of my pussy-whipped father. Roy's mother and my strange mother were the ones who thought becoming a Jehovah's Witness was a great idea in the first place.

The beat goes on.

Roy would love to argue for hours on why Dodges were better than Chevys or Fords. I really didn't care, but it seemed to matter to him. Roy was one of those people who always needed to be right about everything. On the other hand, he introduced me to the wonderful music of Bob Dylan and Joan Collins. My favorites at the time were Simon and Garfunkel.

I was very self-righteous back then. I was a full-time minister for the Lord. I knew everything about everything. I even printed a business card that would tell people how wonderful I was. It said:

"Have Sword will Travel"

Contact

Casarona—Salina Kansas

SS AAA

Have Gun – Will Travel was a 1950s Western TV series. It starred Richard Boone as Paladin, the gun fighter for hire. I thought of myself as a spiritual gun fighter. The word "sword" has been used to mean the Bible at times. As for the SS, it meant Sacred Service. The AAA meant I was only "Available After Armageddon" for marriage. I was so full of myself.

For two years, I dealt with hot Kansas summers and cold Kansas winters. We would spend our days driving down dusty country roads, looking for god's lost sheep. Some of the territories were called "unassigned territories." These were areas that were not assigned to any congregations and hadn't been worked in Field Service for many years. We would roll up to their farms with a cloud of dust trailing behind us. A pack of dogs would come running out from behind the barn. The first thing the dogs would do is piss all over our tires. We would jump out of the cars in our suits and ties and try to tell the farmers about god's coming New World Order. People would tell us about the last time someone had shown up at their door to talk to them about the Bible many years ago. They told us the people had called themselves "Russelites" or "The Bible Students." These were names used by the Jehovah's Witnesses before 1935. They were probably preaching the end of the world to them way back then, too. I met a woman in Salina in the door-to-door ministry that told me, "I had a hard time getting rid of the last Witnesses at my door with their phonograph."

Back in the 1940s, the Witnesses were issued phonographs. They would ring your doorbell and set up their phonograph on your front steps and turn it on. You would then hear "Judge" (self-proclaimed title) Rutherford screaming out how "religion is a snare and a racket." Joe Rutherford was the second president of the Watchtower Bible and Tract Society. If anyone knew how corrupt religion was, it was good ole' Joe for sure, because he lived like a king back in the Great Depression. He had two Packards (these were the most expensive cars built at the time) and most of the time lived in his mansion called Beth Sarim in San Diego.

Beth Sarim is Hebrew for "House of the Princes." Beth Sarim was a ten-bedroom mansion, constructed in 1929.

The Judge had a problem, however; how could he build this mansion and justify it to his followers, many of whom had no jobs in the Great Depression? Joe decided that Beth Sarim wasn't for him. As noted in the Society's publications, it was built for various resurrected Old Testament patriarchs or prophets. Yes, Abraham, Moses, David, Isaiah and Samuel were all supposed to be resurrected together and live with the Judge in his new mansion. Yeah, that's the ticket. In fact, the good Judge even added their names to the title of the house. However, until they showed up, the Judge used Beth Sarim as his personal winter home and executive office for the Society until the day he died.

There were seven small cabins on the property. The cabins were there for his servants and private female secretaries. Two of these secretaries, Berta Peale and Bonnie Boyd, enjoyed many trips to Europe every year with the good Judge. Bonnie Boyd was only sixteen years old when she was invited to Bethel. She was Rutherford's personal secretary. When this young woman arrived at Bethel, she was immediately given a job as Rutherford's personal dietician, although she had no experience or training in that field, and Rutherford already had a man in this position at that time.

Berta Peale, just before her death, confessed in a committee meeting with president Knorr himself, that she and Rutherford had been more than just friends. She said, "He was like a husband to me in every way." Knorr had already known about Rutherford's drunken sexual escapades. Knorr did nothing to Berta and she was told to remain silent. She was one of the Anointed Ones.

Maybe she and the Judge are having a great time ruling like Kings and Priests up in heaven together.

The Judge died before the dead Bible characters could show up and live with him. Rutherford wanted to be buried there at Beth Sarim and rumor has it that he was. The city of San Diego refused the request for his burial on the property. However, they say he is buried under six inches of concrete under the garage floor. Maybe his two Packards are there alongside him, too.

If you don't think he is buried there, just go to his gravesite. The only problem is he doesn't seem to have one. Never mind that the fourth president of the Jehovah's Witnesses, Fred Franz, confirmed in an interview that Rutherford was buried at Beth Sarim. The house was secretly sold off in 1948.

This is just one more reminder of all of the failed prophecies and crazy leaders that have been instrumental in the shaping of this strange religious group. Of course, these have been a huge embarrassment to the Society over the years. Needless to say, Beth Sarim's history is quite interesting. If you are interested in more information about Beth Sarim, just go to the Jehovah's Witness website and type in the words "Beth Sarim" and you will find… nothing.

Even though the leaders of the Jehovah's Witnesses can erase all of the real history of their organization on their website, I'm afraid the internet isn't as kind. God, I do love the age of information!

Meanwhile, back to the farmers in Kansas. From their perspective, it must have been pretty strange to be living in the middle of nowhere and have people like us come to their doors every twenty to thirty years, dressed in our suit and ties, Bible in hand, preaching the end of the world. Don't worry if you are not home. We will catch you again in another thirty or forty years.

Sometimes we would turn off the county road and drive down a driveway over half of a mile long. We would come to some old farmhouse that looked abandoned back in the Great Depression. Rags for window curtains blowing in the breeze. We would poke around and look into the windows only to be scared out of our wits to find someone living there. We met some strange people in those remote rural counties, maybe almost as strange as us. It's all a matter of perspective, isn't it?

The goal of the Field Service was to start Bible studies. The only Bible studies I had in Kansas were with boys whose mothers were Witnesses. Their fathers were nonbelievers. Sixteen-year-old Ralph Martin was one of them. His father, Alfred, had been a Witness for many years and had even gone to prison during the Second World War for being a conscientious objector.

There are a lot of strange circumstances for leaving the Witnesses. Alfred's reason was one of the strangest.

In the ministry school, all the publishers were required to give Bible-based talks in front of the congregation. At the end of the talk, the school overseer would grade your talk in front of the whole congregation. If you didn't master one of the points you were working on, like pausing or gesturing, the school overseer would mark your grade slip with a "good," "needs work" or "weak."

Our ministry school overseer, Brother Smith, looked and talked just like Elmer Fudd. Sometimes, he even had a slight stutter. So, one night, Alfred Martin had a student talk. After he gave his talk and sat back down with his family in the audience, Smith told him he would be marked "weak" on the point he was working on. He would have to work on that point again in his next talk in the ministry school. There would be no next talk for Alfred Martin because Alfred stood up from his seat and pointed his bony finger at the school overseer and said, "How can anyone who talks like you tell me how to talk?" He picked up his wife and kids and left the Kingdom Hall and never came back.

His wife Ida and kids did come back to the meetings, but he never did. I had a Bible study with Alfred's son Ralph in the basement of their farmhouse in Brookville. The rafters of that basement were crammed with guns and thousands of rounds of ammunition. I asked Ralph about all the guns. He told me, "My father put them there for when the great tribulation starts. He wants to be ready. He believes all the Witnesses from town will be coming to our farm for protection." Alfred Martin's farm in Brookville, Kansas, was to become our next Noah's Ark. That never happened, of course. A few years later, Alfred was able to make use of one of his many fire arms. He went into the basement and took one of those guns from the rafters and went out to his barn where he killed himself.

One of my first male role models in the Witnesses was John Norman. He was the head of one of the families that moved to Kansas "where the need was greater." He ruled his family with an iron fist. He was from Houma, Louisiana, and acted like a true Southern gentleman. His wife, Beverly, seemed to adore him. They had five kids. He was a hard man. One of my fondest memories was of us sitting around his potbelly stove in his basement. It was 10 degrees below zero outside with snow piled up around his house. We were drinking Jack Daniels and telling jokes.

Another unusual person I liked to hang out with was Grace Green. Sometimes, when it was over 100 degrees out and I was in the Field Service, I would find a way to be in her neighborhood where a glass of iced tea might be waiting for me. She was a widow with two small children, Matthew and Kimberly. She lived in a small house next to the old Schilling Air Force Base. She didn't have a job. Her husband fell out of a tree onto a concrete patio to his death. I guess she was still living off the insurance money. She was one of the first people I had ever met who loved to explore and examine people's personalities. She could read your handwriting, and she loved personality tests. It was at her house that I first took the Lüscher color test. She was very outgoing and didn't mind talking about anything. She was my first experience with a confident and assertive female.

While I was in Salina, she met and fell in love with Bill Frazier. Bill wasn't a Witness at the time. He had been married to a Witness who had died. He had two children who were raised as Witnesses, Becky and Jetta. Since Bill wasn't baptized, this courtship was highly disapproved of and Grace became the subject of some nasty gossip. Witnesses are commanded in the Bible to "marry only in the Lord," and Bill was still considered a pagan. If Bill wanted Grace, he had to start studying the Bible with Jehovah's Witnesses, which he did. After he was baptized, they were then free to marry each other. I liked Bill. He seemed like a regular kind of guy. Years later, he got stuffy and self-righteous. He hired me to work for him after I got fired from Sandy's. I went from $1.45 an hour at Sandy's to $2.50 an hour working for Bill. For about eight months, things were great. Then Bill and Grace decided to move to Holton, Kansas, to where the "need was even greater" than Salina. It seemed Grace wanted to prove to everyone how Bill was now a spiritual giant by moving to some small congregation in the middle of nowhere.

Years later, Grace and Bill moved to Reno where they both drove school buses to make a living. They both died before god could bring his promised paradise to them.

One of Bill's daughters told me how she and her sister called Bill in the hospital before he died. He was losing his long fight with Hodgkin's lymphoma. Bill hadn't talked to his daughters in years because they both had drifted away from the faith. They gathered up all the courage they had to call him that one last time. The conversation went something like this.

"Hello? Dad, it's Becky and me. We just wanted to call you and tell you how much we love you." All Bill could get out was. "Oh, really?"

"Yes! Dad we really do."

"Well, I don't have time to talk to you now. I'm too busy dying!" Then he hung up on them. Needless to say, the girls were crushed.

Bill was an Elder in the local Kingdom Hall. What a guy. Still, to this day, there are tens of thousands of Witnesses who will not talk to their children because they have left their parents church.

Grace too would have the opportunity to shun her children.

A few years after Bill died, Grace moved back to Nebraska and remarried. For a while, she lived in a home just two doors down from her oldest son, Matt, and his two children and wife. Matt died in his sleep one night.

Because Matt's funeral wasn't in a Jehovah's Witness Kingdom Hall but at the funeral home, neither Grace nor her new husband went to his funeral. I guess she didn't mind living a few doors away from Matt but going to his funeral was just too much for her. What did Matt do to be shunned even after his death? Was he dis-fellowshipped? No. Was he disassociated? No. He just stopped going to meetings. He faded. Yes, you can still be shunned by the Jehovah's Witnesses even if you are dead.

"Love never fails."

It was in Kansas that I started up the ranks of the spiritual hierarchy. First, as a full-time Pioneer, then as a Ministerial Servant. I was given a book-study group to preside over. As book-study conductor, I would be in charge of the book study in a private home one day a week and then lead the group in Field Service on the weekends. I was only 19 years old, yet I was presiding over people who had been in the organization for more than 40 years.

In September 1969, just before I turned 20, I turned in my application to go to Bethel.

After I filled out the application and gave it to my circuit overseer, Don Breaux, he had one question for me. "I need to ask you something."

But before he could ask me his question, I blurted out,

"Forever, of course!"

Confused he said, "What?"

So, I said slowly, "I'll be at Bethel forever!"

"Oh," he said, with a smile on his face. "I need to ask you what your draft board classification is."

"Oh, 4-D (minister classification)." I really wanted to impress Don. He too had gone to Bethel at a young age and served there for five years. He and his young bride, Karen, became special pioneers and went to serve in West Virginia for another five years. He was now in his late twenties and already a circuit overseer in charge of half the congregations in Kansas. He looked like JFK and everyone knew the Society had big plans for him. He was on his way. He was my hero and one of my first real role models for sure.

It was time for me to be on my way too. Things were getting tough for me in Salina. Bill Frazier had moved to Holton, Kansas, so I didn't have a job anymore. Roy had moved, too, so I was on my own, no job and no pioneer partner. Many days, I would be out in Field Service by myself, trying to get in my allotted hours. The snow was blowing and it could be twenty degrees below zero. Sometimes I would do a "back call" (now they are called "return visits") at one end of the town and drive clear to the other end of town to do another one, only to head back to where I had started from again. I knew I was kidding myself. Something needed to change. I was lonely and afraid of my future.

My "privilege of service" in Kansas wasn't looking too bright. I didn't want to go back to California and as the bumper sticker said, "Suicide is redundant if you live in Kansas."

Then the letter arrived in February of 1970.

Chapter 12
Bethel the House of God

I ripped open the letter to discover my Bethel application had been accepted. They wanted me to report to the headquarters of the Watchtower Bible and Tract Society on March 23, 1970. I was thrilled to say the least. My prayers had been answered. My new life at the Lord's House could now begin. Kurt Vonnegut once said it so perfectly: "I went to New York to be born again."

I sold off and gave away everything I owned. There was no need for any of it. A couple of bags of clothing were all I would need. My sister, Carol, got my car. My mother and she had moved to Manhattan, Kansas, the year before to serve where "the need was greater." Mom had wanted my sister to go to her last year of high school in Kansas and not California with all its worldly influences.

I found out years later that she had never told my father about her move to Kansas. He found out after she was on the road heading east. He came home from work one day to find a homemade pie on the kitchen counter. She had made his favorite kind of pie—my mother could be a very thoughtful person. Under the pie was a note. "Carol and I have moved to Kansas. You can do what you want now. Love, Norma." I guess, just like my grandfather, she didn't like to tell people where she was going. My mother knew Armageddon was coming soon and she didn't want to be in Southern California when it happened. It turned out that my mom left my father many times over the ensuing years. She always came back, though, until the final time when she left him and she didn't come back. He always supported her and sent her money no matter where she was living. In his own strange way, he really loved her. However, she treated him like shit for not being the "spiritual head" of our family.

The Salina congregation gave me a going away party. Cake, coffee and a few old ladies were there. My friends Tom and Judy Yahtzee were also there, to wish me well. They had moved to Kansas from Colorado to help out our struggling congregation. Tom had always felt bad because he didn't go to Bethel like his older brother Walter. No glory for Tom, he was just a good Publisher with a wife and two kids. I thought about Tom years later at Bethel, how he had always wanted the glory of Bethel service. It would take a few years at Bethel for me to realize he had what I wanted all along: to be normal, with a wife and a couple of kids. But at the time I felt sorry for him because he had missed out on the grand adventure.

I decided to go to New York a few days early. The reason being Saturday, March 21st, was the Passover or the Memorial of Christ's death. This is the most important day of the year among Jehovah's Witnesses. For many people who still call themselves Jehovah's Witnesses but are inactive, this is the only meeting they still attend. What better place to attend the Memorial than the world headquarters—the home of our president N.H Knorr and the Governing Body. This was the "Holy of Holies."

I landed at La Guardia Airport at about 6 p.m. on Friday, March 20th. There was no welcoming committee. There wouldn't be, since nobody knew I was coming. I was looking forward to my first taxi ride. I must have looked pretty confused standing on the curb in front of the airport. A nice older Italian guy picked up my bags and put them in his cab.

"What are you waiting for?" He asked. "Get in." I did and we were off.

"Where to?" He asked.

I got out my letter. "124 Columbia Heights, that's in

Brooklyn."

"Okay, have you ever been there before?" "Nope," I said.

"So, where did you fly in from, kid?"

"Kansas."

"Kansas? Have you ever been to New York before?"

"Yes. My dad's family are from the Bronx. But I don't know anything about Brooklyn."

"Well, welcome. It's going to be a little bit of a trip, but I'll get you there, buddy."

"Great."

He got me there all right, but it turned out to be the most expensive cab ride of my life. I saw most of Brooklyn and parts of Queens. I think I saw the Verrazano Bridge at least twice.

He talked about his family and crazy wife. I talked about moving to the world headquarters of the Jehovah's

Witnesses. He wasn't impressed at all. I guess he got tired of talking to me because after two hours he dropped me off in front of the building at 124 Columbia Heights. The massive red brick building has a huge three-story watch tower on its top. The building was bought in 1909 and refurbished as a dormitory in 1927. This building symbolized the world headquarters of the Jehovah's Witnesses.

He got my bags out of the trunk and put them by the front door.

"How much do I owe you?" I asked.

$109.50 kid," he said.

I gave him $110 and started walking toward my bags.

"Hey, kid! What, no tip? You're in New York now, not Kansas anymore…you got to tip here!"

I turned around and gave him another $10. He never even thanked me. I had come to New York with $300, and I was down to $180.

Thirty-eight years later, I worked as a cab driver in Portland, Oregon. I would have never dreamed of ripping someone off, like he did to me. The cab ride should have been only twenty minutes and not two hours.

At the time, the cab fare didn't matter. I would have given him everything I had to get to that spot. I was standing in front of the 124 building, the world headquarters. This truly was one of the defining moments of my life. Everything before this was just preparation for what was on the other side of those doors. I made it. The rest of my life would be gravy from here on out.

I grabbed my bags and went through the doors and up a couple of steps. There was a guy on the phone at the reception desk. He seemed about my age. I stood there until he looked up.

He put his hand over the receiver. "Can I help you?"

"Yes, I'm Keith…Keith Casarona."

"Okay, Keith. Can I help you?"

"I'm here to report for Bethel service."

He got a disgruntled look on his face and went back to talking on the phone. "Hey, Tom, I'll call you back later. I got a new boy here I need to deal with."

He hung up the phone and opened a desk draw. He got out a list and started looking at it.

"What's your name again?"

"Keith Casarona."

"When were you supposed to check in anyway?"

"Monday, the 23rd."

He gave me another disgruntled look. "This is Friday the 20th."

"Yes, I know. I decided to come early."

He shook his head. "You decided to come early…great. Do me a favor and grab your bags and wait in the lounge." He pointed straight ahead. "This could take a while."

As I grabbed my bags and walked into the lounge, I thought to myself that "new boy" was a strange term. I dropped my bags into a chair and looked out of the picture windows at the views of the New York harbor and the Brooklyn Bridge. There were thousands of twinkling lights all over lower Manhattan. The lounge looked like something out of the 1940s art deco with its overstuffed couches. There was a big black piano in the corner begging for someone to play some George Gershwin melodies. A group of young men and women chatted in the corner. The happiest moments of my Bethel experience proved to be those first few minutes standing there in the lounge of the 124 building, overlooking the East River. I was home at last.

The Society has owned some of the most expensive pieces of real estate in all of Brooklyn. The Brooklyn Heights area is one of the most upscale neighborhoods in all of New York. Just below the 124 building is the world-famous promenade where dozens of motion pictures have been made over the years. This included *Annie Hall*, *Moonstruck* and dozens of others

Years later, the Society would sell off most of these properties for hundreds of millions of dollars.

Just across the East River, the World Trade Centers were under construction in lower Manhattan. I had no idea at the time, that on the very day those buildings were destroyed on 9/11, I too would lose most of my relatives and all my friends.

I continued to look out the windows until the brother from the front desk came and got me.

"This is Larry," he said, introducing me to another brother. "He'll show you to your room." I grabbed my bags and we headed out the front door and across the street, down about one-hundred yards to the 129 building. This older, rundown apartment building still had some "worldly" people living in it.

"Where you from?" Larry asked.

"California, by way of Kansas."

"Oh, don't tell people you're from California."

"Why not?" I asked.

He smiled. "You'll find out."

We walked up two flights of stairs and came to apartment 33. Larry knocked on the door.

Some guy my age in pajamas opened the door.

Larry looked at him and said. "This is your new roommate." He turned and walked away.

My new roommate had a funny little smile on his face. "Hi

I'm Stanley, welcome to the Ritz. Right this way."

"I'm Keith."

I quickly discovered that the 800-square-foot apartment I was in had only one bedroom and one bathroom. Seven guys lived there, three guys in the living room, two guys in an alcove, and two guys in the ten-by-ten bedroom. The bedroom had two beds, two desks and two dressers. It was so small you had to go outside to change your mind. They put me in the bedroom with a Mexican kid from Texas. It turned out the 129 building was one of the oldest buildings the Society owned and definitely the most run down. It didn't get a major remodel until years later. Many "new boys" with little or no seniority started out there.

I threw my bags on the bed and looked at Gilbert. "I'm starving. Any place to get some food around here?"

"Well, there is a deli a couple blocks down the street if you have money. There is always breakfast tomorrow morning, I guess."

If you have money? Did some Bethelites not have money, I wondered.

This was the first day of my four-year journey, and my head was spinning with all kinds of questions.

Stanley took me back into the living room where I met a couple more of my new roommates.

"Hey guys, this is Keith … the new boy."

Chapter 13
The New Boy

The next morning was Saturday. I was up at 6:30 a.m., threw some clothes on, and headed to the 124 building for breakfast and my first "morning worship." Hundreds of Bethelites swarmed into the front entrance of the 124 building, since that was where most of the dining rooms were at that time. Some came in from underground tunnels from the 119 and 107 buildings. The Society owned about a half a dozen buildings in the Heights at the time and would be buying lots more over the next few years. The final count would be twenty properties before they started selling them all off in the mid-2000s.

Stanley said I could sit at his table since there was an extra space. We sat in the upper dinner room, which was full of tables that fit exactly ten people. Each table had a Table Head and a Table Foot. The Table Head was a Bethel Elder. The Table Foot was usually someone with some Bethel seniority.

I sat in amazement at how organized and perfect all the tables looked with all the cups, saucers and plates of china.

A middle-aged Sister smiled at me.

"Stanley, who is your new friend?"

"His name is Keith Casarona. He just got here."

"Welcome, Brother Casarona. I'm Sister Jones."

"Hi, I just…" Before I could say another word, a voice blared from all of the televisions mounted on the walls. It was none other than Brother Knorr himself, the president of the Society. He began his comments about the daily text. Sooner or later everyone in the Bethel family would have to make their comments about the text in front of all of us. We, too, would be on the text table and get a chance to share our thoughts and wisdom about every six months. Almost two thousand Bethelites, plus the governing body and all Bethel Elders, would watch as you sat in front of the cameras and spoke. Over the years, there would be thousands of different interpretations from the different members of the Bethel family. Some of them were on the strange side for sure.

As Knorr completed his text comments and made the last of his announcements, waiters began serving the food. Breakfast and lunch were the two best meals at the Lord's House, with dinner coming in a very distant third. At the time, most of the food was grown on the Society's own farms. Overall, the food was pretty good. "It's the best food in the world," some said. "Before they cooked it."

Some of the food would be on the tables before we got there. Other food would be placed next to the Table Head. The Table Head would pass the platters down one side first. When the platters were empty, they would pass them out to a waiter. The platters would come back a few minutes later, usually with less food on them. The Table

Head would then pass the platters down the opposite side of the table.

The table you were assigned was a big deal because you were usually sitting there for an hour or more each day. If we sat there longer, we usually had very cold food waiting for us.

Once Knorr's announcements were over, we had a prayer. Then everyone pulled out their white linen napkins that were folded and hidden under the table and put them on their laps. There wasn't much talking at the table as chowing down began. I had a thousand questions, but felt this wasn't the time or place to bring them up. I pulled out my napkin and started to place it on my lap.

The Table Head, who hadn't said a word to me as of yet, looked up from his scrambled eggs. "Brother, you need to put that napkin back where you found it."

"Okay." I folded the napkin and put it back under the table in its place.

Sister Jones piped in. "We all get one napkin a week for our personal use, and no matter where we sit, we don't use other people's napkins."

This would be just one of the hundreds of unwritten laws and codes of conduct that a person would need to know if they were to "dwell together in unity" at the Lord's House.

After about fifteen minutes of eating, everyone got up from their seats and pushed their chairs in. From the TVs, we heard Brother Knorr say a few words of prayer and breakfast was over. Some sat back down and kept on eating. If you worked in the home and not the factory, you had some extra time before you had to get to work at 8 a.m., since you didn't have the twenty-minute walk to the factory. Most everyone else would go to their job assignments immediately after breakfast.

Gilbert informed me that since I had come early, I needed to go to the Bethel office to check in.

Once there, I received my Bethel key, and a packet of documents and the booklet, *Dwelling Together in Unity*. My key number was 499. This key allowed me access to all of the major buildings the Society owned. The key was to be guarded with my life. If the key was lost, the wellbeing of two thousand Brothers and Sisters could be at risk. I looked at the key and wondered how many other people before me had been the proud owner of key 499. This key was also one of the ways you could be identified by other Bethelites.

The booklet, *Dwelling Together in Unity,* was not mine to keep. I had to read it and return it to the Bethel office. It was a private and confidential publication for Bethelite's eyes only. The booklet contained some of the many rules and regulations that a person needed to know. You had two-thousand roommates now. Lots to know. Everything from hygiene to marriage, from vacations to sickness. For example, if you were there less than five years and were sick too long, they would take your vacation time away from you. Years later, some brave soul snuck one of the booklets out and put it on the internet. Check it out. It's written by none other than the president himself, Mr. Knorr.

Even though he's been dead for over forty years, Nathan Homer Knorr is truly responsible for making what the Jehovah's Witnesses are today. He had more influence on the Jehovah's Witnesses than Charles Russel or Judge Rutherford put together.

There were a lot of documents I needed to sign before I could "join the club." I hardly read any of them. I believed there wasn't anything the Society would want me to do that wasn't in my best interest. One document was a bit strange. It was a form that said that the Society would have the right to keep my body, if I should die of natural or unnatural causes. Yes, even if I got murdered or decided to kill myself while at Bethel, Bethel still wanted what was left of me. While I was at Bethel, I did know of Bethelites that were either murdered or who killed themselves. They ended up being buried somewhere on the Watchtower farm.

So, what's the reason behind all this? Your guess is as good as mine.

Maybe the Society likes to spend money on funerals. No, I don't think so. What the Society does like is to stay out of lawsuits. Maybe those controlling your corpse can prevent some kind of legal action. Who knows? It doesn't matter. I signed everything that was put in front of me. I was never leaving Bethel before Armageddon anyway.

Chapter 14

Inwood

It turned out that in the spring of 1970, there were a lot of changes that were being made at Bethel. One of the major changes was that a Bethelite wasn't required to go to Kings County or the Brooklyn Heights congregations for six months before being assigned to a local Kingdom Hall in the New York City area. Since there was no waiting anymore, I was assigned to the Inwood congregation in Upper Manhattan as soon as I got there. It was at the very north end of Manhattan, just before entering the Bronx.

I was assigned there with John Adams, another new boy. We had arrived the same week. John was a quiet kind of guy who always had a strange, confused look on his face. His brother was a Bethel overseer. It was always a good thing, if you had some family members at Bethel. John's brother was a factory-floor overseer. If you were going to make Bethel your career, having family members there in positions of power helped for sure. It didn't help poor John, however. A couple of years later, John had a breakdown and tried to kill himself at the Watchtower farm. Having family around was a good thing as long as you were happy. If a person was not happy and wanted to leave Bethel – or leave the planet – you only received more guilt and shame.

On our first trip to the Inwood congregation, Daryl Christianson met John and me in front of the 124 building, and we headed to the subway station. The trip to our new congregation would take about an hour and it would be my first of thousands of subway rides over the years.

To say most Bethelites hated the subways back than was an understatement. There would be thousands of hours spent in those hot and dirty subway cars. Back in the early seventies, the cars were full of graffiti. Plus, late at night, it could be one of the most dangerous places if you were by yourself.

Once on the train, we met another Brother who was also going to the Inwood congregation. It turned out that this was going to be this Brother's last meeting. He had been at Bethel for four years. He had finished his four-year commitment and was now taking his leave. Daryl had just hit his four-year mark, too, but he was staying. My guess is, they had arrived together like John and I.

I couldn't help but think to myself, why would anyone ever leave Bethel, being so close to the important date of 1975? He didn't say much after we were introduced. I would find out later that guys who had been there awhile didn't have much to say to us new boys. We were in two different worlds. It was just like the guys in Vietnam who didn't have much to say to the new recruits. There was nothing you could tell them that they wouldn't figure out for themselves eventually, if they didn't get you or themselves killed first. He just sat there with his eyes glazed over, looking at the billboards and graffiti inside the subway car. It was one of his last subway rides, and he looked numb. I couldn't help but wonder what experiences he had enjoyed while he was there. His last day was my first day, so it seemed like the changing of the guard, so to speak.

After a few minutes, I had to ask, "So, since you have been here for four years, do you have any words of advice to give a new guy like me?"

He sat there for a few seconds and then looked at my shit-eating grin. With a blank look in his eyes, he said, "Yeah. Just do your work and keep your mouth shut. They don't care about you here." Then he turned away.

Wow, I was dumbfounded. What an attitude, I thought. I knew I would never be like this guy.

The congregation to which you were assigned could make a big difference in your stay at Bethel. Some Brothers had great jobs and shitty congregations; other Brothers had great congregations and shitty jobs. Then the truly lucky guys received great jobs and great congregations. These Brothers were called "Golden Boys." Their stay at Bethel was like a walk in the park.

What constituted a good congregation? First of all, there weren't too many Bethelites in it. Inwood had only four initially: Daryl Christianson, Larry Fisher, John and me. One of the reasons Inwood had fewer Bethelites was that it took almost an hour to get there from Bethel.

At Murry Hill congregation, where I had gone to the Memorial for Christ death, there were over sixty Bethelites.

The odds of being invited to a meal out or receiving any food from the local Brothers or Sisters was about zero. Food was a big deal, too. Because it took so long to get to our meetings, there was no time for most of us Bethelites to go to the dinner at Bethel. We had to leave work, clean up and head straight to the meetings. The wonderful Sisters at the Inwood Hall would make up brown bags full of food. We got the bags at the end of the meetings. We usually had our dinners at about 10:00 to 10:30 at night on the subway train heading back home to Bethel. We got back to Bethel at about 11:00 PM, if we were lucky (Jehovah's Witnesses don't like using the word "lucky"). Then we'd be up again at 6:30 to start the day.

After the meetings on Sundays in Inwood, there was always a place for us at one of the brother's houses for a home cooked meal.

The Inwood congregation had about 50 percent African Americans, 25 percent Puerto Ricans and 25 percent mixed nationalities. It was my first mostly black congregation. After fifty years and dozens of Kingdom Halls, I must say the blacks have the best congregations. They are truly wonderful people. They are the real deal, and if you are real too, they will do anything for you. However, if you are an uppity, self-righteous white boy, they will stay clear of you. They saw lots of us young white Bethelites who were full of ourselves come and go. Some of the Bethelites who had preceded us didn't leave on the best terms.

Two more new boys were assigned to our hall in the next couple years, Dave Paro and Dennis Miller. Many a Bethelite would leave Bethel and marry a local girl from their Kingdom Hall. Dave Paro married a Puerto Rican Sister from Inwood.

Most of the available Sisters in the New York area were either black or Puerto Rican. Ninety percent of all Bethelites were White. The few white Sisters were either very young or already snapped up by the hundreds of Bethelites who preceded you. So, your choice was a 14-year-old white girl, or a good-looking black Sister. If you had a car, the selection was a little better with the proximity of Upstate New York, New Jersey or even New England. But for the vast majority of Brothers, it was the Sisters from good old New York City.

There were a lot of mixed marriages, which, of course, is fine, except there was a few weird ones, too. Like the nineteen-year-old, skinny white kid from Wisconsin, who married the forty-two-year old, three-hundred-pound black Sister from the Bronx. She also had three teenage boys of her own. One of her teenage boys was the same age as her new husband. I wondered what his folks thought when he left Bethel before his time and brought her back home to Wisconsin?

There was an old saying among the Bethel boys about the Black Sisters in the New York City area: The longer you are here, the whiter they look.

If you were looking for available white Sisters over sixteen years of age, you needed to travel at least a hundred miles away from New York City.

Having just got there, girls was the last thing on my mind. I was determined to not get involved with any girls because of the commitment I made.

Brenda, a beautiful redhead from Kansas, wrote me a nice letter after I was at Bethel for just a few months. I think she was interested in me. I wrote her back a fiery letter stating, "What are you thinking? I have made a four-year commitment here, so please don't write me anymore!" What a jerk I was.

Anyway, Inwood was a wonderful congregation; however, there were a few whack jobs there just like in any other Kingdom Hall.

Sister Cornell would come up to me and show me her Field Service report. This is a very private report and people usually don't show them to each other. She would tell me with her thick German accent, "Look at this Brother Casarona. I got twenty-two hours in Field Service, ten return visits, three books and nineteen magazines placed."

"Very good, Sister Cornell," I'd say. "Keep up the good work." She was very overbearing. I felt sorry for her two teenage kids and her ex-husband, who I never met. In her living room, there was a full three-foot-high portrait of her father, dress up in his Nazis SS uniform.

Sometimes when you were giving a talk, the black Brothers or Sisters would speak out with a "Yes!" or "That's right!" without them being called on. Just like in the old tent revival meetings in the Deep South. Can I get an amen!

But, overall, I'm sure the strangest people in the Inwood congregation were us Bethelites.

Chapter 15
The Tour

During your first three days at Bethel, you were assigned to a Sister in housekeeping. Her job was to teach you how to make your bed and take care of your room. You were taught the proper "Bethel way" in all things. Of course, they showed you how to scrub the toilets and the bathrooms the proper Bethel way, too. They even had you squeeze small pieces of soap together to make a bigger bar. Waste was not tolerated at Bethel in any form. I guess every penny mattered when it came to soap but not dishes. More on that later.

After my three days of housekeeping duty were over, I would finally be given my Bethel work assignment. I reported to the Bethel office the next morning. It was then customary at this time to get a tour of both the factory and the Bethel home. At the end of the tours, we would be given our work assignments.

My tour included six other new boys and new girls. Since I had never been in the factory, the tour was nothing short of amazing. We watched as hundreds of Brothers in different departments all worked like bees in a colony.

There was the bindery in building three with the sewing machines, the end sheet gluers, the bindery lines, the gatherers, the case makers and the trimmers.

Building One held the hand bindery, the plate and linotype departments. The fifth floor had an ink room, where they made everything from ink to glue and even hand soap. The fourth floor held the job press for the smaller printing jobs. The third floor was the deluxe Bible department and the second floor was the carpenter shop, where they actually made all the furniture that was used at Bethel.

The most impressive sight was the pressroom in building one. The biggest presses there were on the sixth floor, and they were the mighty Cottrell printing presses. There were three of these mighty beasts, and two of them sat side by side, press No. Six and press No. Seven. The noise was deafening as the *Watchtower* and *Awake!* magazines were pouring out of them. I stood there speechless as the Brothers stopped the press to change the giant, sixty-inch, paper roll. It was a race to see how fast they could change the roll and get the press back online. If the roll change went smoothly, the press was back online in less than a minute. This is the very heart of the factory, and I would have given anything to work there.

The tour continued through the home with its many offices. We saw the waiter crews, who spent hours preparing the tables for the next meal. The kitchen staff, who prepared meals for more than seventeen hundred people at a time. We toured the laundry where Brothers sorted, washed and dried thousands of garments a day.

There was even a dry cleaners and a shoe-repair shop, too. The people who were working in the home acted as the support group for the factory workers. The home was quite nice, but it was just not as impressive as the factory where the actual books and magazines were created. That was where the real action was, or so I thought at the time.

At the end of our tour, the six of us stood in the lobby of the 124 building. Brother Lang came down from the Bethel office with the news for which we were all waiting. He handed each of us a piece of paper but told us what it said before we could read it. Maybe he did this to see our reactions. I don't know.

"Brother Casarona, you are assigned to the laundry."

I don't remember what I thought back then. I did know it was a long way from the factory and the press room. I found out later that once you were assigned in the home, odds of moving to the factory were extremely low. As fate would have it, years later I would be in the factory and not only that, I ended my Bethel career in the press room on a printing press, Hoe 10 the Spanish *Awake!*. I was one of the few Brothers in Bethel history to start in the laundry and end up in the press room. It would be a long and strange road with stops in the sewing department, bindery and building one freight elevator along the way.

Wherever they put me, I was determined to give it my all, and I did from the very first day at Bethel to my last. I did give it my all.

I think I was liked by some and disliked by others, but no matter what you thought of me, I wasn't a "Jack."

If you called someone a "Jack" at Bethel, it meant he was a lazy slacker. No one then knew where the term came from. It was used long before 1970 and is still used until this day. It's just another thing that has been passed down from one generation of Bethelites to the next.

Back then, I wanted to please everybody. I wanted to be liked by everybody. When you are young, you might think you can actually do this. But in truth, this isn't possible and really should not be even wished for. If you are trying to please everyone, what do you believe in? What do you stand for? You really want to be liked by all? Then you better get off this planet. It's not possible.

Years later, I figured it out. I call it the "80-percent, 10-percent, 10-percent rule." It goes like this:

Say you met 100 people or even just 10 people. No matter how you act or what you say, one person out of the ten will love you to death. One person out of the ten will hate your guts for whatever reason. The other eight people won't care about you one way or the other.

You just can't please everyone if you are a real person.

There were many "brown noses" at Bethel back then. I'm sure there are many still there today. People willing to kiss anyone's ass to get where they want to go.

In fact, one of the old timers told me that before he became president, Knorr's nickname back in the old days was "Knorr the Nose." The guy who had his nose up Rutherford's ass would be our next president. What a surprise.

Chapter 16

Just Pee with it for Four Years

Some of the tables where you sat for dining were more fun than others. My first table assignment was in the upper dining room, at Houston Robert's table. It was what is called "a dead table." Not much conversation and definitely no humor. People ate their food and got out.

Houston was the floor overseer of the Linotype Department. I sat to the left of him and across from his girlfriend of many years, Judy. I say many years because at the time, the policy at Bethel was you needed a total of fourteen years of full time service before you were allowed to get married and stay at Bethel. Houston had ten years in and his girlfriend had just three years in – she was short one year. This was the policy Knorr made up. That is why the number one reason most Bethelites left Bethel, was to get married.

Houston looked like a total Bethel geek poster boy with really white skin, big lips and thick glasses. Judy was a cute little brunette. A strange looking couple, for sure. I wonder if they are still together. I didn't know about Knorr's policy when I got there, so I started asking Houston and Judy all kinds of questions about it. Houston's face got beet red. Judy informed me I needed to be quiet and just eat my food. After that, I did just what she said. I ate my food and got out of there.

During your first six months at Bethel, all new boys we were required to attend Primary School. This was done after the Bethel Family's Watchtower study on Monday nights. It was an in-depth study of the entire Bible. In that period of time, we were required to read the Bible from cover to cover. We had four instructors. They were Ed Dunlap, Ulysses Glass, Dan Sydik and Bill Wilkinson. A few years later, two of these instructors were asked to leave Bethel.

Besides Primary School, something new was started with my group of Bethelites. It was called the new boy talks. I'm sure they were called something else, but it wasn't what the Bethelites called them. For the first eight weeks after the Watchtower study on Monday nights, eight Bethel heavies would talk to us new boys. They were having a lot of problems back then, so these talks were designed to get the new Brothers on track, right off the bat.

Each Brother received a different subject. George Couch, the home overseer, talked about our rooms and activities around the Bethel home, like table manners. Doctor Dixon talked about health and hygiene. Knorr's subject was sex at Bethel, or I should say how to deal with the lack of sex at Bethel. He talked about things besides sex, including his long list of pet peeves. I had the honor to be at the very first new boy talk that Knorr ever gave on sex. I would have given one-thousand dollars if I could have recorded that talk because no one would ever believe it. The stuff that came out of our president's mouth about sex was strange to say the least.

There were about eighty Brothers and three Sisters at the lecture. Knorr talked about our vow of celibacy. No sex and no marriage for four years. We couldn't even touch a Sister, and we definitely couldn't touch ourselves. I remember him saying, "I only want you to pee with it for four years." He informed us that masturbation was one of Satan's tools. He went on and on about not being tempted by immorality; however, he said that once we do get married, sexual relations were no big deal. He said, "After you have sex, you would up and paint the walls or go to work." A strange thing to say. I know few people who paint their rooms after having sex. I felt really sorry for the Sisters who were sitting there with their faces beet red. Knorr didn't seem to care. Why should he? He was the most powerful person in our organization.

For Knorr, homosexuality was a big problem at Bethel. He had kicked out over sixty homosexuals just a few months earlier in 1969. So, of course, that subject came up. This was a sin worse than any other among the Jehovah's Witnesses. He read us scripture after scripture about the abomination of "men sleeping with men." He also informed us that blue jeans were something homosexuals like to wear. So of course, they were something that any good Bethelite would want to avoid.

Homosexuality will happen with thousands of guys living together. The subject came up a lot. There was a lot of NPGs (Non-Practicing Gays) at Bethel, too. I roomed with one for a while, though I wasn't aware of it at the time.

Over the next few months and years, it was obvious that Knorr really didn't even like the Bethelites. They were a necessary evil to him. They gave him nothing but grief. I can't remember even one time in four years that he even thanked us for being there. I do remember a time when he thanked a bunch of Elders for giving up two whole weeks of their lives. He mentioned their great sacrifice for having to be away from their wives and families, just so they could attend two weeks of special instruction. The difference, of course, was we *had* to be at Bethel and they didn't.

On the other hand, he loved the Gilead students—the Brothers and Sisters who were being trained for foreign missionary service. Of course, when they screwed up they were thousands of miles away and not at his house.

When someone was dismissed from Bethel for one of the many sins Knorr had listed in his new boy talk, we "had them for breakfast." This meant that after the text comments and before breakfast, Knorr would name this person and their transgression. He would then berate them at the breakfast table. This talk could last anywhere between ten to forty minutes, depending on Knorr's fury. Many times, he would go into graphic details on the nature of the sin. I literally saw foam around his month one time. The Sisters sat there squirming with red faces. There was silence in the dining hall. No one really wanted to eat the cold food that was sitting before him or her after he was done.

Knorr's rants became so bad that on one of his many trips to the South Pacific, he got a big surprise when he returned. For some odd reason, he always took these trips in the wintertime. Around 1973, the Governing Body voted him off his permanent position on the text table. So even the Governing Body was sick of his tirades. They decided the position would be rotated and the entire Governing Body, including Knorr, would have turns leading the text comments.

When he got back to Bethel, you could tell Knorr was pissed. The next week was the Gilead gradation. While he was making the announcements, he informed the Bethel family of the new change at the text table. The non-smiling Knorr said and I quote: "I decided to let them have it!" Little by little he was losing his supreme power.

Funny, I was told before I went to Bethel that all the Bethelites called Brother Knorr "Papa." In the four years I was there, I never heard one person call him that. On the other hand, I did hear many call him "King Knorr."

At the end of Knorr's new boy talk, he asked if anyone had any questions. Everyone sat there stunned for a few seconds. I raised my hand. Knorr pointed his bony finger at me.

"Yes, son."

I stood up.

"I think I speak for everyone here. We just wanted to thank you, Brother Knorr, for taking this time and sharing this important information with us." Let the ass kissing begin.

Chapter 17

My Privilege of Service

The laundry was in the basement of the 119 building. It was moved there in the spring of 1969 from the basement of the 124 building. Why is it that people like to put laundries in basements? The 119 building was the newest of all the Society's properties. This was a state-of-the-art laundry facility for its time. It had washing machines that could handle more than four hundred pounds of clothes in one washing. Steam presses, clothes driers, a press that could iron sheets, the hanky press that did handkerchiefs and napkins, and the infamous shirt press which some of the boys at Bethel there called "the button smasher."

Everyone at Bethel was given a laundry bag that went with the room you were assigned. We would fill out a laundry ticket with the number of items that were in the bag. You would lay out your clothes with shirts and pants, first underwear and next T-shirts, and then socks last. It was all tied together, put in your bag and dropped down the laundry shoot in your building once a week.

When the bags were brought into the laundry, they had to go through a process that was called "check in." All of the clothes were counted. If your bag came down without a ticket, the laundry boys would declare: "No ticket, trick it." Then any garments that didn't have a tag were given one for identification. These were yellow plastic tags that melted onto your clothes. For example, my tag on the front of my underwear would read 499-129-33. This was my key number, building number and room number. From there, the clothes were sorted into different washes: whites, colors, dress shirts, work clothes, etc. The clothes were washed, dried, pressed and folded, and then they went to "check out" where, hopefully, everything went back into the same bags in which they arrived. Your dress shirts and bag of clean clothes ended up back on the top of your bed the next day. If we were in "burn-out mode" where we had to work as fast as we could, we could even get all the bags back to their rooms in the same day.

The laundry room overseer was Ken Dowling. He had "key men" under him: Ron Teleson, Bob Rains, Tony Zimmerman, Jack Sutton and Greg Javens. Greg Javens would meet a female Gilead student at Bethel and go through Gilead, too, to be with her on her assignment in Brazil. A few years later, he committed suicide.

Under the "key men" were the grunts, and under the grunts were the new boys. There was a definite pecking order, and it was important that everyone knew their place just like in any congregation of Jehovah's Witnesses.

I knew nothing about the laundry or taking care of clothes before I went to Bethel. All of my experience was working at restaurants and working in and around kitchens. I stated that on my application. The same week I arrived at Bethel, another new boy was assigned to the kitchen. He knew nothing about kitchens or food. He had worked at a commercial laundry and dry cleaners before Bethel.

Ironically, he was assigned the kitchen, and I was assigned the laundry.

The powers that be didn't want you going to Bethel with any ideas about how things should be done. They are going to train you the Bethel way—their way. Years later, I used to joke around with young Brothers who wanted to go to Bethel. I told them if they wanted to work at the farm, just tell them you had no farm experience whatsoever. It worked more often than not.

However, if you were one of the very few who went to college and was trained in a skill they really needed, you ended up with a really good job, right off the bat. So, by following the Society's recommendation about not pursuing a higher education, you were punished with a shitty job. If you disobeyed the Society and earned a better education, you were rewarded with a better job.

Just one of the many Catch 22s at Bethel.

The Society made it hard on people, because the Brothers running the place knew the death of any religion was education and knowledge. That is why most of the Jehovah's Witnesses of today, who are in their 50s, 60s and 70s, are mostly blue-collar workers with just a high school education.

You were a real rebel if you went to college back then. My last few months at Bethel, I worked under Craig. He was my press operator on the printing press Hoe 10. After Bethel, he went to college to be a chiropractic physician and later he became a full M.D. He told me, years later, that when he was going to college, they hated him in his local Kingdom Hall. *How dare he try and make something of himself. Why can't he just be happy like the rest of us in the janitorial business?* However, after he finished school, it was a different story. The Brothers called him "the doctor," and they loved him. In fact, they wanted him to go back to Bethel to be their in-house chiropractor. They did everything possible to get him to return. Of course, they would have offered him a very nice "compensation package" and a luxury apartment if he would just come back. He said, "No, thank you." Yes, there was a double standard when it came to higher education.

James Pipkorn was in the laundry, too. I met him on my first day at Bethel. We would be good friends over the next forty years until his death in 2016.

The first few days in the laundry, my assignment was folding underwear. There were big tables with mountains of clean white underwear about four feet high. Four Brothers would pick a side of a table and fold. They had rules on how fast you had to fold this underwear, too. We had to fold a pound a minute. I soon found out that the nickname for the men and women's underwear in the laundry was "twinks." Why? Because just like a Hostess Twinkie, if you open them up before you washed them and look inside, there might be a "surprise in every package."

One day, they put this short, fat kid from Alabama on the table. His name was Danny Stewart. We were behind on folding underwear. We were in what they called "burn-out mode." We were folding underwear as fast as we could. This was done so we could get the laundry bags back to the rooms on time. Danny had two speeds: slow and stop. We were folding about four times as fast as he was. One Brother looked over at him and said, "Hey, Danny, can you pick up the pace here. We need to get this load out!"

Danny just kept folding the same way he had for the last hour and said, "Anything I fold, you don't have to fold."

"You're just a Jack, Danny." He didn't seem to mind being called the worst name you could call a Bethelite. I guess he thought he had four years to go, so what's the big hurry.

The key men trained me on quite a few jobs in the laundry. I operated the hanky press for a while and even did some delivery. Delivery was probably the best job in the laundry for many reasons. You were able to leave the hot laundry, where overseers were breathing down your neck. You got to go all over the Bethel home, delivering clean clothes. Speed was always the most important thing there, too. One day, I was waiting with my rack of clothes in front of an elevator, and I happened to be talking to a young housekeeper. We talked for no more than a minute or two as I was waiting. One of my fellow delivery boys came around a corner and saw me talking to her, and that was the last day I delivered clothes.

Nothing was ever said to me back at the laundry, but the next day I received a job change.

That day, I learned something they didn't tell you in the *Dwelling Together in Unity* booklet. I learned that not only are there lots of Brothers at Bethel, but "Big Brother" was definitely there, too. Yes, it was a paradise for snitches.

Most everyone there was on a vigil, looking for any minor or major infractions of the many written and unwritten laws.

Why would they do that? For brownie points, of course. By going to your overseer with information about another, you were, in essence, saying, "Look at me, Brother Overseer. I'm looking out for you and our department." Eyes and ears were everywhere, snooping for just one wrong action or statement.

Ever wonder why they call them brownie points? Because the color brown is the same color you would find on many people's noses at the Lord's House.

After you were there awhile and people got to know each other, there seemed to be a separation between those who were self-righteous snitches and those who weren't. The snitches were identified and avoided. In fact, the guys in the laundry came up with a code word to be used when someone who was looking for brownie points showed up before others could notice him. The code was using the number 52 in a sentence.

"Hey, we need 52 more garment bags over here." In other words, look around we have company. Brother Snitch is among us.

Chapter 18
Look, Ma, No Hands

By the time the summer rolled around, the overseers decided to put me on the dryers. It was hotter than hell in the laundry by then. Either the air conditioning didn't work or they decide not to use it to save money. It was anywhere from 110 to 115 degrees down there in the basement, which some called "the hole." Of course, the dryers were one of the hottest jobs there. It was so bad, many of us were taking salt tablets. The person training me—this ugly Polish kid from Chicago, Jack Pachocko—made the job even worse. He was probably the first person I met there that I didn't like besides the snitch in the delivery department. He was a terrible instructor. He wasn't kind, and he was always hoping you would screw up so he could bring it to your attention. He was perfect Bethel overseer material.

Finally, after about six months of being moved around the laundry, they gave me a permanent job: the steam press next to the dryers. I was pressing and ironing men's pants and women's garments all day long. I worked by myself, sweating my ass off.

I remembered my mother spending one day a week ironing the family's clothes. I thought about how boring this must have been for her now that I was doing it six days a week. A couple of years later, I would have begged to be put back in the laundry, ironing clothes or doing any other job there, after I discovered the machines in the bindery.

After being at Bethel for about a year, I just didn't feel right about some of the things that were happening. There was an undertone, a pretense of love and concern as outlined in the Society's publications. But at the core, it seemed to be missing. There were things said and things done that just didn't add up. Plus, most of the guys who had been there many years didn't seem all that happy. Many guys that hadn't been there very long were already counting the days until their time was up. It just wasn't one thing. It was lots of little things that added up to one big thing. As much as I didn't want to admit it, there just wasn't the care for each other that you would have expected in the headquarters, the spiritual paradise of God's only true religion on Earth.

Of course, the old timers there knew lots of secrets at the headquarters, but no one would talk to the new boys about such things. I wish I had gone to the Bethel library more and read some of those older publications. There were hidden secrets in those old books there that could have revealed just how wacky my religion really was.

However, many of the pieces of the puzzle began falling into place. Little did I know back then that it would take me another thirty years before this giant puzzle would be complete and the mystery revealed. For me, the last piece of the puzzle would fall into place on September 11, 2001.

The curtain would be pushed aside to reveal who the great and powerful Oz really was.

One day, when I was working in the laundry, I came over to help fold underwear on the "twinks" table with a couple of other guys. At the table was a short, stocky guy whose nickname was Stub. He was folding underwear along with the rest of us. He had been at Bethel for about three years. Stub had worked on the home cleaning crew, which was a great job.

"What are you doing in the laundry? Visiting?" I asked.

"No," he said. "I turned in my thirty-day notice. The Bethel office told me I needed to go to the laundry for my last thirty days here. I guess they wanted to punish me for leaving early."

Wow, I thought to myself. They told us that every job at Bethel was "a privilege of service." Yet, they obviously didn't really believe that. So, for me, the laundry was "a privilege of service," but for Stub it was supposed to be some kind of punishment.

Less than a month later, this fact was proven once again with Gary Kennedy. Gary and his brother James (Jimmy) were very interesting people. Gary and I would be best of friends for the next thirty years until I decided to leave the religion in which he was raised. I had arrived at Bethel within a couple of weeks of his brother Jimmy's arrival. Gary had arrived six months before both of us. Their father had been in show business in Hollywood and had many celebrities as friends. He even claimed to have "witnessed" to Clark Gable right before Gable made his last movie, *The Misfits*. James Kennedy Senior was well liked and very connected to the powers that be at Bethel.

Gary and Jimmy were always doing crazy things before they arrived at Bethel. It didn't stop once they got there, either. They were always daring each other, egging each other on. Their last adventure finally got Jimmy killed.

Months after both Jimmy and Gary had left Bethel, they thought it would be fun to climb up Ruby Falls in Georgia. They thought it would be more interesting to climb up inside the actual waterfalls. The one-hundred-and-fifty-foot climb included water cascading over slippery rocks.

Their families, along with Jimmy's three-month-pregnant wife, were all below in the campground, preparing lunch. They were waiting for their men to return when they heard what sounded like a large log careening down the falls hitting the rocks as it went. To their horror, they found it wasn't a log at all, but the mangled body of Jimmy Kennedy at the bottom of Ruby Falls.

Years later, Gary told me that Jimmy was his parent's favorite son, and his death almost destroyed them. Gary spent the rest of his life trying to prove to his father that he was worthy of his love. He and his father would have fun during the public talks they gave. They would have contests on who could get the most people crying in the Kingdom Hall by the end of their lectures. Gary had many lines that would get the audiences sobbing. One of his favorites was the one about the dying child. "The small child lay in its mother's arms, dying. He looked up into the heavens before he died and said, Jehovah be praised."

There wasn't a dry eye in the place. Just like so many of the Brothers, Gary and his father were both show boaters and loved to entertain.

One of the many ways Gary loved to garner attention after he left Bethel was by getting out of bed in the morning and, wearing his pajamas and bathrobe, head down to the local grocery store. He would walk through the store, shopping in his robe and slippers and watching people's shocked expressions as he traipsed down the aisles looking like he had just woken up. For many years, he would do the same thing when he and his wife were invited over for dinner at a friend's house. He would show up in his bath robe. Who knows, maybe he thought he was Hugh Hefner.

Sometimes, he would be in Field Service, open up his book bag, pull out some dog biscuits and start munching away.

The words I would use to best describe Gary would be: Look, Ma, no hands.

Gary told me how, as youngsters, he and his brother would hop freight trains in Georgia and see how far they could get in just one weekend, before they had to be back to school on Monday morning.

Usually at the international conventions, the Brothers would read telegrams from all over the world, basically patting each other on the back for a job well done. In 1969, Gary and his brother sent a bogus telegram to the international convention headquarters in Atlanta that was read in front of about sixty thousand people from some made-up country.

When I first met Gary, I really thought all the stories he told me were just that, stories. There was no way a person could do all the things he said he did. However, the longer I got to know him, the more I came to realize he really had done all of the things he said he did.

Gary was the first person I ever saw who wore his baseball cap on backwards; this was way back in 1970. I really think he invented this stunt.

He was the Jerry Lewis of Bethel. He always seemed to have a smile on his face. He was a wonderful, wacky and funny guy. He was truly a free spirit. Rules to Gary were inconvenient obstacles.

Of course, this was a big problem at Bethel. The last thing they wanted there were free spirits. Conformity was everything; the individual meant nothing. The pressure to conform would prove to be too much for him and so, Gary ended up leaving Bethel before his four years were up.

Years later, Gary listed Bethel as his higher education on his Facebook page. I would have to agree with Gary. Bethel was certainly an education.

Gary had been at Bethel almost a year when he showed up in the laundry. He had been on the waiter crew and destroyed a full cart of china serving plates and bowls worth about $300. That was a lot of money. It would take a Bethelite over a year to make that kind of money. What he was doing at the time of this crash was probably another version of "Look, Ma, no hands." I never got a clear story. I guessed he had destroyed china on other occasions as well.

The bottom line was the overseer of the waiter crew wanted Gary gone.

I could never figure out why the whole Bethel family ate on breakable china in the first place. Between the dish duties and the waiters, thousands of dollars of fine china were broken every year. Even back in the 1970s, they made unbreakable dishes.

It's just strange that such a stingy organization would be willing to look the other way when it came to their dishes.

Even the Bethel housekeepers were required to squeeze four or five thin layers of bath soap bars together to make one larger bar. These people were tight.

After I was at Bethel a couple of years, I happened to be sitting next to the headwaiter in charge of the dining rooms, David Martin, one Saturday at lunch when it was open seating. We heard a glass break at the other end of the dining room. I looked over at him and asked, "Are a lot of dishes broken here every week?"

"Lots," he said.

"So why don't we use plastic glasses or buy CorningWare, something sturdier?" I asked.

He had a funny little look on his face. "Because Knorr likes china."

"Oh, Brother Knorr likes eating on fine china?" "Yes," he said with a smirk on his face.

"I got an idea," I told him. "Let's give Knorr his china and the rest of us will eat on CorningWare. We'll save the organization thousands of dollars every year."

"Good idea, but it will never fly."

I guess the powers that be didn't mind their dishes breaking. They just didn't want people to break too many of them all at once.

The Bethel office felt it was time to send Gary to "the hole" for an attitude adjustment, just like they did with Stub. Gary got a job change and was reassigned to the laundry. This now confirms the fact the laundry was considered the penal institution of the home.

Gary had made a name for himself, which is one thing you never want to do at Bethel. Once you were no longer just a number and the powers-that-be discovered you had a name, you were on their radar, and Gary definitely was on theirs. It turned out Gary had been on their radar from the very beginning of his Bethel stay.

On their radar meant: "What's that brother's name? I think I've heard about this person before! Wasn't he just in the Bethel office for some other infraction?" This was never a good thing.

It seemed that if the people that checked in your laundry bag found anything that was outlandish or "worldly," they were required to bring it to the attention to the overseer, Ken Doweling. That's right, they would even snoop through your dirty clothes looking for who knows what.

A couple of weeks after Gary arrived at Bethel, the laundry found a wild pair of flowered bell bottoms pants in his laundry bag. This resulted in him getting his first "service talk" right off the bat—not good. They had laid these pants before him and asked him what he was thinking when he got them. He told them that he was in a dramatic play at the international convention and had to act the part of a worldly kid. The district overseer there had told him to buy the most outlandish set of clothes he could find to play the part. He told them he was going to wash the pants and then give them away. This turned out to be true.

But that didn't matter. By the very fact that Gary was in the Bethel office, he was already guilty. This would be his first strike. The dishes were his second strike. Gary was on thin ice. He was getting a reputation. I think they would have kicked Gary out of Bethel at that point if it hadn't been for his well-connected father.

A well-connected or powerful family member made a big difference in how they treated you. They would give Gary one more chance in the laundry. Of all the guys I saw at Bethel, Gary was one of the hardest workers there. He could "burn out" like no one else and did so all the time.

Chapter 19
"Gary Will Die, of Course"

After Gary was sent to the laundry, Ken Dowling had a talk to all of his key men. My roommate was at this meeting also. Ken basically told them to watch for anything Gary said or did that was against company policy. In other words, the "fix was in" and it was now snitch time. Of course, we all needed to do our part.

As I said, I liked Gary and we started hanging out, at work and after work, too. Ken Dowling must have noticed this because he pulled me aside one day. It was one of the few conversations we ever had. This conversation would change my direction at Bethel. It proved to be another piece of the giant puzzle this religion had become. This conversation would show me some months later how the Watchtower Bible and Tract Society actually deals with real problems in their organization. The conversation went like this:

"Brother Casarona, you seem to be a hard worker. This laundry needs hard workers, too. However, I'm a little concerned about who you've been hanging around with lately. You know there can be bad associations, even here at Bethel." "Yes sir, I know."

He pointed over at Gary who was just a few feet away, working the check-in area. "Gary has a hard time respecting authority and following the rules here at Bethel.

If he doesn't change and obey me in every way, he WILL DIE at Armageddon. You do believe that, don't you, Brother Casarona?"

I knew some Bethel overseers thought that way, but to say it out loud? The *Dwelling Together in Unity* booklet said that Bethel overseers were the supreme authority in all matters when it came to our Bethel service. I sold my soul to the company store that day and lied.

"Yes sir, of course."

"You must report to me anything Gary says or does that is against Society policy."

"Yes sir!"

I hated Ken Dowling after that. I hated myself after that, too. I began to question myself. I began to question the things they asked us to do. How far was I willing to go? Was I willing to turn in my own friend just so I could look better in their eyes? Was Gary really going to die at Armageddon because of his attitude? Gary was a hard worker and a good friend. I was very confused.

I was taught growing up in the congregation to not have "fear of man." Yet, it was here at Bethel, the house of God, where I would truly learn what it meant to be in "fear of man."

It's sad to say, but to this day the organization still believes its leaders are the direct representation of God's will on

Earth. If you are not in alignment with their rules and regulations, you will be cast out, and everyone knows what happens to those who are cast out of God's organization: Death at God's own hand at Armageddon.

I told Gary what our overseer told me. He was, of course, crushed. It seemed to make a difference though, and he started to make a better effort to comply and fit in. Who knows? Maybe he thought Ken Dowling's words were true somehow.

Of course, it wasn't what Ken Dowling said that was the problem. Anyone can say stupid things. The problem was how the Society handled this matter and other discrepancies. In just a few months, the leaders of the organization and the president himself would have an opportunity to show hundreds of Bethelites how things like this are handled in Jehovah's house.

Ken Dowling was a short, stocky, bald guy with glasses. He was definitely no lady's man. However, I have never met anyone before him who had more self-confidence. He was totality in love with himself. He loved to flirt with the Bethel Sisters and Gilead students who were assigned to work in the laundry. He, of course, wanted to make sure they knew that he was the overseer.

One day, he was standing by the 119 elevator with one of his key men. A Sister who was blessed with ample cleavage walked by him. After she was gone, I heard him turn and say to his friend. "That sister is like a cow in heat. She wants it bad!"

Maybe people think things like this, but to say it out loud to someone else? These were just a few of the many things he said and did that seemed inappropriate for a Bethel overseer.

I felt it was time for this bad attitude to be brought to light. And I wasn't the only one in the laundry who felt the Bethel Elders would want to know about Dowling's behavior. Ron Telleson, Jack Sutton, James Pipkorn, myself and three other Brothers from the laundry knew the powers that be would want to know about his attitude and the misuse of power by one of their overseers.

Ron Telleson, one of Ken's key men, told an ex-circuit overseer what was happening in the laundry. This older ex-circuit overseer said a lot of these things were going on in Bethel and someone should step up and say something. He and two other ex-circuit overseers felt the same way because of some of the injustices they also witnessed. They were the three Freds: Fred Barnes, Fred Fredeen and Fred Hilmo. These were great men who had a vision of truth, righteousness and fairness. But in the world of religious politics, those qualities often don't mean much.

The word went out. The three Freds asked anyone who had a problem with an overseer to come to the Towers library. Over one-hundred Brothers showed up and started telling their stories. You couldn't believe some of the nasty things some of these overseers were getting away with. Dowling was just one of many overseers who were misusing their power. After all was said and done, Fred Hilmo spoke.

"We need to inform Knorr about all of this so they can straighten this out."

Fred Hilmo requested a meeting with Brother Knorr. This was the appropriate action, just as Brother Knorr himself stated in his booklet *Dwelling Together in Unity*. "Every member of the Bethel family or missionary home, no matter where he is located in the Lord's organization, should feel perfectly free to any complaints if he is mistreated by another individual. These complaints may be registered with the branch servant in charge or directly to the president."

Of course, Knorr was willing to meet with Fred Hilmo. Knorr was very interested in anyone who had any complaints about him or Jehovah's organization and the overseers who ran it. After this meeting, Knorr decided to call a meeting with all of the Bethel overseers and the other Brothers with concerns (otherwise soon to be known as the rebels and troublemakers) to have a discussion about these matters.

You know what he was planning to do. He was going to play Jehu and bring us altogether so fire could come out of the heavens and consume all of us! He was going to "clean the house of God." Not of the wrong doers, nope, just the people who were trying to report it.

Chapter 20

Black Thursday: The Day the Music Died

It was in September, 1971, that Knorr gathered all of the Bethel overseers and Governing Body to the Kingdom Hall in the 119 building. The three Freds and about fifty Brothers showed up. That's right. Only fifty showed up out of the one-hundred who were at the first meeting. The other guys chickened out; they knew it was going to be a blood bath. I was there with six others from the laundry. No turning back now. I was sure God's organization and His holy spirit would deal appropriately with these matters.

They brought the Brothers into the auditorium in small groups or one at a time. We were not present for the testimony of the different Brothers, but we did hear about some of it later.

It started out with Dan S. who wasn't even thirty years old and partaking and thus claimed he was one of the anointed. Meaning he thought he was part of the little flock or the anointed ones. As mentioned before, these are people who are supposed to be chosen directly by God. Dan told all of the overseers about how Max Larson told him, in no uncertain terms, that there was no way he was one of the anointed ones.

Max was the head of the entire factory complex. He was one of Knorr's best friends. They would dress their wives up and go dancing together at the Rainbow Room in Manhattan. I always wondered how they were able to afford that on our small monthly allowances.

Max, at the time, was just a member of the "great crowd or other sheep," and thus was not one of the anointed, which really pissed him off. Of course, the question was, how could God pick this kid Dan S. over Max? Especially since Max had been at God's house for more than forty years?

Sometimes I wondered how God picks those anointed guys anyway. God can be strange sometimes.

Guess what? Years later, Max decides, by way of God's holy spirit, that he is now one of the anointed also. What a surprise! God changes His mind once again.

Back at the meeting, the Brother's stories of misconduct and abuse of power by Bethel's Elders kept flowing. They were shaking the pillars of the organization. Knorr knew this and got madder and madder. By the fire in his eyes, I'm sure he would have loved to have killed us all on the spot! Everyone knew these men were above the law. How dare we? Where the hell is Jehu when you needed him?

Then it was our turn to share our information about our dear Brother Dowling. When some of the Brothers from the laundry started telling us about Ken's escapades, Knorr went off on all of us. In the middle of his rant, something crazy happened. All of a sudden, Fred Franz stood up and said, "These men are appointed to their positions of responsibility and power not because of their spiritual qualifications, but because of their secular abilities!" The room was silent. What did this mean? No one really knew for sure. But this statement stopped Knorr dead in his tracks.

After a few seconds of silence, Knorr said. "We'll look into these matters later." That was the end of the meeting.

Years later, Jack Sutton told me that as he and Jim Pipkorn walked back from the meeting, Jim looked over at Jack and asked him how he thought the meeting went. "Well Jim, I think this is the end of our Bethel careers." He was right.

What happened after Black Thursday? Basically nothing. There was only one committee meeting. It was for the laundry overseer, Ken Dowling. At the meeting, there was some damning testimony from seven different people about Ken's spiritual immaturity and abuse of power. What was the judicial outcome of this meeting? What did Bob Lang and George Couch decide to do with Ken? Since George Couch had promoted Ken to the position of oversight, it would be a bad reflection on George if Ken was removed.

After the meeting, they could do only one thing. In a matter of weeks Ken Dowling was promoted to, where else but the Bethel office. They rewarded Ken and promoted him into one of the most powerful positions in the Bethel Home.

The Holy Spirit has kicked in one more time.

Ken was a company man, and company men always take care of their own. Just look at the Elders in any local Kingdom Hall. After fifty years in the organization, I saw this kind of favoritism take place on many occasions.

Oh, something else did happen to about one-hundred-and-fifty people back then. We all lost heart. We found out that when it really came down to it, the leaders and the head of the organization had little or no desire to really clean things up in the organization. They truly were above the law. They were untouchable.

Come to find out this wasn't the first time that sincere people tried to approach Knorr and the Governing Body with information of unscriptural behavior, and it wouldn't be the last. Just a few years later, one of the top leaders of the Governing Body would be dis-fellowshipped because he, too, had information they didn't want to hear—information about a major misstep the Society had made. This information would have created a mass exodus from the mother ship.

Of course, nothing happened to any of the other Bethel overseers that were in question on Black Thursday. It would be business as usually again.

My guess is Franz and Knorr got together and decided to sweep the whole thing under the rug. Why? They couldn't afford a scandal. How would it look if dozens of their overseers were removed or reprimanded for their indiscretions? The news would have got out, for sure.

Funny how this was reminiscent of what happened to my parents back in 1961. Could there be a pattern here? If there was, I couldn't see it at the time. I really didn't want to see it, for sure. After years in the organization, I have to say this was no coincidence. It was just the voice of "Christmas future."

Brother Knorr, I'm sure, was hoping the three Freds and their wives would just quit and leave Bethel. He couldn't really kick them out. They didn't do anything wrong. How would that have looked?

These guys weren't going anywhere. They were in their late-fifties. They had invested their entire lives in this organization. They were career men, but the powers that be made sure their careers were now over.

I find it quite interesting that there has never been a retirement program for people who served the organization for forty, fifty or even sixty years. These are people who have been circuit overseers, district overseers or even Bethelites. I guess somehow, they believe Jehovah will provide for them in some mysterious way or something.

Back to the three Freds. The powers that be didn't kick them out for their transgressions. Looking back, it would have been kinder if they had. Instead, they tried to break them and humiliate them in front of the whole Bethel family. They made their lives a living hell. Yes, they wanted to make an example out of them.

They even put Fred Barnes, who was well into his fifties at the time, on a machine in the bindery called "the gather." Why did they call this machine "the gather?" Some people jokingly said, "Because you had to gather all strength just to work on it." This was a machine that even healthy 19 year olds had a hard time keeping up with.

Fred had a heart attack. What a surprise.

By this everyone will know that you are my disciples, if you love one another. John 13:35

This has proved to be true, for there was little or no love at the world headquarters of the Jehovah's Witnesses. This would prove to be just the tip of the iceberg.

The rest of us laundry boys were also screwed, as were the other Brothers who showed up at the Black Thursday meeting. We were all marked. We had done the unforgivable. By bringing up the wrongdoings of the Bethel overseers and the pillars of the organization, our Bethel careers were over.

Our files were noted. Of course, there were files on everyone. Dwayne Wilkie (one of the factory overseers) had a system where he would actually judge you with an A, B, C, D and F for your spirituality. One person in a back room could now decide based on a piece of paper how "spiritual" you were. After Black Thursday, I wondered what our grades were now.

Whether it's at the world headquarters or your local Kingdom Hall, the Brothers in power judge all Witnesses. Whether it's noted on a piece of paper or discussed in a "private" conversation among the Elders, everyone is judged. Yes, Big Brother is alive and well.

It was apparent after Black Thursday that there was only one thing left to do: serve our time and get out.

It was at about this time that the movie *THX 1138* came out. The people of the future had no names, just numbers, like Bethel. The movie was about a future Society where sex was forbidden, just like Bethel, and everyone worked at monotonous jobs, just like Bethel. They were all drones. Fiction imitates reality.

It was one of those hot New York City summer nights, when it was still 90 percent humidity at 11:00 p.m. It was one of those nights where there was no brown paper bag with dinner in it. Sister Iirizary forgot that it was her turn to make us our dinner. I got off the subway train from my congregation meeting with my book bag in hand and loosened the tie around my neck. My suit and clothes were drenched with sweat. Most of the trains in the early 1970s didn't have air conditioning. Other Bethelites, whose congregations were over an hour away, climbed up the long staircase from the Clark Street subway station. At the top of the stairs, we got a blast of cooler air. God did that feel good! Another day was over.

Two blocks away from the subway station was the Plymouth Deli. Some of the guys with money went in to get a hero sandwich for a couple of bucks. It was the end of the month. I had no money for food. I had just enough money for subway tokens to get me to and from the congregational meetings for the next week. I walked back to the 129 building, got to my room and just started tearing up for no reason. I went to the kitchen and opened the refrigerator door to see a bottle of Cold Duck I had bought a week earlier. I have no idea why I bought something as foolish as that. I guess it sounded interesting. I grabbed the bottle and started drinking. The cold wine tasted like heaven. Before I knew it, the whole bottle was gone. The room started to spin. I laid down on my bed. After a few minutes, I threw up all over the bed and myself. I just lay there crying. It was the first time I had ever gotten drunk in my life.

My roommate came into the room and asked, "Are you okay?"

"Yes," I told him. "I'm sick."

I was sick. I was sick of heart.

I thought, it really is true. They really don't care about us here.

Chapter 21
The Machines Conquer All

After the fiasco of Ken Dowling's committee meeting, many of us received job changes. Some were moved out of the laundry and some even out of the Bethel home. I guess they wanted to bust up the troublemakers. At the time, they were asking for volunteers for a night shift in the factory. They didn't usually send the "home boys" to the factory, but they sent many of us. Most of the guys who worked in the Bethel home wanted to stay there. They loved to be able to sit around the dining room table and have that extra cup of coffee before they had to be back at work. Besides, they had heard the stories about the factory.

I had no idea what was waiting for us over there, just a few blocks away.

If the laundry was the penal institution of the home, then the bindery was the penal institution of the factory. The only difference was the bindery made the laundry look like heaven.

I was sent to work on the night shift in the sewing department. The Smythe sewing machine was a machine that was designed by the devil himself. You would sit on this chair and throw thousands and thousands of paper sheets called signatures over a saddle where they were sewn together. They would later become books when the bindery lines got through with them. The good thing about working on these machines is you could always stop them.

On the other hand, on the bindery lines, there was no stopping the machines. You were like Charlton Heston, the galley slave in the movie *Ben Hur*. Everyone rowed together and no one stopped. If one person stopped, the whole line could go down. It was just like the movie except there were no drums beating and it was always ramming speed.

The night shift in the sewing department was rock bottom for me in the winter of 1971-72. I tried to sleep during the days and dragged myself to work at nights. I was in a fog most of the time.

After many months on the night shift in the sewing department, it was time for a job change. I was sent to the bindery on the 5th floor, building 3, bindery line 5.

Welcome to Hell. Abandon all hope, ye who enter here. They didn't put the sign above the door like Auschwitz's slogan "work sets you free," but they might as well have.

You had to stand in the same spot, between two different machines. Your job was to take a book out of one machine, "the rounder," and turn it upside down and shove it into another machine called "the back liner."

In the eight-plus-hours shift, you stood there, doing this same motion between 15,000 to 17,000 times a day.

There were days in that factory that felt like eternity. You would look at the clock and it said 2:13, then a lifetime would pass, and you would look back at the clock again and it said 2:28.

You tried to keep your mind active by thinking about different things. Your first week, you thought about all of the important events in your life. The next week, you would think about places you wanted to visit. The next week, you would think about all the movies you ever saw. The next week, you thought about girls. The next week, you thought about all the mistakes you ever made. The next week…

After a few months, you would have a strange, blank look on your face. Someone would walk up to you and ask what you were thinking about. "Nothing," you'd say as you stared off into the distance, because you were brain dead. The lights were on but nobody was home.

If you begged your line overseer, he might give you a five-minute break to go to the bathroom every four hours. That meant he would have to take over your position. Since he didn't want to be standing between two machines either, you needed to get back to your spot as soon as possible. There was no time to even shake it twice. Of course, they could have bought a machine that did the same job for about $5,000, but it only cost them $22 a month for a warm body like me to do the same job.

If it wasn't for Knorr's white china habit, perhaps the money saved from unbroken dishes and reformed bath soap could have paid for one of those machines.

One time, an Army general came through on a tour of the factory. He shook his head in astonishment when he saw the people on the machines. The tour guide said, "I'm sure you could get your troops to do the same thing."

The general replied, "Are you kidding? No way."

Only the insane or religious zealots need to apply.

My friend Jim Pipkorn ended up in the factory, too. He got shafted to the bindery also. He was on the "end sheet gluer." In the bindery, he became so depressed that for months he would come back to his room at night and make himself some dinner and then just go to bed at about 7:00 p.m.

I asked him why he was doing that. He said, "It makes the days go by quicker."

We were counting our time. It was just like Vietnam. You would ask a new boy how long he had left. If he said something like, "Three years and two months to go," we would reply, "You poor bastard. That is after 1975." You should have seen the look on his face.

Of course, there was no racial prejudice in the Lord's house. Even though Pastor Russel wrote about the inferiority of African Americans in many of his publications.

About 10 percent of all Bethelites were black. However, about 60 percent of the guys working in the bindery were black. It seemed odd to me how disproportionate the numbers were. I couldn't help but ask Calvin Chyke about this one day as we were walking to the factory together. He was in charge of factory personnel at the time. He told me, "The black Brothers had a natural rhythm that fit in well with the machines."

I guess this was one time when natural rhythm wasn't an advantage.

Ronnie Klineman from Ruston, Louisiana, told me my favorite story about Brother Lyman Swingle who was on the Governing Body. Ronnie sat at Lyman's table. There happened to be a new black kid from Detroit assigned to Brother Swingle's table. Of course, as a new boy, he was feeling pretty good about himself as most new boys do when they first arrive.

Lyman glanced over at him at lunch one day. "Boy, would you please pass me the potatoes?"

The black Brother looked at Lyman with disdain and fired back. "I'm not your boy!"

To which Lyman said, not even batting an eye. "Nigger, pass the potatoes."

Hard to believe, isn't it? Yes, Bethel was not the place to try and be uppity. Black or white, we were all just boys in their eyes and, of course, they could say and do anything they wanted to us. Was this kid going to go and complain about something a member of the Governing Body said? I think not.

This was the early 1970s and the Black Power movement was just starting to happen. Some of the black Brothers at Bethel had a little bit of an attitude before they got there. If they didn't, many picked it up after a few months in the house of God. I can't say I blame them. It was a white man's organization with very few black overseers. The "Brothers" there weren't all "Brothers."

There are many terms used in this book that might sound foreign to those not familiar with the Jehovah Witnesses. There are many words or terms used at Bethel that are unique to just their organization. Here are some:

The Family/ Bethel Family – These are Jehovah's Witnesses who are called Bethelites, the workers at the world headquarters and branch offices around the world.

A Jack – Someone who is a slacker or just lazy.

A pot licker – This term has been used for many years but its connotation is unclear. It is basically used in the same way as "A Jack."

New Boy – Someone who just got to Bethel and doesn't know the ropes.

A Golden Boy – Someone who has a great job that isn't on a production line. He is assigned to a great Kingdom

Hall that has few Bethelites in it and is just a short distance from Bethel. He never gets into any trouble. If he does something wrong, someone else is usually blamed. A Golden Boy is a very rare occurrence at Bethel.

G Job – Work done outside of Bethel for monetary gain.

Gleaning – Many of the Sisters use this term to refer to the gathering of leftover food from the dining room after the breakfast or noon meal is over. There was nothing worth taking after the supper meal.

Hopper Shopper – People who get most of their garments out of the clothes hoppers that hold all the donated and second-hand clothing.

Mugger Money – Cash you keep somewhere on your person in case you are ever mugged. The reason for this money is to prevent you from being beaten. The mugger or assailants have gone through a lot of trouble to rob you. You will really piss them off if you don't have anything to give them. They will be convinced you are holding out on them and they will proceed to beat the shit out of you. Because who really walks around New York City with no money?

Burn Out or Tour Speed – Work that is done at a much faster pace than normal. Many times, this activity was incorporated when people were coming through on a tour. We would work extra fast to impress them.

Short Time – Someone who left Bethel early, before his or her tour of duty was up.

Morning Worship – This is the morning activity (except on Sunday) of discussing the Daily Text. The Bethel family would listen and watch five to six Brothers or Sisters on television give their comments about a scripture that was picked out of the "Year Book" for that day.

S R or a Ricky Righteous – Someone who is self-righteous or a super zealot. Many new boys are afflicted with this attitude. This person thinks of himself or herself as the right hand of God. They might feel it's their right and duty to impose their perceived concepts of God's will onto other people.

A Privilege of Service – This is how Bethel Elders will describe any job assigned to you, no matter how lowly or demeaning it might seem. It is your privilege and honor to work on this job assignment, however, there is a catch. This same job or "privilege of service" could be considered to be a punishment. This is the case if they reassign you to a shitty job because of some minor infraction. Then your new "privilege of service" has turned into what is commonly known as "the shaft" at Bethel.

The Shaft – This can happen if you are reassigned to a job that isn't as prestigious as your previous one. Not only is it not prestigious, it could be so physically demanding that you think you are going to die. You are obviously not moving up the company ladder. You are now going in the opposite direction. "The shaft" is applied when the powers that be want you to leave Bethel. However, instead of asking you to leave, they figure they can take advantage of you for a while before you break down or just give up. These same overseers will tell you there is no such thing as "the shaft" at Bethel. This obviously is not true. Just ask Fred Barnes or hundreds of other Brothers who have experienced "the shaft" at Bethel first hand. Since Bethel is just like any other organization that is run by politics, "the shaft" is used liberally and is inserted when you are bending over.

Service Talk – Usually given to you by an overseer or Bethel Elder. However, any fellow Brother at Bethel could give you this talk if he is an "S R." This talk is usually conducted in a back room somewhere and is administered if it seems you have stepped out of line or somehow broken one of many written or unwritten laws at Bethel. These talks are usually not done for serious offenses. That would require a judicial committee. Even if you did nothing wrong, don't try and defend yourself. The person giving you the "service talk" doesn't want his mind confused by any facts. "The old Indian Navajo" trick (explained later) is best applied here. Sometimes you might receive a job change after your "service talk" to teach you a lesson. The job change would then be considered "the shaft."

Bad Attitude or B A – This is someone who is on the opposite end of being an "S R" or a "Ricky Righteous." This person has some doubts about Bethel and the Bethel system. He may have seen or experienced some unchristian behavior by the powers-that-be. Or maybe someone who didn't like him has given him "the shaft." He may decide to verbalize these disappointments or thoughts to others. If this attitude is noted, he may receive a "service talk."

G B or Governing Body – These are the supreme leaders of the organization, usually ten to fifteen members. They are the leaders who control the "heavies," the "company men," the Bethel family and the rest of the world of Jehovah's Witnesses. Their numbers vary a lot because they are older men who keep dying off. There are currently eight members.

A Bethel Heavy – One of the four to five dozen people who are either running Bethel or are in a position of prominence.

Company Man – Someone who is staying past his commitment and loves Bethel and wants to make

Bethel his career. They are the new future leaders of the organization. Of course, the goal here is to be a "Bethel heavy" one day.

Having someone for breakfast – This is done when someone leaves Bethel in disgrace, or has been kicked out for a serious transgression. The Governing Body will inform the Bethel family of this person's sins and sometimes describe these sins in graphic detail after the Daily Text and before breakfast starts. The only time they didn't do this was when a pedophile and Governing Body member was asked to leave Bethel. That story and cover-up is in chapter 24.

Family Night – When the Bethel Family would volunteer or take turns getting up on a stage. They can perform skits, sing or tell jokes. Of course, this is highly regulated. They didn't have this when I was at Bethel.

These are important terms people should know when they first arrive at Bethel. Sadly, most people find out about these terms the hard way. Maybe they should have a complete discloser for the new boys about these important items in their *Dwelling Together in Unity* booklet.

However, complete disclosure really isn't their style.

Chapter 22

"Catch 22"

In September 1970, about six months after I got to Bethel, Roy Baty, my old pioneer partner, showed up at Bethel. Roy had a Bible study in Kansas with a mother and her daughter. Roy had fallen in love with the daughter, Mary Lynn. The problem was, she was only fifteen years old. Roy knew sometime needed to pass before they could get married, so four years at Bethel seemed like a good idea.

When he got there, he was so self-righteous, he made me sick. He reminded me of me, when I first arrived. I told him, "I can't say anything to you right now. Roy, come back in about six months and we'll talk again." Of course, he looked at me like I was crazy.

If you had been there any amount of time, you wanted to stay away from the new boys. A self-righteous new boy could be quite dangerous. A few months on the machines would show him where the true "Shekinah Light" in the Holy of Holies really was.

When I was a new boy, I tracked down Mark Bivins at Bethel. He had been in the Glendora congregation when my family was there back in the 1950s. His father had been the congregation overseer. For some odd reason, he wasn't happy to see me. He certainly didn't want me to come back in six months to see him again, either.

There is a funny and strange story about Mark and why they asked him to leave Bethel. Mark met a girl while at Bethel, and they got engaged, as many Bethelites will do. But in Mark's case, somewhere in the engagement he realized that this girl wasn't the love of his life. Mark broke the engagement off. The girl and her family were very upset and contacted the Brothers at Bethel. Bottom line: Mark was asked to leave Bethel. Why? Because he broke a vow or scared oath. I guess back then the Society felt it's better to marry someone you're not compatible with and be miserable for the rest of your life than break an engagement, causing everyone a lot of grief.

It makes perfect sense. We know how much the Society hates breaking their promises.

Anyway, back to Roy.

Poor Roy got off to a bad start, just like my friend Gary Kennedy. The good thing is at least Roy didn't end up on their radar like Gary did.

They put Roy in a room in building 124 with Eugene Alcorn, a Black brother from Michigan. Eugene had a real attitude. Roy had been at Bethel only a couple of weeks before he got a taste of "Bethel justice." It seems he and his roommate Eugene fought over the radio one night. Eugene wanted the radio on. Roy wanted it off, so he got out of bed and turned it off. Eugene got up and turned it back on. Roy got up and turned it off. Eugene turned it on…you get the idea. Words were exchanged before the brawl began. In the wrestling match that ensued, the sink in their room got busted. Now, usually most of the guys would cover for each other. Instead, Eugene went straight to the Bethel office the next morning and told the Brothers about his white roommate who didn't like black people. He went on to say that they had a disagreement and then Roy beat him up. In that process, the sink in the room got busted.

They hauled Roy into the Bethel office. How it works at Bethel is whoever gets there first with the story usually wins, pretty much just like in the Kingdom Hall. The reasoning is only the righteous ones would naturally report the behavior of the unrighteous ones. By the time Roy got to the Bethel office, the decision was already made.

Eugene ended up in the pressroom. Roy's job assignment was the bindery.

I never did like Eugene. He had a reputation for having the foulest mouth and one of the worst attitudes in the factory.

He is now serving as an Elder in New Jersey.

Besides working about 48 hours a week, you also had dish duties and watchman duties. Because the waiters worked from about 6:00 a.m. to about 3:00 p.m., others needed to do the supper dishes. Every few weeks, some of the Bethel family had that privilege. I say some because you never saw any of the Bethel heavies do any dish duties. It was only the new boys and those who were there less than four years. Yes, we are all equal, but some of us were more equal than others.

The dish duties were not fun, especially in the summer time. The worst job on dish duty was working on the "hot end" of the dish washing machine. Two Brothers loaded the front end and two Brothers took the 150-degree dishes off the back end. Your hands were on fire. You couldn't wear gloves or the dishes would slip out of your hands and break on the floor.

I first met Dave Borga on dish duty. He was Jim Pipkorn's best friend and roommate from Wisconsin. Dave was in charge that night. He put me on the hot end by myself because we were shorthanded. Of course, he could have helped me out, but he just sat up on a counter, laughing. It was like the *I Love Lucy* show where Lucy was in the factory pulling candies off a conveyor belt. Except the candies weren't 150 degrees.

I did dish duties there for about a year. Then I figured out that since the Bethel heavies didn't want to do them, why should I? I prayed to Jehovah to get me off dish duty. A week later, I met Allen Richards. Allen would do any dish duty for a half-gallon of Canadian Ace beer. It was the worst rot-gut beer in New York City at the time. The good news is it only cost eighty-nine cents. So, thanks to Allen, you could get out of two hours of hell for less than a dollar. I often wonder how Allen's liver is doing.

Besides dish duty, there was night watchman duty. If you lived in the Towers Hotel, you would get a watchman duty every four to six weeks. This was because most of the people living in the Towers Hotel were worldly people. The Society started posting guards on each floor every night.

Beside Towers watchman duty, once every two to three years in the Bethel home, you pulled an all-night watchman duty. It started at about 9:00 p.m. on a Saturday night. The regular watchman would get the day off and you would fill in. It was very creepy. It was dark and you had to walk through all three buildings (119, 107 and 124) and the basements. A person had to do this loop three times in all three buildings. He was required to punch a time clock at different locations.

On a hot Saturday night in July 1971, I was assigned all-night watchman duty. Many hours later, toward the end of the night at about 3:00 a.m. Sunday morning, I was in the dark basement of the 124 building and all of a sudden, this guy jumps in front of me and screams. I thought it was the ghost of Charles Russell. I could have died. Guess who it was? It was Scott, the regular night watchman. He said he couldn't sleep and wanted to have some fun with me. What a jerk. About a year later, he was asked to leave Bethel. He was actually kicked out. We had Scott for breakfast because it seemed he liked to sneak into the women's bathrooms in the 107 building in the middle of the night. They only had one bathroom per floor—Knorr's idea on how to save money, I guess. Scott would lock the toilet door and wait until some Sisters came in to take showers. He got quite a free peep show.

It seems all those long nights working alone finally got to him.

The good news is that Scott is an Elder in Salem, Oregon, now. He happened to be the overseer that I was assigned to work under at a district convention in Corvallis, Oregon, many years ago. He was in charge of cleaning the women's bathrooms...just kidding.

There was another guy who was just as weird as Scott. He would sneak into a married couple's room in the middle of the night, lie on the floor next to a guy's wife and try and get a free feel.

If you were a strange person before you went to Bethel, you became even stranger once there.

In the winter of 1970, I saw a movie that changed my life forever. I probably could have received a service talk for seeing it. Why? Because the Watchtower Bible and Tract Society condemns all R-rated movies, and you could get into serious trouble for seeing one.

If you are thinking about joining the Jehovah's Witnesses, keep that in mind. That doesn't change the fact that tens of thousands of Elders and publishers still see R-rated movies every year. They just don't get caught. That is the Catch 22 about seeing *Catch 22*.

Catch 22 was such a great movie. After I saw it, I went out and bought the book. When I read the book, I had tears in my eyes because it was so funny yet so painfully true.

The story was about a bunch of guys living together in an institution and the institution was the United States Army Air Force. The movie was Bethel incarnate.

It started off with two officers talking as they are walking down a runway. As they walk, a plane crashes, killing everyone on board. The two officers don't even look to see what had happened – officers and overseers who didn't give a damn.

People like Major Major Major in the movie were all around Bethel. Introverted people who were promoted not because they were spiritual or even for their qualifications as good managers but because they were the oldest guys in the department or they knew how to kiss some serious ass. Of course, these people have no idea how to handle others and hated the fact that people wanted to talk to them. If you ever had a meeting with them, "He would be out, unless they were in and then he would be really out."

The best part was at the end of the movie when they were finally going to let Yossarian go home after they did everything they could to destroy him. They told him he could finally leave. However there was a catch. "There is one thing you have to do for us in return." "What would that be?" Yossarian was afraid to ask.

"Like us!"

"Like you?"

"Like us! Say nice things about us. Tell the folks back home what a good job we are doing."

Have you ever wondered why most Bethelites don't talk much about Bethel once they go back home? If you have nothing good to say about the place, best to keep your mouth shut. Besides they know that no one would believe them even if they did tell the truth.

It's just like the old saying: "Never teach a pig to sing. It's just a waste of time and annoys the pig."

Deep down, Jehovah's Witnesses really don't want to know what Bethel is like. Why destroy the myth?

Of course, there were an insane amount of catch 22s at Bethel. It happens when they say things they really don't mean and mean things they really didn't say. Where the unwritten law takes precedence over the written laws. The book *Catch 22* was Bethel. It had everything in it, the double standards, the politics and favoritism. The biggest thing that stood out was the hypocrisy.

Yes, Bethel is one big giant catch 22. They give you a service talk because you weren't wearing a tie for your book study, yet on the other hand, they let the pedophiles go free and even paid them off.

Looking back at the movie and Bethel, they have one other thing in common: They are both comedies. Dark comedies, that is.

However, neither Yossarian nor I were laughing at the time. The joke was, indeed, on us.

Chapter 23

Feed the Rounder

I was dying every day on the machines. I prayed every day: "Please god, get me out of here." There was no way I could do this another two years. I was losing my mind.

I happened to find a picture of an old man with grey hair praying. In the picture, on the table next to the old man were a book, a loaf of bread and a bowl of gruel. It was a cheap print of Rhoda Nyberg's famous painting called *Grace*. I have no idea why, but I hung it up in my locker for all to see. I didn't know it at the time, but I'm convinced that picture saved my life, because a miracle happened.

One day, my floor overseer, Phill Gookenbiel, saw this picture and said, "What is this, Brother Casarona? This guy is not a Jehovah's Witness! Because that is not a New World Translation Bible on his table."

"I thought he was a Witness," I replied. "I thought he was one of the anointed ones, celebrating the Passover behind the Iron Curtain and that was the only Bible he could get." All Phil could say as he walked away was, "Hmmmm."

A miracle happened, because I got a job change two weeks later. I had tears in my eyes when they said I was being transferred out of the bindery. I walked up to my line overseer and blew him a kiss. He and the rest of the guys on bindery line 5 hated my guts. I couldn't blame them,

I would have too, if someone else had escaped the slow death that was happening in the bindery. I'll never forget the sad look in their eyes, as I walked away from them and their machines. I smiled to myself, as I walked across the sky bridge and out of Hell.

My new job was operator of the east freight elevator that was in building one. It was the oldest building of the four factory buildings. I thought I had died and gone to heaven. I could walk around and even go to the bathroom anytime I wanted, and I didn't need permission to do so. Plus, I could even spend more than five minutes doing my business in there. I was my own boss and loving it. Maybe there was a God after all, I thought.

The factory complex consisted of four large buildings. Each building was one full city block in size. My job was to move people and freight from the different floors in building one. I also moved freight in front of the different elevators to other buildings by way of the sky bridges that connected all four buildings.

In my building, there was the hand bindery on the ninth floor where they did small, customized book bindery. This was where a lot of the older Sisters who didn't want to work as a Bethel housekeeper worked. Brook Miller, the wife of Harley Miller, was there also. Harley, who was in charge of the entire service department, for some reason he couldn't handle his own alcoholic wife.

The eighth floor was storage.

The seventh floor was the linotype and plate department. This is where they made the plates for the rotary presses that churned out dozens of magazines and books. The overseer in the plate department was Warren Manns. The overseer of the linotype department was Houston Roberts, my first table head.

The sixth floor was the pressroom—the heart of the factory. The pressroom guys knew they were the cream of the crop. They knew all the other jobs at Bethel were there to support them. Like the laundry, it was always hot in the pressroom. This was because the ink needed to be warm in order to work correctly with the paper. Because of this, most of the guys wore shirts with the sleeves ripped off of them. Their clothes were full of oil, ink and sweat. They wore these rags like red badges of courage. That is where I met some of my best friends. Some called them the "pressroom animals." They were great guys. The overseer there was Richard Wheelock.

Just below the pressroom was the fifth-floor ink room. This was considered the "M.A.S.H. unit" of the factory. These guys got away with murder. These guys even took as many coffee breaks as they wanted. They even had a place where they could hide, where one of them could take a nap as the others were on lookout. The overseer there was Norm Brekke. I thought he was a really cool guy; that is until Jimmy Olson killed himself (more on that later). Norm Brekke would go to bat for his boys, "the inkies," which he did on more than one occasion.

The fourth floor was the job press. This was for the small jobs like invitations, handbills, assembly programs, etc. The overseer there was Tom Combs, another self-righteous company man. Tom always had a smile on his face. The smile was as fake as he was.

On the third floor was the deluxe Bible department. Many overseers passed through there. It was another great place to work.

The second floor was the carpenter shop where Bethel made all of its own furniture: beds, dressers, tables and anything else you could think of. The overseer was Richard Kimble.

The first floor was also a storage area. There were only three of us down there in the basement: Dennis, the elevator operator on the west freight elevator, an old man named Davis who ran the giant diesels that supplied all of the electricity that ran the factory and me.

The three of us all had lockers together in the basement. The old man didn't say much. I don't think he said more than a dozen words to us in the two years I was there. He just grunted mostly. I'm sure he had stories, but he wasn't sharing.

I did stumble onto one of those stories after I had been on the elevator for about a year. One day, when things were slow, I decide to clean my half of the basement. It hadn't been done in years and there was junk down there from the time of Rutherford. I started sorting things out. After

I had moved out a bunch of old oil drums, I found a pallet with what looked like ten old artillery shells. They were about two feet high. It turned out they were brand new pistons for our giant diesel engine. They were buried in the corner of the basement and looked like they had been there for many years. After asking around and going to the machine shop, I found out that they were a ten-thousand-dollar mistake. It seemed that many years earlier, the diesel needed new pistons, which had to be custom made. Someone sent in the wrong measurements and the pistons were too big to fit the diesel cylinders. They were now on the basement floor, gathering dust. I asked Russel Mock, head of the machine shop, if I could get rid of them. The answer was, "No."

"Will they ever have any use other than as paper weights?" I asked.

"No," he said, "They are just scrap metal now."

It kind of reminded me of some of the Jehovah's Witness beliefs: They don't fit, but we can't get rid of them, either. I bet they are still down in that spiritual basement waiting for "new light."

I remember looking at those pistons and thinking about a little old lady in Salina, Kansas, trying to scrape together a dollar to put in the contribution box. Sorry, I guess we will need ten-thousand little old ladies to cover this mistake. It would take one Bethelite almost 38 years to earn that kind of money at twenty-two dollars a month.

A few months passed. I was getting comfortable again, maybe a little too comfortable. I was starting to lose some of my fear of man. However, I knew that the bindery was just one building away over a sky bridge.

Sometimes I would have to go to the bindery to deliver freight. I would walk past some of my old friends like Roy and Jim Pipkorn. They looked at me and never said a word – their eyes said it all. We all knew what it was like to be married to the machines. I was glad I made it out. Jim would make it out too, just before he left Bethel, but Roy never did. He served his entire time in the bindery.

When the tour groups came through, it was a different story. It was shoulders back and smiling faces. We were Bethelites and damn proud of it. Even if the bastards there were trying to kill us. We were there for God, not man.

I worked hard. There was no way I was going back to the bindery. I wanted to be the best elevator operator they ever had. I found out later that they usually only left a person on the elevators for one year. The reason being, many of the guys would start flaking out after a while. I ended up on the elevators for more than two years. I would have been there longer if I hadn't said something.

After about a year on the elevator, I found a small sign that read: "Happiness is not a destination, but a daily way of travel." With so many of us counting our days, I thought this would be nice to hang in my elevator. Years later, I finally figured out what those words really meant.

One day, I was by the glue room, which was on the other end of the ink department, standing with Mike Stillman and two other guys. (As luck would have it, I ended up marrying Mike's sister two years later.)

Mike waved around a big wooden paddle about six feet long. He started to beat the hardened horsehide glue with it. It made a sound like a whip hitting bare flesh. He yelled out, "Feed the rounder." The rounder was the cruel machine I had worked on, while I was in the bindery. Then Mike slapped the glue again.

"Feed the rounder!" ....Slap! "Please don't beat me, brother overseer!"

"Feed the rounder!" ....Slap!

We all laughed and laughed. Just then, walking up from behind us from the sky bridge was none other than "Liver Lips" Linderman, the overseer of all of building three and the entire bindery! He stood there for a minute, quaking, and finally said, "Just what do think would have happened if it was a tour group that had come over that bridge instead of me?"

Mike just stood there with his paddle over his shoulder and said with a deadpan look on his face, "Well, I guess they would think we were normal, like everyone else!"

Rule No. 1: Never face down an overseer.

Rule No. 2: Never defend yourself.

Mike's words were words no overseer wanted to hear. I couldn't believe he'd actually said it!

Linderman stood there with smoke coming out of his ears and with a hateful look. He clearly didn't know what to say. How dare we stand up to him? He finally said, "You, you…have done a very bad thing." He turned and walked off.

We are totally screwed, I thought.

That was it, bindery here we come. Back to hell!

But no, Norm Brekke, the ink room overseer came through and saved us from all getting shafted to the bindery. I'm sure Mr. Linderman would have loved to have gotten his hands on us and put us on one of his machines for a real attitude adjustment.

That is what is so nice about Bethel – it's the love!

There is an old Bethel story that goes like this:

Phone rings in the fifth-floor bindery. New boy picks it up and says, "This is Stewflouten's sweat shop." (Stewflouten was the bindery overseer before Linderman back in the 1950s.)

The voice on the other end of the phone says, "Do you know who this is?" New boy answers, "No!"

"This is Max Larson, the factory overseer!" New boy says, "Well, do you know who this is?" "No!" Says Max. New boy says, "Good!" and then hangs up. True story.

Chapter 24
Lola La-La-La Lola

I'm not sure where I met Steve H., but it was love at first sight. Not physical love, though looking back, I don't think he would have minded that.

I was in love with the fact that he had been there for almost two years, and he had enough seniority to get us a better room in the Towers Hotel and out of our seven-man room in the rundown 129 building.

The Society had rented three floors in an old rundown hotel in Brooklyn Heights called The Towers Hotel. These rooms all had their own bathrooms. They went up for bid. If these rooms had been in the 119, 107 or 124 buildings, you would have needed at least ten-years seniority to secure one. The rooms in The Towers Hotel were two blocks from the main complex and still had a bunch of worldly people living in there. So, none of the older Bethelites wanted to live there. New boys, however, who wanted a decent room and didn't want to live with six or seven other guys, jumped at the opportunity. Plus, because of all of the old timers in the 119, 107 and 124 buildings, you had to always be on your best behavior.

Steve H. and I were part of the first group of guys to move into The Towers Hotel. We got room T-211. It had a beautiful view overlooking ventilators directly over the Towers ballroom. Some Saturday nights, the bed would almost vibrate from Carlos Santana's music down in the ballroom. Those Puerto Ricans knew how to have fun at a wedding reception, that's for sure.

Another fond memory from that room came from a hot July afternoon. I was trying to get some sleep because I was on the night shift. Everyone had windows open, trying to catch a little breeze. Back then, none of the rooms at Bethel had air conditioning. Some homesick new boy next door played John Denver's *Country Roads* sixty-seven times in a row.

I remember seeing two guys walking down a street in Greenwich Village and kissing each other on the lips. I was totally shocked. I was twenty-one and really knew nothing about homosexuals. I'd never met any growing up and even if I had met one, I wouldn't have known it.

To say we were homophobic is putting it mildly. A group of Bethelites even beat up a couple of gay guys one night in the Heights. They felt bad about their actions the next day and went to home overseer, Brother George Couch, to confess their unchristian behavior.

George sat there with a smile on his face and told them, "Don't worry about it boys, just don't do it again." The story spread like wildfire through Bethel. Basically, if you wanted to beat up some homosexuals, no big deal; the powers that be are looking the other way.

Their attitude was: Since God is going to kill them all off pretty soon, why should He have all the fun.

We were taught that homosexuality was the ultimate sin and worse than fornication. It was the reason why Sodom and Gomora were destroyed by God himself.

Before I go on, I must say that because I was raised a Jehovah's Witness, I was a stanch homophobic for most my life. I'm not that person now. My heart goes out to the thousands of gays who have left the Jehovah's Witness organization and thus lost their families because of their sexual orientation. They are part of our society and should be accepted as such. However, I don't feel the same way about pedophiles.

The Organization will tell you that there is zero tolerance for any pedophiles and homosexuals in the Jehovah's Witness organization. That is why all known gays had been kicked out and dis-fellowshipped before I arrived. Of course, one would think that obviously all gays and pedophiles would be kicked out and dis-fellowshipped if found there in the future.

Sorry, I should say *most* homosexuals and pedophiles were kicked out in disgrace. Unless the president and his buddies liked you. Then you could leave Bethel with no disgrace and even pioneer! Hell, they might even send you a check every month, too. You had to be in their club, of course. The good old boys club, that is.

Which homosexuals did they like? How about two members of the Governing Body? Remember, the Governing Body? These were the top leaders of the

Watchtower Bible and Tract Society. At the time, there were seventeen members on the Governing Body, two of whom were gay. That meant that more than 11 percent were gay. Since these men were all appointed by God's Holy Spirit maybe God liked gays more than the Society would like to admit.

Governing Body member Ewart Chitty (born ca. 1898) entered the London Bethel in 1921, began to work in the office and by 1938 held some sort of official position. By 1942, Chitty was secretary of the International Bible Students Association (IBSA), the Societies' British equivalent of the Watchtower Bible and Tract Society of New York, Inc. Somewhere along the line he was appointed as Secretary Treasurer of the IBSA, a position he held until his appointment to the Governing Body in November 1974. He wasn't a member of the Governing Body for very long because he resigned in 1979. However, Chitty remained in Brooklyn working in Writing Correspondence, so it seems he was certainly in good standing. According to close acquaintances, Chitty was drinking heavily by 1979. This likely contributed to him being dismissed from Brooklyn Bethel and reassigned to the London Bethel a few years later. There he worked on an assignment with little responsibility, but he was appointed an Elder in a local congregation. Chitty died about 1993. As to Chitty's homosexuality, he certainly made some remarks in his 1963 life story in The Watchtower that leaned in this direction. By then, he had roomed with the same man for 30 years. When in Brooklyn, Chitty seems to have preferred younger men as roommates. In 1979, an actual charge was brought to the Governing Body against Chitty by a former roommate (not his thirty-year boyfriend) and involved some sort of inappropriate conduct. The powers-that-be concluded that Chitty had homosexual tendencies, whatever that meant, and asked him to resign from the Governing Body. Chitty could hardly do anything but comply with the rest of the Governing Body's wishes, since his only alternative would have been to leave Bethel at age 81. He had been there for 58 years. It may well be that the Governing Body didn't view Chitty as guilty of homosexual activity, since he remained a Bethel member in Brooklyn or London. But it may also be that they made a deal – Chitty would remain quiet about where "the dead bodies" (secrets) were buried as long as the Society cared for him in his old age.

If he hadn't been guilty of molesting his roommate, why would he have ever resigned as a Governing Body member?

Our next Governing Body member was not just a homosexual but a pedophile also.

Leo K. Greenlees entered the Toronto, Canada, Bethel in 1936, eventually becoming Treasurer of the Canadian branch and of the IBSA of Canada. In 1964, he went to Brooklyn Bethel, and in 1965, he was elected as a director of the Societies' New York Corporation. As a director, Greenlees automatically became a Governing Body member when that body was formally instituted in 1971. He often spoke at Gilead graduations and was the concluding speaker for the day at the Watchtower Centennial business meeting at Three Rivers Stadium in Pittsburgh, Pennsylvania, on October 6, 1984. A 1982 Watchtower publication mentions him as being on the Teaching Committee of the Governing Body. Leo Greenlees was last mentioned in Watchtower publications in the December 1, 1984 Watchtower issue where he is said to have passed out diplomas at the September Gilead graduation.

In late 1984, Greenlees was convicted by the other Governing Body members of molesting a ten-year-old boy. The boy's parents had complained to the Society and it took action. Greenlees was a friend of the family and often visited them.

Leo Greenlees was the overseer of the Green Point congregation in Queens. He was a Bethel Elder and Governing Body member. He was a homosexual and pedophile. He really loved the Brothers, especially the younger ones.

He raped young Mark Palo when he was just ten years old. Mark was just one of many others. Mark, in an interview on YouTube, mentions he had been abused by Leo and another Jehovah's Witness.

How did the powers-that-be deal with this pedophile when he was caught in 1984? What punishment was administered? What example did they make of one of their own?

They gave Leo a "golden parachute" and asked him to leave. That's right, could you please just go someplace else? He wasn't kicked out and wasn't dis-fellowshipped. They even let him special pioneer, so of course he got an allowance from the society every month like all special pioneers do!

After he left Bethel, Leo became a special pioneer in the New Orleans area for a while and then moved around to many different congregations over the next few years. Just like most pedophiles do until they're stopped. However, Leo was never stopped. He proved to be untouchable. He had unlimited "get out of jail free" cards.

I ran into him in Mexico in the late 1980s, when I was there on vacation with my wife. I had known him at Bethel because he was my roommate Jack Sutton's presiding overseer.

Leo was a special pioneer in Mexico at the time. I didn't know his history back then. As we were having a cup of coffee together at my hotel, I do remember thinking to myself, why would someone who was on the Governing Body (which is, of course, the highest possible position a person could obtain in the organization) be a special pioneer in Mexico now? This made no sense to me and was very strange indeed.

However, now the pieces of the puzzle fit together so nicely.

I also remember him telling me how he had many Bible studies, mostly with younger boys. Big surprise.

For Leo, the only reprimand he ever received was the announcement at the world headquarters one morning in 1984 at breakfast: "Leo Greenlees is no longer a Bethelite. End of the matter."

Of course, they wanted this to be the "end of the matter." They swept him and his predisposition for young boys under the rug and wanted him as far away from them as possible.

Oh, yes, the Society even admitted they had a problem with their leaders. A January 1, 1986 Watchtower article (p. 13) stated: "Shocking as it is, some who have been prominent in Jehovah's organization have succumbed to homosexuality and child molesting."

In the Watchtower article, they didn't disclose the rest. What they should have said is this: "Shocking as it is, some who have been prominent in Jehovah's organization have succumbed to homosexuality and child molesting and we have done NOTHING about it!" That is the "shocking" part they conveniently left out of the article, not that people could do this, but that the leaders there would do nothing about it.

Who was the article talking about? For some odd reason, they didn't go into any details or name any names. Big surprise.

Yes, they spoke out and condemned it in their publications, but they let it slide when it really mattered. The funny thing is, I knew nothing about these matters when I was a Jehovah's Witness. Yet all of this information is out there in plain sight.

Now, of course, for the big question: Why would they let Leo go free and endanger the welfare of who knows how many young people in their organization and elsewhere?

Maybe there is another story here that we are not seeing. The bigger picture, as they say. Let's follow the money. After Leo left Bethel, he was a special pioneer. Leo was being paid directly by the Society every month up to the day he died. Leo was not in disgrace and enjoyed his position of prominence for the rest of his life. Yet, he was buggering young boys moving from congregation to congregation. Why wasn't he stopped? Why did they turn a blind eye and paid him off as well?

What was Leo's position at Bethel? He was the secretary treasurer of the whole Watchtower Bible and Tract Society. This was one of the most powerful positions there. Meaning he knew everything about the Societies' finances. My guess is he had them by the balls, and they knew it.

He had so much dirt on them that if any of it came to light, he would have blasted their Watchtower Bible and Tract Society back to the time of the great Miracle Wheat scandal of 1911. This was when Brother Russell was selling ordinary wheat that sold for about ninety cents a bushel for sixty dollars a bushel. Of course, the real "miracle" indeed was that people were stupid enough to buy it at that price.

My guess is, when Leo was caught, he told them what his terms would be. They of course had no choice but to agree with them and play ball.

There are only two options here. Leo Greenlees was in the good old boy club and he had a get out of jail free card. Or maybe he wasn't. He was just another pervert at Bethel who had a lot of nasty information about the Society and their corrupt dealings. He played his ace, and threatened to use this information on them. In which case, he got the same get out of jail free card.

Either way, The Watchtower Bible and Tract Society of New York and Pennsylvania are blood guilty. They have hidden pedophiles in their organization in the past. They are hiding them today, and they seem to want to continue this practice into the future.

The A&E Channel made this painfully clear in 2018 on their show *Cults and Extreme Beliefs*, season one, episode two: *Jehovah's Witnesses*.

There are hundreds of cases on the Internet of Elders who have turned a blind eye to these sexual predators. These young people are now coming forward and saying, "No more!"

The Watchtower Bible and Tract Society have put their own self-interest ahead of the wellbeing of their people and their people's children – the "flock" they are supposed to be protecting. I guess they don't mind if a few lambs in their flock get screwed along the way!

The leaders of the organization (the good shepherds) tell their followers they should all be just like "sheep." Why would they say that? Well, because we all know sheep are always afraid of wolves; however in the end, it is actually the shepherd who eats some of them, while he fleeces the rest of the flock.

Of course, most Jehovah's Witnesses don't know that The Watchtower Bible and Tract Society was being fined $4,000 a DAY by the State of California for not turning over the names of all the active pedophiles in their organization.

The Witnesses will be quick to point out: "We don't hate the people, we just hate their actions." Really? In Leo Greenlees case, I guess they hated neither the person nor his actions.

They did dis-fellowship a member of their Governing Body a few years earlier. His name was Raymond Franz. He was Fred Franz's nephew. When I was at Bethel, Ray was considered one of the most approachable members of the Governing Body. He was a very humble person and loved by many. What was his crime?

Raymond Franz, Ed Dunlap and Lyman Swingle were doing research as writers for the new *Aid to Bible Understanding* book. They researched the time lines, which were based upon the cornerstone date of 1914 as being the end of the Gentiles Times. This was the time period supposedly running for two-thousand, five-hundred-and-twenty years since 607 BC. Franz tells of how he sent his personal secretary Charles Ploeger to visit the New York City libraries to try and substantiate this date for the destruction of Jerusalem. No such evidence was forthcoming. Instead, the date 587-586 BC was reinforced. Later, in 1977, a Swedish Elder sent a great deal of documentation based upon over ten-thousand cuneiform tablets found in the Mesopotamian area that dated back to the time of ancient Babylon, which substantiated that the destruction of Jerusalem was not 607 BC, but twenty years later. After Ray Franz left Bethel, he wrote a book, *Crisis of Conscience*. In it he states, "Much of the time and space under the *Aid* book heading of 'Chronology' was spent in trying to weaken the credibility of the archeological and historical evidence that would make erroneous our 607 BC date and give a different starting point for our calculations and therefore an ending date different from 1914."

Franz and his secretary even took a trip to Brown University in Rhode Island to interview Professor Abraham Sachs, a specialist in ancient cuneiform texts, in an attempt to find a weakness or flaw in the historical evidence. Not one possibility existed of such evidence being erroneous. Yet, Franz felt obligated to write the article in the *Aid* book without revealing all of the facts. He was forced to do this by the rest of the Governing Body who had refused to reconsider this important matter.

To destroy the credibility of 1914 as the invisible return of Christ would truly devastate the entire authority structure of the Governing Body. They could not be pointed to as the "appointed channel" of communication between God and the rest of their followers.

A shock wave within the organization was inevitable. No matter how tight the security, sooner or later the evidence that destroyed the authority of the Governing Body would leak out.

What do you think happened? Do you think the leaders were happy to hear how their organization had been wrong for over one-hundred years? What would happen to them and their church if everything concerning the cornerstone date of 1914 were wrong? All of the preaching about the "lasts days" and the "Generation" that saw those things in 1914 were incorrect.

The Governing Body felt it would be a good time to go to Jehovah again and pray.

What should we do, God? We have a serious problem here. This problem is definitely bigger than the pedophile problem. Should we listen to those devoted men in the writing department who have researched this subject thoroughly? Men who already have written dozens of books and publications for the Society. Men who all have over forty years of full-time service and have been faithful to you and your organization?

If we do listen to them, it could be the end of the church as we know it. We could lose the prestige we get from millions of our followers, from people who think you are talking to only us.

We could lose our lavish lifestyles and our fancy apartments overlooking lower Manhattan. Then there are all those free trips we get to exotic places for our speaking assignments. This is a tough one, for sure!

God answered. Fred Franz, the president, along with Leo Greenlees (who was still a member of the Governing Body back then) and the rest of the Governing Body made their decision. Ray Franz and Ed Dunlap would be dis-fellowshipped. Before they were dis-fellowshipped, however, the Governing Body pleaded with them to ignore the facts and maintain the Society's present understanding for "the sake of unity." However, the two men stood firm on what was right.

The term "the sake of unity" means this: Sure, we are wrong about this one, however, we need to shut our eyes and stick together and keep our mouths shut, for the sake of the greater good! What is the greater good? The myth that we and our organization *are* the greater good!

Dozens more left the Bethel family or were disfellowshipped in the months to come, as they apparently "knew too much." While members of the Bethel family heard regular denouncements of the apostates, few knew about the events that had really occurred. The great cover up was working once again.

Lyman Swingle saw the light and gave in for the sake of unity. He rejoined his country club lifestyle.

On April 30, 1980, Karl Klein of the Governing Body stated to the whole Bethel family: "If you have a tendency towards 'apostasy,' get a hobby and keep yourself busy to keep your mind off of it. Stay away from deep Bible study to determine meanings of the scriptures."

So, there you have it. More "new light" from the Governing Body for the Bethel family. "Stay away from deep Bible study." If you dig too deep, you just might find out how wrong we have been with the many false prophecies and incorrect dates we have used for over a hundred years in this organization.

Raymond Franz's book *Crisis of Conscience* has a lot of fun information about the inner workings and clouded history of the Watchtower Bible and Tract Society, things that only someone who was on their board of directors could possibly know. The book contains a lot of classified documents. There you will find what is really behind the screen of the great and powerful Wizard of OZ.

Who knows, maybe even Leo Greenless read Ray's book! He must have laughed out loud thinking to himself how he beat the organization. Unlike Ray, Leo could act with impunity. Ray was dis-fellowshiped whereas Leo never was. The difference is Leo had no problem threatening blackmail, whereas Ray was too much of Christian to do that.

So, if we look at the Governing Body members Leo Greenlees and Ray Franz and what happened at Black Thursday, there seems to be a definite pattern here. It seems like the society likes to protect and promote the wrong doers in their organization and chastise and reprove the people who want to bring this wrong doing to light. Or is it "New Light" or is it any light, or maybe there is no light. I'm confused!

In the end, Leo was doing the same to the little boys in Mexico as the Governing Body had been doing to all of us Bethel boys for years.

Chapter 25

Something Jesus Would Do

Life is strange, and what happened to David, a friend of mine, in December 1972 couldn't be any stranger. David worked in the carpenter shop. One day he ran his hand through a table saw almost up to his wrist. He cut off his middle finger and destroyed two others.

They took him to the emergency room in Brooklyn, his hand wrapped in a bloody towel. He was in all kinds of pain. The nurses moved him out of the waiting room into a smaller room.

David told me it went something like this. An orderly, who was helping him get into a gown, told him, "We need a urine sample." David was about to pass out because of the pain and blood loss. The orderly was grabbing David's penis for the urine test when a second orderly came in and saw what was going on.

"Jerry, you sick fag!" Cried the second orderly. "What the hell are you doing? This guy is bleeding to death and you are trying to get a free feel?"

My poor friend David was getting screwed over by everyone. The orderly wanted a free feel and he would soon find out Bethel wanted him gone.

The good Brothers at Bethel told him it would be best for him (not them of course) if he left Bethel. Why? Because he was no longer a twenty-two-dollar a month asset. He was now a ten-thousand-dollar liability. It's always best to send the wounded soldiers home, I guess.

He and his family had no money and no insurance for the many operations he would need on his hand in the months to come. He begged them to let him stay at Bethel. After many talks, they finally gave in and let him stay. This was one of the few times that I saw the organization open up their wallets and pay for a person who was injured at Bethel.

On December 26th the same day that David ran his hand through the table saw, some worldly guy who I guess didn't like the way his Christmas went that year jumped off the roof of The Towers Hotel and committed suicide. He hit a parking sign on the way down and exploded on the sidewalk below. I didn't really see him hit the payment, but I saw parts of him for weeks after he died.

His blood and tiny little bits of his flesh were still on the sidewalk. No one cleaned it up, and he was there for months until the New York snow and rain washed away what was left of him.

One thing wonderful about being at Bethel and New York City, you never know what is going to happen next.

Hey, it's New York. As the saying goes, "Forget about it."

My new roommate, Steve, also had all of the characteristics of someone who was leaning towards the NPG (non-practicing gay) way. He had all of the mannerisms and was very clingy. Let me put it this way, I wasn't going to do any rum and Cokes with him on a Saturday night and see what happened next.

He would say things like, "So, what are we going to do together this coming Saturday after work?"

I don't know Steve, I would think. What *are* we going to do together? I started to ditch him after work. Steve moved out of the room. I guess I wasn't friendly enough. Maybe he found a roommate who was more NPG friendly. I was able to keep the room in The Towers.

My new roommate was my old buddy Jack Sutton, one of the guys I worked with from the laundry. He was from Phoenix and I was from California. We became good friends at Bethel and have remained friends for almost fifty years. I was the best man in his wedding and he was the best man in mine. Jack is very intelligent, so of course he left the organization many years before I did.

Anyway, Jack and I decided to decorate our room in a western motif. We had some old western posters on our walls and a poster of a bullfighter and a bull from Mexico.

One night at about 7:00 p.m., we heard a knock on the door. It was Curtis Johnson, the newly appointed home servant to The Towers Hotel. This guy looked and talked just like the Nazi with thick black glasses and the shit-eating smile in the movie *Raiders of the Lost Ark*. He was bald and about five feet and four inches tall – a real dweeb and the perfect company man.

We told him he was welcome to come in. You could tell he felt very uncomfortable. "No thanks, Brothers. I'm here to talk to you about your room."

"Our room?"

"The decorations in your room."

"Okay, what about them?"

"We don't like them."

"Who is we?"

"Well, you know, the Bethel office."

"Really?"

"Really!" He said as he was twitching.

"We don't like your bull-fighting poster on your wall. A tour group might think we like killing animals."

"Brother Johnson," I said. "No tours come through The Towers Hotel and besides, we don't even look at the poster in that manner."

"Never mind about that. We want it down!"

"Alright," we said. "We'll take it down."

We never said when we would take it down, though. So, we did take it down, about a year later when we moved to a different room. I'm sure our files were noted.

I'm afraid we hadn't seen the last of our dear friend Brother Johnson. More on him later.

The organization didn't seem to mind their top leaders having sex with young boys, but our bull-fighting poster was just too much of an offense for their finer senses.

Kool-Aid, anyone?

Before I talk about sex at Bethel, it would be good to talk about the history of sex in the organization. The organization would say that it started with Adam and Eve, but the real Jehovah's Witness organization is less than 150 years old. In reality, it's an 1800s' religion, with 1800s' morals and mentality. You know, since it started back in the Victorian period.

Anyway, back in the Garden of Eden is when the real problem started, in the organization's mind anyway.

The first real question ever posed to man had nothing to do with universal sovereignty, as the church would have you believe. Adam had a decision to make: everlasting life with god or really good sex with a perfect mate for a few years.

You know how Adam voted. No offense god, but I think I'll take the great sex for a few years, thank you!

Remember, the Bible said, "The man was not deceived!" He knew what he was doing; in his mind the choice was clear. Would he choose everlasting life with a god? A god who, let's face it, really wasn't all that friendly and who was invisible? Or he could choose a few wonderful years of bliss with the woman of his dreams, the love of his life – a beautiful, visible woman.

Adam was the first man to die for love and really good sex. What a hero! I say really good sex because who would give up everlasting life for bad sex? God didn't create a fool. What he did create was a perfect man and a perfect woman, with a perfectly normal and healthy sex drive.

Most churches think that Adam should have chosen god over his wife and the Jehovah's Witnesses are no different. Religions are about control and most religions are run by self-righteous men with control and sexual issues. Men who want to suppress women and use sex for control and power.

Many of the churches of today like to quote the Bible where it says, "The head of the woman is the man." God never wrote that. Man wrote that! Men have been using it against women for thousands of years to gain power. The Garden of Eden thing is pure urban myth anyway.

So, back to sex and Bethelites. Most of the people who are called to Bethel are single young men who are at their sexual peak. Back then, they signed a four-year contract to stay at the house of god, no matter what. That meant no sex, no matter what, during that time period. So, clearly, some very interesting things would go on there.

Where to start? We already talked about the gays and the NPGs (non-practicing gays). There were plenty of those. The rest of the guys at Bethel fell into different groups:

Guys who had girlfriends before they came. They asked the girls to wait for them. The odds of them still being together at the end of four years was almost zero. I knew of only one guy who was able to keep the girlfriend he had before he went to Bethel.

Guys who got girlfriends in the New York area while they were there.

Guys who got together with Bethel Sisters and married them.

Guys who found girlfriends back home when they were on vacations or met a girl when they were going through on tour of the Bethel home or factory.

Guys who hired a hooker on 8th Avenue.

Guys with no girlfriends but who just masturbated a lot.

Straight guys who were not gay and didn't like women or sex.

Since the Governing Body and most of the leaders at Bethel were enjoying sex, the average non-gay Bethelite wanted sex, too.

That was tough for guys like Roy Baty with girlfriends back home, because you only received two weeks of vacation a year. Since you received no vacation your first year, you really earned a total of only six weeks in four years. Many guys, like myself, only received four weeks in four years. The reason being: Instead of taking our last two weeks of vacation, we would just shorten our four-year tour of duty by two weeks. I came in on March 21, 1970. Now I could leave on March 7, 1974. The thought being that any day not at Bethel was a vacation!

There were all kinds at Bethel. There was a guy in the service department who ran off with the district overseer's wife. There were old married Sisters who left their husbands for single young Bethel boys. You know, all the stuff you would see in any Kingdom Hall.

Love is a strange thing and what it does to people is even stranger.

My friend Tom Plank met a girl in upstate New York. Her name was Babe. He was totally in love with Babe. She had a lot of good-looking Bethel boys chasing after her over the years. She said she was done with all of the games and thought Tom was the real deal, so she chose him. Tom was the real deal, too. They called him "The Animal" in the pressroom, but he had a huge heart and was one of my best friends for over thirty years, until I left the organization.

Tom was in heaven with Babe for a while. However, Tom wasn't the best-looking guy on the planet. He looked a lot like the old movie star Wallace Beery. Tom started getting nervous. Why would a beautiful woman like Babe be interested in someone who looked like him? So, did she end up dropping Tom? No, he dropped her and even worse, he started going out with a friend of hers who was in the same clique. His new girlfriend, Nina, was the least attractive girl in this group and could cuss like a drunken sailor. Why did he do this? I guess he felt she was safe and was all that he really deserved.

I asked him if he was crazy. I told him what my father told me: "Always go after the prettiest girls. They are just as lonely as the ugly ones." He realized his mistake and tried calling Babe. She wouldn't return any of his phone calls. He finally asked me to talk to her and apologize for his actions. He was willing to do anything to get her back, including groveling.

I called her and set up the meeting. She came to Bethel and we talked. I told her Tom's sad story. That he had realized his big mistake and he would do anything she requested just to have her back in his life. I told her how amazing Tom was and how they could be perfect for each other.

She sat there and after a few minutes she confessed. "It was bad enough that he dropped me in front of all of my friends. I thought I was finally over all of the games guys like to play. But Nina? Really? Let me tell you something Keith, I will never be back with Tom – ever! A woman can handle almost anything except one thing in a man. That one thing is indecision. A man must know what he wants and be unwavering!"

Years later, Tom confided in me that he still thought about Babe and that she will always be the love of his life.

Bethel tours were nice, but most of the time, they were very sad. You would see these great-looking Sisters go through on tour. They would give you the eye. You would give them the eye. Then they would get on the bus and leave. There was no way to meet them. Sometimes you would see them later that day in the Bethel home, hanging around with some nerd from their hometown. Sometimes they would ask if the nerd knew other Bethelites. Sure, they did, but their friends were Bethel geeks, too.

Sometimes it worked out great. I saw Debbie Stillman, the lady I would marry, standing in front of the ink room in the summer of 1972 on a Bethel tour.

So, why did our President Nathan Knorr get married to Audrey Mock in 1953? Did he get married for companionship? No. He had more than 1,500 Brothers for companionship. He could always do things with them: sit around and talk about the Bible, go to a movie or play chess. There were plenty of brown noses for that. Did he get married to have children? No. It was forbidden to have children at Bethel. If you got pregnant, you were required to leave immediately. Did he get married to be with that one special person forever? No. He was going to heaven and Audrey wasn't. She was part of the "great crowd," and she had no heavenly hope. In fact, after Nathan died, Audrey remarried. So, she knew she would never be seeing Nathan again, for sure. So, why did Knorr get married?

It sure looks like it was for good old fashion SEX.

"Love makes the world go "round" was a popular saying back then. At Bethel, we new boys had a saying of our own. "If god created anything better than sex, He kept it for himself!"

How would we know if sex was that great? Most of us had never had it. But that didn't stop us from talking about it, fantasying about it and dreaming about it. We couldn't have it, so we glorified it. We were in our twenties and virgins. Some of us were in our thirties and forties and had never known a woman. We had some raging hormones going on.

Jehovah's Witnesses are forbidden to have sex in the following situations:

Sex out of wedlock.

Sex with someone besides your spouse.

Sex with someone of the same sex.

Sex with your own children or other people's children.

Of course, there would be no sex before marriage and sadly in some cases there was very little sex after marriage, either. Usually the only person you'd have sex with is the one and only person you ever had sex with. That meant there was plenty of sexual incompatibility going on. That is, in part, why more people are kicked out of the Jehovah's Witnesses every year for sexual violations than anything else.

Yes, sex continues to be their biggest problem at the world headquarters and in the local Kingdom Halls.

Strange that most of the Governing Body members were Germans in the formative years of the organization. Knorr, Franz, Swingle, Suiter, Henschel, Groh, Fekel, Schroeder, Potzinger. Sorry, no women and no blacks. White men of German ancestry, in most cases. These were hard men with lots of rules.

However, even the Germans like sex. I found that out after Knorr's new boy sex talk. Knorr and his buddies were able to enjoy that privilege. I say privilege because not everyone was permitted to have it. Knorr came up with the new rules for having sex at Bethel. He did this after he surprised the whole Bethel family by returning from a vacation in 1953, married to Audrey.

New rules for the boys: If you wanted to get married and stay at Bethel, the two people would be required to have a total of fourteen years of full-time service. You were forbidden to get married for the first four years at Bethel, no matter what. If you wanted to stay at Bethel, you had to add another six years. Plus the person you wanted to marry needed a minimum of four years of full-time service also.

I didn't say forbidden, did I? I guess I did. But the Bible clearly states "That only those that have fallen away from the faith, would be forbidding others to marry!" 1 Timothy 4:1-3.

That can't be right. They would be disregarding information set out in the Bible. The old double-standard rule kicks in again!

If you objected to these rules, the powers-that-be would say, "Well, you signed an agreement!" Yes, you're nineteen years old, and you should have known what you were signing, right? In most states, a contract isn't even legal until you are twenty-one.

Some would say that you could always leave before your time. Yes, if you didn't mind the reproach and the shame of being a "short timer."

There was also the punishment aspect. Yes, you could be punished if you left Bethel and got married before your contract was up by being forbidden to pioneer for six months. This may not seem like much of a punishment, but these loving Brothers who thought up this punishment were brilliant.

If you couldn't pioneer, you would lose your 4-D classification. At that time, it meant that you would go back to a 1-A classification. It was the height of the Vietnam War. If you got called up to the draft board, guess what? You were going to jail!

Why would you be going to jail? Because being a conscientious objector was the only option for a Jehovah's

Witness. Back then, refusing to serve in the military was automatic jail time.

The bottom line was that if you left before your time, you could be heading to a real prison. Not the one in Brooklyn Heights.

Of course, they could have thanked you for the two or three years of service you had given them. All the time you spent working long hours for basically no pay.

That's not their style. There was no gratitude for your time served. Instead, get your prison uniform ready and grab your ankles. This was the thanks you got.

Really, don't you think a loving organization would have people's best interest at heart? As in: "Oh, Brother we are sorry to hear you are having a hard time here at Bethel. So, you would like to leave? Go my friend and be in peace. May god be with you, and thank you for the time you did spend here with us. Of course, you can pioneer if you like." Maybe if those words had been spoken to Jimmy Olson, he would still be with us today.

That statement sounds like something Jesus would say. But it doesn't appear that Jesus was anywhere near the place, and he certainly was not running things there at Bethel, the house of god. Did he ever?

Did I say loving organization? The Bible states at John 13: 35, that by their love you would be able to recognize true followers. Boy, isn't that the truth! But there was no real love at the world headquarters or in the Society. This lack of real love and apathy started at the very top of the organization with Knorr and worked its way down to the local Kingdom Halls.

Yes, there is a pretense of love, but at the real core there is something altogether different.

A friend of mine, Ted Devink, from the Pressroom wanted to leave Bethel before his time was up. I told him, "Ted, just leave, what can they do to you?"

Ted said, "They won't let me pioneer – for six months." "Oh, really?" I said. "Do you mean they won't let you go out in Field Service?"

"No, they will."

"So, they won't let you go in Field Service for 100 hours a month?"

"No, they will."

"Oh," I said. "So, you can't be called a pioneer?"

"Yes, that is right."

"So now you would be classified as 1-A again? Very interesting."

"Yes, I'm screwed." He said.

Ted went to Richard Wheelock after he had turned in his thirty-day notice. He asked Richard if he could have a couple of hours off to go to a job interview because he was going to need a job after he left Bethel. Richard went nuts. How could Ted ask for this? What was he thinking? Richard ripped into him for trying to steal two hours from Jehovah.

What Richard should have said to Ted, but didn't, was: "Sure, Brother. Whatever we can do to help. By the way, thank you so very much for the two years you did spend here and the sacrifices you made, though we paid you practically nothing and treated you like shit the whole time."

All the double standards and unwritten laws – it was just too much for most of us. The vast majority of the people left Bethel at or before their four years were up. They couldn't wait to leave what the Bethel leaders called the "spiritual paradise."

I say most of us felt that way. However there were some who loved it. A very small percent stayed after their contract was up. This small group of people wanted to join the country club, too. They liked the way things were done there. They loved the politics and power trips. They soon would fit right in with the cold-hearted bastards who were running the place.

Chapter 26

A Hero and a Quart of Beer

On top of working forty-six hours a week at Bethel, Monday nights were the Watchtower study and primary school, and Tuesday and Friday nights were meetings at the Kingdom Hall. Sundays were for Field Service in the mornings and meetings in the afternoons. Basically, the only free time you had were two weekday nights and Saturday afternoons and evenings. That came to only about 15 to 17 hours of free time every week.

Guess what many of us Bethelites did with all that extra free time? We got another job.

Those at Bethel called those outside jobs "G-jobs." No one really knows where the name came from. But a G-job is any job you worked to make more money, more than the seventy-three cents a day or the twenty-two dollars a month Bethel gave us. We spent about nine dollars a month, just on subway tokens to get back and forth to our Kingdom Halls. So, after those necessary traveling expenses, we were really only making about five cents an hour.

I heard a story about a guy who was mugged in New York City. The mugger put a gun to his head and said, "Give me your money or I'm going to blow your brains out!" The man said, "You better shoot. Because I know one thing about New York: You can live here without brains, but you got to have money!"

Many of the guys at Bethel had families that couldn't send any extra cash for the basic necessities. That meant earning even ten or twenty bucks extra a week could make a big difference in making life a little more comfortable.

When the Sisters forgot your dinner at the Kingdom Hall, with that extra cash, there could be a slice of pizza in your future. Once or twice a week, you could get a hero and a quart of beer down at Plymouth Deli. If you were really rolling in cash, you could buy a chuck steak at 69 cents a pound and some frozen French fries, add one onion and cook it up in your room on an electric skillet. A cheap steak and a quart of beer and life was good.

For really special occasions, there was a restaurant that was a Bethelite's idea of a real paradise. If one of our buddies "made his time" and was leaving Bethel, the restaurant of choice was Steak & Brew. For about $7.95, you could buy a complete dinner consisting of an appetizer, a steak, veggies, a baked potato, ice cream and coffee. But, most important to us Bethelites was the promise of *unlimited* beer, wine or sangria. Of course, it was the cheapest rot-gut beer you could get in New York City at the time, but we didn't care. Just say the words Steak & Brew and a Bethelite's eyes would light up.

Yes, just a couple of extra dollars a month could make a real difference there.

There were many different types of G-jobs the Brothers were willing to do for a little extra money. Believe it or not, most of the extra money we made went to food.

Some guys in the pressroom ran a paper route. It started at 3:00 a.m. on Sunday mornings. You would run through apartment buildings delivering this massive Sunday edition of the newspaper to people's doorways. I did it once. Not for me.

Some lucky guys got jobs at the Fleur De Lis catering hall in Brooklyn as waiters at wedding receptions. That job provided great tips, plus you could keep all the half-drunk bottles of wine when it was over. You might have to pick out a cigarette butt or two, but what the heck? There was a waiting list to work there and it was very tough to get hired on there.

Some guys found jobs painting apartments. Anything for a buck.

My friend Jim Pipkorn worked at a funeral home in the Lower East Side of Manhattan. It was always fun visiting him at his place of employment. One Saturday afternoon, I went to his funeral home to pick him up to go to a movie in Times Square.

"He is downstairs in the basement," the owner told me. I looked down the stairs and shook my head no. "It's okay," he said with a smile. I, on the other hand, really didn't want to go down there. Jim must have heard us upstairs talking. "Keith, come on down here. They won't hurt you." I slowly walked down the stairs to the basement.

As I expected, there were dead people down there. Two guys in white aprons were hunched over an old dead guy lying on a porcelain table. There were tubes and needles everywhere and blood pouring down the table into a waiting bucket. There was another old dead guy on an embalming table next to them as they worked. He was naked with a strange look on his face. This dead guy also had a sixteen-ounce can of Rheingold beer perched in the middle of his chest. As the undertakers were working, the oldest one would reach over and take the can of beer off the dead guy's chest and take a swig from it. I wondered what this dead guy's relatives would have thought if they could have seen their dead grandpa with a can of beer on his chest.

Another time I visited Jim at the funeral home, he was alone in the basement. He showed me a large refrigerator where they kept the dead people. He opened one of the drawers and rolled out a dead black pimp. The guy had been stabbed about twenty times. He then rolled out a dead woman in her twenties. There wasn't a mark on her body. She had no hands and no head. The missing limbs had been surgically removed.

"Why?" I asked Jim.

"Because whoever killed her knew that if she could be identified, the killers could be caught. She had no birthmarks or tattoos, yet the police still identified her. How do you think they did that?"

"I don't know, feet marks?" I said.

"No such thing. She had an IUD that had a serial number on it."

One of my first G-jobs was as a dishwasher. I washed pots and pans in a high-end restaurant three blocks from Bethel. I was a true "pot licker."

To this day, I will not order turkey and dressing in a restaurant. The restaurant served little miniature loaves of bread. People would eat half of them and then put out their cigarettes in what was left of the bread. The waiters would bring what was left of the loaf of bread to the kitchen and throw them in a dirty cardboard box on the floor. Next week the bread in that box was the stuffing for the Thursday turkey-and-bread-stuffing special.

I also worked in two liquor stores, one in the Inwood area and one in Brooklyn Heights. Hey, one dollar and seventy-five cents an hour seemed like good money. I was only making five cents an hour working for Jehovah. I guess Jehovah doesn't believe in minimum wage. Some nights, I wouldn't bring home any money. Instead, I traded my earnings for two of my best friends: Jack Daniels and Johnnie Walker.

At this time, Dave Borga, the waiter who showed me the hot end of the dishwasher, worked in the pressroom.

Dave would go down in Bethel history as the king of all G-jobbers. They still speak about him to this day, forty years later, in the new boy talks. While working at his Bethel job, he also had a full-time job working the night shift at a toy factory in New Jersey. That's right, he was working almost eighty hours a week! He was getting by on just three to four hours of sleep each night. Needless to say, he didn't last long, working at that pace. But he was able to buy a newer Ford Mustang before he had to leave Bethel.

Dave finally left the religion and had been out for almost thirty years. However he has recently rejoined the church and is very happy being back into their fold.

Al Pacino once said. "Just when I thought I was out… they sucked me back in!"

One weekend, Jack Sutton and I painted a whole apartment for only one-hundred-and-fifty dollars. Seventy-five dollars apiece. Of course, it would have taken us almost four months at our Bethel jobs to make that kind of money. We knew we had under bid the job when the alcoholic owner came home with over a hundred dollars' worth of booze. He loved us.

Chapter 27

"New Light" on Ear Infections

As I have mentioned before, one of the problems with breakfast was when Knorr went off on one of his many rants. Whatever food that was supposed to be served hot or warm turned ice cold – not good for scrambled eggs or what we called vulcanized eggs. To make vulcanized eggs, the cooks placed hundreds of raw eggs on large cookie sheets and then baked them. The eggs had the consistency of rubber – barely edible when warm and like shoe leather when cold.

Whatever was left to eat after prayer was up for grabs. Sisters would jump up after the prayer with their Tupperware containers in hand and load up. Before you could blink an eye, a Sister could clean off three tables of leftovers. This was an important activity if you wanted anything decent to eat at night.

The reason being that the dinners there were a real joke.

Of the 1,600 Bethelites, maybe about one hundred showed up for dinner. Were we not hungry? Of course we were. We were twenty year olds, working hard all day in a factory.

So, why would so few show up for dinner? The food was either nasty combinations they threw together, like squash stuffed with mystery meat (some called this dish "monkey butts"). If the food was decent, there really wasn't enough of it to go around to feed even the ten hungry guys on one table. Plus, we only had fifteen minutes to eat dinner before the final prayer. The waiters served the food for about ten of those fifteen minutes, because sometimes it would take five minutes to get the first platters passed out. Most of the time, the waiters came back with hardly anything on them. At other times, the food ran out ten minutes into the dinner.

I remember many times leaving the lower dinner room and still being hungry. I couldn't help but think of the line in *Oliver*, "Please sir may I have some more?"

The Brothers were sending us a message, and I received it loud and clear. *We really don't want to feed you guys at night. You better figure out something else to do.* I'm sure not feeding us saved the Society thousands of dollars every year. Excuse me, I meant pretending to feed us.

After a while, I also noticed a glaring fact. It was that if you looked around the dining room, you never, and I mean never, saw any of the Bethel overseers or elders going to dinner. They knew the food was shit and stayed away too. So after six months there, I decided I would help out the society and save them yet even more money and stopped going to the dinners altogether.

The last week I was at Bethel, I don't know why, but after boycotting the dinner there for over three years, I went to dinner. It was the Last Supper for me. A bunch of the guys there stood up and gave me a standing ovation. I had no idea that my lack of attendance was that noticeable. It was very funny and very surprising and yes, the food was still nasty that night.

Given the terrible situation with Bethel dinners, your choices were to scavenge leftovers after lunch, which was hit or miss, or on Sunday afternoons, they put out bread and cold cuts. This was great, but since most Bethelites didn't get back to Bethel until Sunday evening, because of being at their congregations all day, they missed out on the free food. Of course, you could buy food with your own money. This was yet another reason to get a G-job.

I knew there was going to be trouble from the first day that I was assigned to Doctor Dixon's table. The icicles were hanging from the silverware.

The good doctor's table was the first table in the upper dinning next to the staircase. I was assigned there after I got my job on the freight elevator in the factory of building one. The reason being, I had to be out the door and one of first people back at the factory after lunch and breakfast. The elevator was hand operated and required someone to take personnel up to their different departments.

I sat across the table from an old bat named Esther Lopez. It was war with her, from the first day I sat at that table. Our first conversation went something like this.

Me: "Hi, I'm Keith"

Ester: "Where are you from, Keith?"

Me: "I came here from Kansas." (I never thought it was a good idea to tell people I was from California at Bethel. For some odd reason, Brothers from California weren't really liked at Bethel and had bad reputations. Maybe we were too liberal. I really don't know. It was just another one of those strange unexplained attitudes.)

Esther: "Where were you raised in Kansas?"

Me: "Ah no, California"

Esther: "It figures!"

Me: "Wow, you can really feel the love at this table!"

Esther: "Sometimes the loving thing to do is correct your Brothers when they need it."

Me: "Well, SISTER Lopez, I think I'll let the Brothers do that!"

Talk about a bitter old woman. No matter. As soon as prayer was over, I was out of there.

Another thing about Dixon's table was that he screwed us over with the food distribution. The protocol at a Bethel table for Table Heads was if you passed a platter of food down the right side of the table, then when that platter was empty and filled with more food, it would be passed down the opposite side of the table. This was so all people on the table could get a chance at some of the food.

The doctor had a better idea. Ninety-five percent of the time, the food went to his wife first and to Esther Lopez second. Esther was one of Audrey Knorr's best friends. Yes, the good doctor liked to do a little ass kissing himself.

Many times, the platters never made it to the end of the table. So, if you were in the last two seats on the left-hand side, you were screwed.

One time, we were served fried chicken. The first large platter of chicken came to our table. The doctor, of course, helped himself and his wife to the best parts. Then he passed the platter down the right side of the table. When the platter of chicken reached me, only chicken backs were left. I took two backs and passed it on. The platter was sent out for more chicken and came back half full. Dixon again took the best parts and passed the platter to his wife. Again, by the time it reached me, only backs were left. So, I took two more backs and passed it on. The platter went out again for more chicken. This time the platter came back with all chicken backs on it. So, what did the good doctor do? He is full now, so he finally sends the platter down the left side. I took three more backs. At the end of the meal, my plate was stacked high with all the bones from the chicken backs. Dixon looks over at me and all my chicken bones and says, "Well, Brother Casarona, you sure made a pig out of yourself today."

I never really liked Doctor Dixon. He was a pompous ass. He and his wife had their own plush apartment and plenty of money. We were living in two different worlds. He and his wife were privileged and in the good old boys' club and I wasn't. Again, it also showed me how they rewarded people with a good education. No, he didn't listen to them and skipped a college education, and because of that, he was rewarded for it.

Catch 22.

One day at Doctor Dixon's lunch table, the whole upper dining room was pretty quiet. One table was really loud; it was the tour table with visiting Brothers and Sisters. The good doctor kept looking over and giving them dirty looks as if to say, "How dare you disturb my lunch?"

I said, "You can tell they're not Bethelites." Meaning they were happy and joyful.

He knew what I meant and said, "I think you have a bad attitude about Bethel."

I said, "I have a bad attitude about New York City."

He said, "Are you kidding? Look at all the great things you can do here. You have all the plays and the fine dining!"

I said, "Brother Dixon, I don't know the New York City you're talking about. A poor Bethelite's New York City is a hero sandwich and a quart of beer once a month, if we are lucky."

He gave me a disgusted look and turned away.

What Bethel needed was a general practitioner as a doctor. Doctor Dixon was a surgeon, so he had the bedside manner of a goat with little or no empathy.

One time a young Bethelite was complaining about bleeding from his rectum. The good doctor told the Brother that it was no big deal, that he probably was just wiping his ass too hard with toilet paper. The Brother didn't like the diagnosis and paid a worldly doctor for a second opinion. After many tests, they found he had a bleeding ulcer.

There was little or no tolerance for sick people at Bethel. If you were sick too much or started costing them money, they would send you home.

When I was at Bethel for three years, I started to have problems with my wisdom teeth. I went to the Bethel dentist. The first question he asked after looking at my teeth was, "So, how long have you been here at Bethel?" I told him three years.

Then he said, "Are you planning to stay after your four years?"

To which I said, "No."

The dentist said, "Your teeth are fine!"

Yes, I could have lied. I was raised to tell the truth. That god, my god Jehovah hated lies. Yet I was living in the house of lies.

Six months after I left the house of god, it cost me hundreds of dollars to get all my impacted wisdom teeth removed.

If you were sick, you would stay in your room. When the housekeeper showed up to clean your room and found you there, she reported you to the Bethel infirmary. The nurse, who looked like one of those German SS matrons from the prison camps, would come in with a frown on her face and take your temperature. Then she would ask you a bunch of questions with less empathy than the doctor. They never said it, but the feeling was "we know you are not really sick."

When sick, you got half a piece of toast and a cup of soup (not a bowl) that day and that's all. They felt starvation was the best cure for any illness. I guess they were right, because nine times out of ten, you were back on the job the next day.

In the four years I was at Bethel, I only took two days off for being sick. I didn't want my rations cut or any more guilt trips.

This is my favorite story about dear Doctor Dixon.

By the time, OSHA (Occupational Safety and Health Administration) got to the Jehovah's Witnesses, it was too late for most of us. The noise levels in the pressroom were deafening. Because of that, some of the pressroom personnel started to wear ear protection. Of course, they had to pay for these earmuffs with their own money.

Maybe they felt pretty strongly about this since they were taking a whole month's pay to protect their hearing.

Factory visitors noticed that some of the workers were wearing earmuffs, but most were not wearing any ear protection.

People on the tours would question their guides about this.

"Is there a problem with excessive noise in the pressroom?"

Now the Society had a real dilemma. What should they do to keep visitors from being concerned? Should they spend hundreds of dollars on earmuffs or should they stop the Brothers from wearing them?

They had to decide between the Brothers' health and the Societies' money. What would they do? Good question. I'm sure they prayed on the matter again and again. They really needed some Divine guidance here.

Here's what they did: In the summer of 1973, the Brothers in the pressroom got "new light" on the matter of ear protection. This term "new light" is one that the Jehovah's Witnesses like to use. When the light is dim, clear understanding of a problem or issue is not possible. At the point in time (could be many years later) when god's Holy Spirit kicks in and turns up the light on the problem, they can see it in a whole new light. This means if the leaders of the Jehovah's Witnesses are ever wrong about anything and need to change their minds about a policy or doctrine, they can just say we have "new light" on the matter.

Of course, the leaders of the Jehovah's Witnesses can never say they were ever wrong about anything. The reason for this is that the leaders have told everyone a thousand times over, including in their publications, that this organization is run directly by god Himself. We are told that the Governing Body receives all of their information directly from god. How else could god's only true religion on Earth be run? That is why, in their 150-plus-year history, there has never been an apology. (Even with the 1975 debacle, they blamed the publishers for "reading too much into the date" rather than point the finger at themselves.) More on this soon.

However, despite god running the place, the leaders have screwed up and changed their minds and policies over the years. They have done this on dozens of occasions.

Since god can never be wrong, they had to come up with the term "new light." The old light isn't wrong of course. It could never be. It's just that the new light is much better and brighter than the old light. Very clever don't you think?

Here are some of the few examples of how the new light has come into play or, as they say, "the light has gotten brighter" over the years.

On whether or not the gay men of Sodom would be resurrected to the paradise Earth:

1879: These men will be resurrected.

1952: The light gets brighter. These men will not be resurrected.

1965: More new light. These men will be resurrected, for sure.

1988: Jehovah apparently changed his mind once again. These men will not be resurrected!

How about the separating of the "sheep and the goats" (the good people and bad people) during the judgment period?

1919: It will take place after the time of tribulation.

1923: It is taking place now, before the tribulation.

1995: Guess what? The light gets brighter. It will take place after the time of tribulation.

Then you have the "Lord" in Romans 10: 12-16

1903: "Lord" refers to Jesus.

1940: The light gets brighter? "Lord" refers to Jehovah.
1978: The light gets dimmer? "Lord" refers to Jesus.

1980: The light gets brighter once again? "Lord" refers to Jehovah.

These are just a few of the hundreds of things on which the Society has changed its mind over the years.

They say they are directed by god himself, and they say he never lies. So, why would their god Jehovah give so much false or misleading information over the years? How and why would he flip flop so many times?

Seems like the light from god might be on a dimmer switch sometimes.

But who knows? Maybe it's not god changing his mind about all this stuff. It's just a bunch of confused old church leaders, just like in the other religions in the world who all claim god is only talking to them.

If this new light stuff is pretty confusing, just ask Jehovah's Witnesses about it. They won't be able to explain it either.

This is the reason that if you go to the Jehovah's Witness official website, you can't research most of the Society's older publications. There are hundreds of them permanently removed. If you could find them somewhere, you would discover for yourself all of the mistakes, discrepancies and false prophecies and lots of the old new light they would like to bury away forever.

Recently, I started doing the same thing that the Watch Tower Bible and Tract Society does when they make a mistake. I never say I'm sorry or apologize anymore. I'm using their great idea and I say, "I got new light." Of course, people look at me like I'm crazy when I say it, as they should.

Yet eight-million Jehovah's Witnesses don't think their church leaders are crazy for using that term. It makes total sense to them. So that, my friends, is the new light about the new light.

Anyway, back to the new light we received about ear protection from our good doctor.

Every month, the entire factory would have a fire drill. We would all gather in the basement of building one, and Max Larson, our factory overseer, would give us new information. At this meeting, the subject of ear protection came up. He said, and I quote, "I have a letter here from Doctor Dixon, and he says that earmuffs are not good to use because they could cause ear infections."

There we have it, the new light about earmuffs! We, of course, had to stop wearing them immediately for the sake of our ears and the new company policy. Plus, it stopped the tours from asking those inconvenient and embarrassing questions about our health.

I'm sure it went down something like this. Max Larsen called up Doctor Dixon.

"Hey, Doc, I'm getting all kinds of flack about some of these guys wearing ear protection. I really need to nip this in the bud and stop this. I was wondering if you could whip out a letter telling everyone how harmful earmuffs can be."

"No problem. I'll have it over by tomorrow."

"Good, I'll have a case of that fine Spanish Brandy sent to your room."

Well, thanks to Doctor Dixon, some of my friends from the pressroom are now wearing hearing aids (at relatively young ages).

Yes, I guess I was getting a bad attitude because they were pissing on us and calling it water.

I heard about a guy named John who must have figured this important fact out also. He worked in the bindery. He left the factory one day, like hundreds of us boys did for the noon meal. However he never went to lunch that day. Instead he went to his room and got his bags and got a cab and went to the airport. There was no thirty day notice for John. For John the light bulb came on over his head and he discovered some "new light."

It was at about this time that Bethel history was being made. An unknown Brother would have the honor of the shortest stay ever at Bethel. This record hasn't been broken in the last 150 years. His total time of serving at Bethel would be only about forty-five seconds.

Brother Lang was walking across Columbia Heights Boulevard one sunny spring day. He was heading from the 124 building to the 107 building. As he was crossing the street, a Brother drove up on his motorcycle and stopped in front of Brother Lang. I heard from a friend it went something like this:

It just so happened that Bob Lang was the first person this new boy talked to. "Hey, my friend," said the new boy, "I'm looking for 124 Columbia Heights."

"This is it, why?"

Smiling and excited, the new boy said, "Well, I'm reporting in for my Bethel service!"

"Really?"

"Yes!"

"Well," said Bob Lang, "is this your motorcycle?"

"Yes, it is."

"You can't have a motorcycle here at Bethel."

"Are you sure?"

"Of course, I'm sure. I'm the assistant home overseer!"

"Okay, bye." The new boy was down the street and gone forever.

Lucky bastard. He could spot in less than a minute what would take most of us years or the rest of our lives to figure out. He was our hero, for sure.

Chapter 28

My Dollar Car

On Saturdays, many Bethelites would take the subway to Times Square and Seventh Avenue and walk around looking for a good movie to see. Of course, some guys were looking for hookers, like Pat who was the elevator operator in the 129 building.

Some guys would walk all the way down to Flatbush Boulevard in Brooklyn. It wasn't unusual to walk down there to find there wasn't a movie worth seeing and walk all the way back home. With little money, there wasn't much to do in the city.

Bethel didn't give you a vacation during your first year. In your second year, you received eleven vacation days. Besides vacations, the only time I got out of the city was to go to the district conventions. In 1970, I went to Virginia Beach, Virginia. In 1971, Jim Pipkorn, Dave Borga and I went to Montreal, Canada. In 1972, Jim and I went to Scranton, Pennsylvania.

Owning a car at Bethel meant you had the freedom to leave the city. Without a car, your whole life was either Bethel or your Kingdom Hall. Unless you knew someone with a car, you were stuck in the city for months on end.

A car could change all that.

Some guys had nice cars, too. Jim Pipkorn first had a 65 Ford Mustang Rag Top. Then he got a 1967 GTO. Mr. G-job King, Dave Borga, had a 1969 Mach 1. A guy on the waiter crew had a 1968 396 Rag Top SS Camaro. All those cars spelled one thing: freedom!

These car owners did have their problems. One of the biggest problems was parking. There were none for the average Bethelites back then. The Bethel heavies had parking spaces, of course. There was plenty of parking after the Society bought the old Squibb property, but it would be many years later that they finally decided to give the Bethelites some free parking. They really didn't like the average Bethelite having a car. That extra freedom can be dangerous stuff.

Sometimes the only option there was to park illegally. You just didn't have a choice sometimes. Many guys parked illegally, and sometimes they got lucky and weren't issued a ticket. If not, the fine was ten dollars. The fine was twenty-five dollars if they parked too close to a fire hydrant.

The Kennedy boys, Jim and Gary, found a way to beat the system. They brought their Thunderbird up from Georgia. Instead of driving their car around for hours, looking for a parking place at night like the rest of the guys had to do, they just parked their car wherever they wanted. They figured since it had out-of-state plates, they were home free. It worked for about six months. One day, they went to where they had parked their car the night before. It had been next to a fire hydrant, but now it was gone.

They figured it had been stolen. So, they called the police. The police informed them the car had been impounded because of $600 worth of parking tickets. The police said they were welcome to come down and pick up their car. Just bring their checkbook. The boys said, "You can keep the car!"

The other problem was break-ins. If you had a convertible, you never locked your car. The reason was that if a thief wanted in, he would just take a knife and cut your roof open. Best to always leave the car doors unlocked so the thief could get in. Most of the guys at Bethel used a heavy-duty chain around the steering wheel and brake pedal with a big padlock on it. Sure, someone could hotwire the car and maybe even drive away. However, there would be no brakes or steering unless the thief had bolt cutters. Some guys would install a kill switch or chain the hood down so no one could steal the battery. Another thing guys would do is leave the glove box open to show there was nothing of value in the car. If you didn't leave your glove box open, many times your side mirror would be broken by the next morning. That way they could break into your car and see what was in your glove box themselves.

We often saw new cars parked on the street in Brooklyn Heights. In six months to a year, they looked like junk because of the way New Yorkers liked to park their cars. They parked by sound. They backed in, until they heard a crunch, then they moved forward until they heard another crunch and then they backed up and heard the final crunch. Now they were parked.

After two years, I met the love of my life. She wasn't pretty, but she was cheap. I bought a car for only one dollar. That's right, one buck! My roommate Jack Sutton's girlfriend, Hedy, had a 1968 Ford Fairlane. The car was totaled in a crash. The insurance paid her off and gave her the car, too. She sold it to me for only one dollar. The car looked like something out of *Mad Max*. It was a complete wreck! Every quarter panel was trashed. It had been rear ended at about 40 miles per hour. The trunk, which was originally five feet long, was now only three feet long. It looked like shit, but it ran great. It was the perfect car for New York City too, because you could park it anywhere and not worry about it.

I would drive down FDR Drive with my radio on, and Elton John singing *Rocket Man*. Driving this wreck of a car was like the parting of the Red Sea. A quarter of a mile ahead of me, cars would start moving into the other lanes. Drivers knew someone was coming – a man who had nothing to lose.

As Bob Dylan once said, "When you ain't got nothing, you got nothing to lose!"

I was driving my piece of shit car in The Bowery in Lower Manhattan one Saturday afternoon. I pulled up to a stop sign and this tramp walks up and starts trying to clean my windshield with a rag that looked like he blew his nose in it a few times. After fifteen seconds, he asked me for a buck.

I saw the irony in this, and I had to say, "Are you crazy? You need to give me a buck!"

He said, "Why should I?"

I said, "Because I bet you make more money than I do. How much money do you make a month?"

He said, "I don't know. With my VA check, maybe three to four hundred dollars."

I said, "I make twenty-two bucks a month. You need to give me a buck buddy!"

He didn't believe me. I'm not sure I believed it either. A homeless person was making more money than we were each month.

With my car, I drove the guys from Bethel to the airport for five dollars – good money. I also drove Bethelites who were assigned to my Kingdom Hall to the meetings. Instead of the one-hour-plus train ride in the hot subway, we could do it in just about twenty minutes. They gave me their subway money for the ride. Five people at seventy cents per person was good money.

And last but not least, my car could get me very far away from the wonderful House of god on weekends.

In the two years that I had my car in New York City, people broke into it and tried to steal that piece of junk three times.

Back then, hundreds of cars were stolen in the city every day. The *New York Post* said that the average life span of a

Corvette Stingray (sports car) parked on the street in New York was only 24 hours!

One time, coming back from Rhode Island at 2:00 a.m., I had to get off the expressway because of some construction. I ended up in the South Bronx. That was not a place you wanted to be in the day, let alone at that time of night. While I drove around trying to find my way back to the expressway, I could see the glow from the cutting torches. People were cutting up the cars they'd stolen the day before, right on the street. I prayed to god to get me out of there and fast. Finally, I found my way out.

Sometimes we would see cars broken down on the Brooklyn Bridge the night before. They had been pushed to the end of the off ramp. We would pass them on our way to the factory at 7:45 a.m. The cars had no tires. Then we passed them again going to lunch. The cars had no trunk or doors. When we would pass by on our way home that night, there was no engine or seats. The next day, it was just the shell sitting there.

A Brother in my Kingdom Hall got a flat tire on the Brooklyn Queens Expressway. The highway back then had so many potholes in it, you would swear mortars had shelled it. Anyway, he got out of his car and started jacking up the back end to change his flat tire. Just then, a car pulled up in front of his car and stopped. Four black guys jumped out and before the Brother could say a word, they started jacking up the front end of his car.

"Hey! What are you doing?" He asked.

"Hey, motherfucker," one of the black guys said, "you get the back two and we'll get the front two!"

"But this is my car!" The Brother yelled back.

"Yeah?" They looked at him with confused looks.

"Yes, it is," said the Brother. In ten seconds, the black guys were back in their car and down the road, looking for more "free" auto parts.

Bethelites didn't always have to work on Saturday mornings at Bethel. An ex-Bethelite told me that back in the 1950s some Bethelites jumped in their car on a Friday night after work and tried to drive all the way to Chicago and be back for breakfast by Monday morning. They didn't make it. They crashed their car and three of them died. Of course, Knorr figured that if they had been working, that would have never happened.

We had "new light" now. We all worked on Saturday mornings. That man was a genius.

My soon to be brother in-law, Mike Stillman, had a 1946 orange Chevy pickup truck with a camper on the back. The camper door looked like an old outhouse door. It was made out of old barn wood and even had a half-moon cut out of it. Above the door were the words "Keep on Trucking."

Calvin Chyke, one of the factory heavies, hauled Mike into his office one day and told him that he was a disgrace to the organization and how dare he put "Keep on Trucking" on his truck. Calvin told Mike that everyone knew the term really meant "Keep on F...king!"

Mike never took the words off his truck. He was in the ink room and good old Norm Brekke would protect him. He was bulletproof.

As Bob Dylan said, "Some of us are prisoners, and some us are guards."

I walked by my parked car on the way to the factory one morning in the winter of 1974. Some kids had spray-painted my car with the words "Fuck you" in red on the front fender. I thought, did they really mean "Keep on Trucking?" I laughed to myself. I wished I had painted it on there instead of them. Because that was how I felt.

Oh, yes! I waited until someone said something before I took it off.

One day, I was walking to the factory and passed my car parked next to the park. I noticed that someone had taken a ball-peen hammer to my windshield, right where the driver sits. I looked down the street. All of the parked cars, new and old, had their windshields smashed. I looked up the hill. Every parked car in sight had a smashed windshield. I counted 53 cars with smashed windshields that morning. Someone had fun the night before!

Well, that was the deathblow for my baby. It would cost eighty-five bucks for a new windshield. There was no way I could put another dollar into that car. I drove it up to Rhode Island one Saturday in January 1974. One-hundred-and-eighty miles with no windshield. It was only twenty-five degrees with a wind-chill factor of colder than who knows what. I drove with the heater blasting, hoping the cops wouldn't pull me over. I parked the old girl at my soon-to-be-in-laws house.

I sold the car's parts because I didn't want to replace the windshield. I sold the transmission and rear end to a friend, keeping the engine and tires for myself. I sold the gas tank to Roy Baty, and he welded it into his van so he could buy thirty-five gallons of gas at a time. This saved him waiting in the many gas lines caused by the 1973-1974 gas crisis.

In the end, she looked just liked one of those cars at the bottom of the Brooklyn Bridge. R.I.P. sweetheart. My first real love!

Owning a car in New York City. What a trip.

Chapter 29

1,500 Bottles of Brandy

When I still had my car, I was driving back towards Brooklyn down FDR Drive late one Sunday afternoon. I was taking an old timer back to Bethel after he had given the public talk at our Kingdom Hall. He had been at Bethel for more than forty years. After a couple of minutes of silence, he pointed over to the Schafer Brewery Company and said, "Son, if they ever shut down that factory," he smiled as he pointed over at Bethel, "they would have to shut down our factory, too."

To say that Bethelites like their booze would be an understatement.

The story goes that three guys are sitting around, each drinking a large mug of beer. A Publisher, a Pioneer and a Bethelite. Just then, three flies fall into all three of their mugs of beer. The Publisher pushes the glass away and says, "I can't drink this now." The Pioneer picks the fly out of the beer, flicks it away and keeps on drinking. The Bethelite picks up the fly by its wings, holds it over the glass, and says, "Spit it out. Spit it out!"

There was one guy at Bethel who didn't spit it out. Dwayne went with me and a few other guys to Jack Sutton's Polish wedding in Green Point. Now, the Polish know how to put on a wedding! It was what they called a "football wedding," the kind of wedding Bethelites dream of because each table had two bottles of booze: a bottle of Scotch on one end and a bottle of whiskey on the other end. Well, needless to say, Dwayne and many others there had way too much to drink. We took Dwayne back to Bethel that night. He lived in the 124 building, which was called "The most holy," because that is where Knorr and most the other Bethel "heavies" lived. My friend Dave took Dwayne to his room and put him in bed. But as soon as Dave left him, Dwayne decided to go to the men's bathroom down the hall. As soon as he hit the door to the men's room, he passed out face down on the floor. At about 4:00 a.m., a new boy went to the bathroom and found him there in a pool of blood. Oh my God, thought the new boy. This guy is dead! He called Doctor Dixon and told him about the dead guy in the fifth-floor bathroom.

The doctor examined Dwayne and said, "He's not dead but will wish he was when he wakes up." Of course, Dwayne was in the Bethel office sitting in front of George Couch the home servant the next day with a big bandage on his head. He did the Old Indian Navajo trick. It worked; he only received a verbal reprimand. They don't tolerate much at Bethel, but if they kicked everyone out for drinking too much, the place would have been a ghost town years ago.

The Jehovah's Witnesses have many restrictions placed on them, however, alcohol has never been one of them, and it is a big problem in most Kingdom Halls.

If you were stuck in a repressed, antiquated religion that was started in the late 1800s, a religion that is waiting for the world to end on any day, you, too, might drink a little too much.

There are tens of thousands of alcoholics in their organization. Even though it's a dis-fellowshipping offense, in the fifty years I spent in their organization, I never saw one person ever get dis-fellowshipped for being an alcoholic.

The leniency on this matter in the organization started at the very top and has worked its way down. There are many stories about Bethelites in the 1920s, 1930s and 1940s who would be found passed out on the sidewalk on a Sunday morning in front of the 124 building. They would just be dusted off and brought inside. No big deal.

Maybe the reason for this was the fact that everyone knew Rutherford was a raging alcoholic. During prohibition, the good Judge made sure there was no shortage of alcohol in the Lord's House. I guess that was of one of "Caesars laws" that didn't need to be followed.

Yes, to this day, booze and Bethel go hand in hand. The old timer said it perfectly: Shut down one factory and the other would follow.

For Knorr, it was his twenty-year-old Bells Scotch. He enjoyed it by the case. Of course, he never had to buy any of it. His supply always came in the form of gifts by his many admirers.

I'm sure even tight-ass Nathan Knorr could have sex after a nice bottle of Scotch. I could just see him chasing Audrey around his tenth-floor penthouse, wanting to do to her what he was already doing to the rest of us.

Speaking of cases of booze, here is a true story that few people know about. The story of how 1,500 bottles of fine Spanish Brandy was stolen at Bethel.

It was the summer of 1973. There was an International Convention in NYC. It was called The Divine Victory International Convention. Brothers were flying in from everywhere. Two 747 jets full of Jehovah's Witnesses flew in from Spain alone to attend the assembly. All of these Spanish Witnesses of course wanted to visit the Bethel home and factory. My friend Armando, who spoke Spanish, led one of these groups through the factory. It happened to be the tour group that included the Spanish Overseer in charge of the entire delegation.

At the end of the tour, the Spanish overseer spoke to Armando. "My friend, we have a gift for you and all the other Bethelites here at the World Headquarters. All of the Brothers and Sisters from Spain have chipped in to buy you and all the other hard-working Bethelites a bottle of fine Spanish Brandy, and this is your bottle."

As Armando accepted the bottle, the Spanish overseer asked, "So, who would we talk to about how to distribute the other 1,500 bottles to the rest of the Brothers and

Sisters?"

"Well, I guess that would be George Couch, the Bethel Home overseer," said Armando.

That night, Armando came over to our room, and shared with us some of his fine Spanish Brandy. As we sat there, he told us the story of how he got the bottle and about the other 1,500 bottles that would be distributed.

As you probably guessed, it's been more than forty years, and I still haven't seen my bottle of Brandy. Oh, those 1,500 bottles did get passed around, and you have a good idea who got them. We even spotted some of those bottles at a number of local Elders' homes in the New York City area. About thirty guys, the Bethel heavies and their friends, received them all!

Isn't it stealing when you give something to a person to give it to another but keep it for yourself?

So, this brings us to the absolute worst possible thing at Bethel. A Bethelite who steals from his fellow Bethelite! Stealing from some poor Bethelite making seventy-three cents a day should be a stoning offense. We had three thieves (not counting the guys who stole our Brandy) in the four years I was there. These guys would always wait until we were paid. We were paid in cash at breakfast once a month. Then, later that day, they opened our unsecured lockers when we were working and ripped us off. It never happened to me, but I had friends who had to borrow money to buy subway tokens because of what these so-called "Brothers" did to them.

One of these guys was one of the most self-righteous new boys you ever saw. He would walk around the factory with an *Aid to Bible Understanding* book under his arm. He gave a text comment one time and said, "I have walked the floors of the 124 at night, and I have heard the devil's rock 'n' roll music coming out of the Brothers' rooms." This guy thought of himself as god's own mouth piece. Sure enough, six months later, it was announced at the breakfast table that the self-righteous Brother Leroy has been dis-fellowshipped for stealing.

Isn't that always the way it is? The more righteous ones are the ones you need to keep an eye on the most. Just like in the local congregations.

Chapter 30

The Old Navajo Indian Trick

In my four years at Bethel, I had the privilege of performing the Old Navajo Indian Trick three times. There was a fourth time I should have used it, but didn't. I just didn't care anymore.

What is the Old Navajo Indian Trick? This was not a term used at Bethel. That's because Jack Sutton made it up. The first time we got into a jam playing penny ante poker, I asked Jack what are we going to do. Jack said, "It's time for the Old Navajo Indian Trick." "What is that?" I asked. He said, "It's begging the pony soldiers not to shoot you. Simply put, it was begging and screaming for one's life." In this case, the pony soldiers were the leaders in the Bethel office. We didn't want them to punish us anymore. Please don't shoot.

The first time we employed it was in 1971. Jack and I were bored and restless, so we started playing cards on Saturday afternoons. We bought a poker table and put a bedspread over it. On one Saturday, we invited a couple of guys over to play poker with us. This poker game was a low-stakes, penny-ante game. After a couple of hours of playing, Ron Telleson got up to leave. We counted up his chips and told him he owed us one-dollar and thirty-four cents. He said, "You guys are kidding, right?"

"No," I said. "We were playing for real money."

Ron said, "We can't be playing for real money."

"We can't?"

"No, god hates gambling of any kinds!"

I looked over at Jack and said, "Okay, let's forget the whole thing. We'll never do it again and keep your one-dollar-and-thirty-four cents, too."

Ron said, "No way, you guys need to turn yourself in to the Brothers, and if you don't, I will!"

We didn't know it at the time, but this wasn't the first time Ron had turned people in for perceived indiscretions. The Brothers were always looking out for god and the organization. It reminded me of the secret police in Nazi Germany. We must keep "zee organization" clean from the penny-ante poker players! So, we turned ourselves in.

The key to turning yourself in was to carefully choose your confessor. Usually the choices fell somewhere between a self-righteous tight ass and someone who might believe in a little bit of mercy. We chose the latter: Brother Merton Campbell. He thought the whole thing was kind of humorous and told us to never do it again and yes, we needed to get rid of the poker table. We sold the table to Dave Borga the G-Job King. Next week, Ron asked us, "Did you turn yourselves in?" "Yes sir, we did." Sieg Heil!

Another time we had to beg for mercy was in August of 1972.

John Brayton from Providence, Rhode Island, and his gang of followers/groupies (including his on-again-off-again girlfriend, Linda) came down to Bethel from Rhode Island. We had a big party in my room, and Linda was clearly trying to make John jealous by throwing herself at one of my friends. I told Linda and her cousin Patty that I wanted to talk to them about the games Linda was playing. We went to The Towers library and talked for about 45 minutes. When we got back to our room, John had left. I guess the little egomaniac jumped to the conclusion that we were talking about him, so he decided to teach them a lesson and drive back to Rhode Island without them. He left the girls high and dry. They had a car but no money. Plus, it was too late for them to try and find a gas station and their way out of Brooklyn, let alone back to Rhode Island. And there was no money for a hotel. So, Jack and I decided to let the girls stay in our room for the night.

We asked everyone to leave. As I was leaving the room, I noticed a guy sticking his head around the corner at the end of the hall. I went back to the room and told the girls to lock the door and open it to no one. Jack and I spent the night in Pipkorn's room on the third floor. The next morning, they were gone.

Two months later, Jack and I got a letter from Linda and Patti. The letter said that their conscience had been bothering them about being in our room that night. They knew it was against Bethel policy for girls to be in a Bethel Brother's room all night.

They sent one letter to us and another one to the Bethel office. Next thing we knew, we were in George Couch's office. As we were sitting there, sweating bullets, George said, "So, Brothers, just what do you think those two Sisters were doing all night in your room with those two Brothers, anyway?"

"What?" We asked together.

"What do you think they were doing?"

"What do you mean?" We asked again.

"We found out that Brother Robinson and some other guy went back to your room after you boys left, and they were in your room all night long!" You can imagine the looks on our faces.

Apparently, a bunch of people got screwed that night, and we were the ones who never even received a kiss. It was time to employ the Old Navajo Indian Trick yet again. The Bethel office could have kicked us both out for letting unauthorized people use our room without permission, but for some odd reason, they didn't. Maybe because we begged and screamed for our lives.

The week of the missing 1,500 bottles of fine Spanish Brandy was the same week of the famous Grease Gun Fight of '73.

Most of the overseers were at the convention or on vacation, so it was a loose ship in the factory. That week, we had the most tours going through the factory that I had ever seen, one tour after the other. Thousands of people were going through the factory every day.

The grease-gun fight was between the pressroom guys and the ink-room personnel called the "inkies." We were bored and stupid, so there wasn't going to be a happy ending here.

I think it started with someone putting a gob of grease in some other guy's shoes. It soon escalated into a full-blown grease gun war. The grease guns were used to grease the presses and other machinery. They worked by a lever action, and they could shoot a thick gob of grease about 15 feet. At one point, the inkies high-jacked my elevator for about 30 minutes. I found the elevator in the basement, ten floors away. I finally got it back and headed for the ink room. The inkies then flipped the safety switch, so when I got in my elevator and shut the door, the elevator was dead. They looked in the little glass window in the door. I was trapped like a rat in a cage. Laughing, they put their grease guns in three tiny holes and shot me head to toe with grease. Then I finally remembered the safety switch and got out of there. I went up to the pressroom for reinforcements. Tom Plank and I grabbed our grease guns and went down to the 5th floor. We hit the door of the ink room with grease guns blazing. I chased Mike Stillman through a side door of the ink room. As the door flew open, I shot gobs of grease at Mike's head, but the gobs whizzed past Mike's head and into a tour of about ten Brothers and Sisters. I had nailed two Sisters' dresses with grease! I was screwed.

The door shut behind Mike. Some people on the tour thought it was funny. We knew it wasn't going be. The new boy tour guide turned us in. There was only one thing to do: turn myself in and do the old Indian Navajo Trick.

Yes, I begged them to not kick me out of Bethel, the house of god. Funny, isn't it? I begged them not to kick me out even though I was miserable. "Please, Brothers, don't stop the beatings!"

A year later, we were too fed up to use the Indian Navajo Trick. I received a call to come to the Bethel office immediately. We were shorthanded in the factory at the time, but I finally received a replacement to work my elevator. I showed up at the Bethel office with my roommate, Jack Sutton. Bethel Elders Bob Lang and Curtis Johnson were there. Curtis told us what a "reproach to the organization" our room was, with dirty dishes in the pantry and junk under the beds…blah, blah, blah. Our bullfighting poster was gone, but it didn't matter; they were pissed.

We listened to them rant for about ten minutes. That was it! We had enough and we did the unforgivable: We defended ourselves. If they wanted to kick us out because our rooms were a mess, so be it. We just didn't care anymore. We told Curtis Johnson that if he had a problem with our room, why didn't he just come to us like a Brother would have, as it said in Matt.18:15. "If your brother sins against you, go and tell him his fault, between you and him alone. If he listens to you, you have gained your brother."

We told them the truth, that we Bethelites were hanging on by a thread, and we were tired of all the nitpicking. The whole world was coming apart and Armageddon was going to be here any day and all these people could think about was if our rooms were clean enough. They sat there with their mouths open and stared at us like how dare we talk to them that way.

That was it; we figured it was time to pack our bags. But nothing happened. I think the only reason they didn't kick us out was because they were shorthanded. At that time, the average stay was only eight months on a four-year contract. Brothers and Sisters were leaving in droves.

Is the old Navajo Indian Trick still used today? Absolutely! It's used not just at Bethel, but also at thousands of Kingdom Halls all over the world! Of course, most people call it something else when they are begging and pleading for their lives.

This trick isn't just used for minor infractions, the way we used it back at Bethel. Now Witnesses use it for more important things, like having sex out of wedlock and committing adultery. You could even be a pedophile or having sex with farm animals. The old Navajo Indian Trick works on any transgression if executed properly, and it has been working for thousands of Witnesses.

This is why the Societies' system of justice is so flawed.

The difference in whether you are dis-fellowshipped and shunned in a Kingdom Hall or just get a slap on the wrist is really based on how well you can perform this trick. Things are NOT done unilaterally in the organization. There are two other factors that come into play that will determine what will happen to you. These are favoritism and politics.

That is why two different people could do the exact transgression/crime in every detail and even in the SAME Kingdom Hall. One person will be dis-fellowshipped and the other person could get just a private reproof.

For example, my old friend Gary Kennedy from the laundry left Bethel before his time was up and married a wonderful woman, Ann Marie. Gary wasn't into working that much, so he pioneered and became an Elder and decided to go to almost every quick-build Kingdom Hall in the country. Quick-builds happened when hundreds of Jehovah's Witnesses from all over the country would show up and build an entire Kingdom Hall in just one weekend!

Being an elder and pioneer, all the Witnesses loved him. He gave amazing public talks that had people crying for joy in the audience. His wife ended up working full time to support his glory-seeking spiritual habit. This went on for over twenty years.

One day, Gary's wife received a phone call from a man from their Kingdom Hall. The man and his wife were both in their early twenties. They had two small children. They hadn't been Jehovah's Witnesses very long. It seemed Gary had taken an interest in this new Brother's wife, who was twenty years younger than him. The man told Ann Marie that his wife and Gary were having an affair.

Ann Marie wasn't that surprised. In fact, she was relieved because she had been in an abusive relationship for many years with Gary. Because of Gary's adultery and the Jehovah's Witnesses rules about adultery, she was now free to cut him loose.

Everyone was shocked in the congregation. There would, of course, be committee meetings. Gary, who had been an Elder for many years, had himself sat in on numerous committee meetings and knew how to play the game. He knew exactly what the Elders were going to be looking for. He informed his new mistress how to work the old Navajo Indian Trick.

He told her that tears, begging, groveling and what looked like true heartfelt repentance was going to be needed. Even though this destroyed two families, Gary and his mistress were both let off the hook and neither one was dis-fellowshipped.

A real Academy Award performance, for sure.

His mistress left her husband and married my old superstar friend. End of story? Not quite.

Gary was even kind enough to adopt her two small children.

After a few years, she, too, discovered who her showboating husband was and left him *and* the religion too. End of story? Not quite.

The wonderful thing about being a Jehovah's Witness is you can move clear across the country and start fresh where no one knows you.

The pedophiles in their organization have enjoyed this little glitch for many years.

Gary moved back to the east coast and started up his show once again. Pioneering, quick builds and kissing more Elder asses. Of course, Gary's first two wives, who saw through his charade, are no longer Jehovah's Witnesses.

Good news: Gary is now remarried and an Elder once again. He is back in the club. He and his third wife are pioneering in Ecuador, looking for more little brown babies to turn into Jehovah's Witnesses. And the show goes on!

Yes, Gary was a master of the Old Navajo Indian Trick.

Talking about Indians reminded me of when my ninety-year-old father came out to visit me a few years ago. He rented a giant RV and towed a boat with it. He was taking his girlfriend from Thailand and her parents all over the west coast, showing them all the sites: Disneyland, Las Vegas and the Grand Canyon. Of course, he never took me on any trips growing up.

Anyway, he took a wrong turn down a one-way street while visiting me. The RV and boat got stuck. Eight cars were honking, trying to find a way around him. The police showed up, my father rolled down his window and the cop said, "Hey, old man, didn't you see the arrows back there?"

My father said, "Hell no. I didn't even see the Indians!"

There were lots of Indians around. I think they were Navajos.

Chapter 31
Jerking Off on the Subway

The first guy I ever saw who was really pissed off with the Jehovah's Witnesses – and especially with Nathan Knorr – was a man we called Mr. Frog. We called him that because he always wore a green suit. He would stand in front of the 124 building just before lunch while hundreds of us Bethelites swarmed around him. His clenched fist would be raised to the heavens, and he would scream at the top of his lungs on the evils of Knorr and his organization. He wasn't looking for justice; it was too late for that. His life had been ruined by the organization in which he had invested his whole life. He was even a Gilead student at one time.

To an ordinary person who was not a Jehovah's Witness, this scene of insanity was quite a sight to see. There were hundreds of us drone workers swarming around Mr. Frog on our way to lunch. We glared at him with hate-filled eyes. We had no empathy for him. Many of us new boys wanted to kick his ass. Of course, we didn't know the whole story about the fellow drone gone mad. We wouldn't have cared even if we did. Why would we? How dare he speak out against our beloved president Knorr, our faithful leader?

Mr. Frog was really Bill Norris. The story goes that he went through Gilead but didn't graduate. While he was there, he met the love of his life (another Gilead student). Bill wasn't able to graduate Gilead, but he still got engaged to the Sister. Knorr was not happy about this at all and sent Bill's betrothed out on assignment to some place in Africa, thereby splitting up the couple forever. Of course, the girl could have chosen Bill over her assignment, but we all know what the organization can do to normal human emotions, feelings and attachments, all things that must be put behind us for the sake of the organization and furthering "kingdom interest."

At any rate, Bill married another woman. However, flunking out of Gilead and then losing the love of his life all took a toll on his new marriage. After having two children, he left his wife and moved to New York to make a career out of tormenting Nathan Knorr and the Society. The funny thing is that his ex-wife remarried in the 1970s and by the mid-1990s, she, her husband and Bill's son all left the organization.

There was also this one crazy old woman who we called Lady Margret. She was fat and ugly and looked like she hadn't taken a bath in years. She lived in the Margret Hotel before it burned down, which was next door to the 107 building.

She would follow us Bethelites down the street, yelling obscenities and calling us every foul name you could think of. "You motherfuckers," she would yell out. Every sentence out of her mouth had a curse word in it. About a month before I left Bethel, I was walking to the factory with a friend and there she was, standing on the corner. She pointed her finger at me and with a strange look in her eye said, "You boys want any soup? You boys want any soup? You boys want any soup?"

I looked over at my friend and said, "I don't believe it. It's the first time in four years she hasn't cursed at us." The very next second, she said. "You black bastards want any soup or not?" We just laughed.

The things that would totally shock any new boy became things that we didn't even give a second thought after a few years.

Yes, we saw it all in New York and especially on the subways. Late one night, I saw an old guy sitting just a few feet away from me. He was dressed in rags and looked insane as he was talking to himself and masturbating. He was in his own little world for sure.

One late night, coming back from a double feature on 42nd Street, I spotted a really big black guy getting on the train. He looked totally crazed and was wearing only a pink tutu. You just knew he wasn't going to a costume party. It was hard not to stare, but you never wanted to make eye contact with those people. Subway rule No. 36: Do not stare at the crazy people.

Don Breaux, the circuit overseer who I admired so much, was one of the few golden boys at Bethel. Before he was a circuit overseer, I found out his job at Bethel was the 124 building receptionist. His job was to welcome all the tour groups. He was able to check out the cute Sisters who were coming to check out the Lord's House. No factory or machines for Don. I told him years later, "Don, you were never at the REAL Bethel." He smiled; he knew what I meant.

Just a week before Don left Bethel to get married, he did make eye contact with the wrong guy. It cost him a broken nose. He told me that while he was sitting on the subway one day, he glanced up and caught a guy's eye for a split second. A moment later, the subway pulled into a station. The guy jumped up out of his seat and swaggered over to Don. "What the fuck are you looking at?" Before Don could say a word, the guy hit him as hard as he could in the face. He got a broken nose. It was probably the only time while he was at Bethel that he wasn't golden.

Just like the Mormon missionaries, we Bethelites stuck out like a sore thumb. How could we not? Where else are you going to see dozens of white twenty-year-olds dressed in suits and ties carrying overloaded book bags? Even in New York City, you could spot us a mile away.

We were hated by many of the locals in Brooklyn Heights. The locals and the crazies all agreed they didn't like us in the area. Sometimes people not in the Heights hated us too.

Ronnie Kleinman was sitting on a subway train coming back from a meeting one night. This big black guy with his five-year-old kid by his side stood up and walked over to

Ronnie. Then he stuck his finger in Ronnie's face and said to his little boy, "Son, this is whitey. You hate whitey!"

There were lots of beggars on the trains too. One black lady could role her pupils back in her head so all you could see was the whites of her eyes. She had a cup in one hand and a cane in the other. She made great money.

To my relief, I was never mugged in New York. The rule of thumb was if you were there for four years, you would get mugged at least once in that time period. I came very close a few times.

The factory area was a very scary place late at night. If you couldn't find a parking space close to the Bethel home late at night, you might end up over by the factory. Walking back from there through Cadman Plaza Park could be a real adventure, to say the least. The key was to walk really fast, and to keep scanning at least two blocks ahead. If you spotted a group of strange people on a corner, you would walk five blocks out of your way to put as much distance between you and them.

One of the best defenses is looking and acting totally nuts! One time, when it looked like I was going to be cornered, I started acting crazy and mumbling to myself. I had some saliva running out of my mouth, too. My head was doing crazy gyrations. I swear that saved my life.

No one wants to mess with crazy people. If you are going to mug someone, you want someone who isn't going to give you any problems.

Another time, I was on a subway car by myself. Three teenagers came into my car. Two from one end and one from the other end. There was no escape. It was going to be the old squeeze play. I was by myself and looked like easy pickings. They started walking toward me. It was winter time, so I was wearing an Army trench coat. When they were about ten feet away, I put my hand under my coat, looking like I could have a gun on me. I grit my teeth and stared at them straight in the eye, as if to say, "You want to party? Let's go!" They looked at each other and just kept on walking.

Sometimes on the subway, we acted like we were crazy just for fun. A couple of times, late at night, we had fun with the commuters. Two or three guys would chase one guy from one end of the subway to the last car. We would corner the guy running and pretended to beat the crap out of him. People would, of course, be in shock. He would lie in a heap on the floor for a minute or two and pretend he was unconscious. No one would try to help him, of course. It was New York City. Then the guy on the floor would get up like nothing had happened. He would take a bow and walk off the train at the next subway stop.

Besides almost being mugged a couple of times, the closest I came to getting hurt while at Bethel was in the summer in 1972. I was at the Scranton, Pennsylvania, Divine Rulership District Convention. After a day of spiritual enlightenment and more new light, Jim Pipkorn and I wandered into a college bar for some beers. Some college kids had their whole table full of little empty eight-ounce green bottles. They looked just like the little bottles of ginger ale we used to drink as kids. So, after having a few beers myself, I glanced over at them and said, "Hey! What is Rolling Rock? Some kind of soda pop?" These four jocks stood up, strutted over to our table and grabbed me. They would have beat the shit out of me if it wasn't for Jim saying, "He is just a fool and an idiot. Please leave him alone."

I met a beautiful sweet girl named Gayle in Scranton at the district convention. I have often wondered what would have happened if I had picked Gayle instead of Debbie. Gayle's mother didn't seem to like me, let alone Bethelites. I took the fork in the road that went to Rhode Island and met Debbie instead. I did it because it looked easier. What a mistake because Debbie's mother turned out to be the Wicked Witch of the East.

The funny thing is, Gayle is the only Jehovah's Witness who hasn't shunned me out of the hundreds I have known (even my ex-wife will not talk to me after eighteen years). We still talk and care for each other. But of course, I can't live in her Jehovah's Witness world and she can't live in mine. I love you, Gayle, and always will. Yes, all those forks in the road of life and where they take you.

One time, Jim and I went to the San Gennaro Festival in Little Italy. It's the festival that was in the movie *The Godfather II*. Jim was standing next to a doorway, and I was sitting on a stoop, watching everything that was happening.

There were wall-to-wall people. I was looking out at the crowd and said, with a smile on my face, "These are my people! You know, I'm Italian too. I love all these short, old, two-hundred pound women with their mustaches!" Just then, I felt this liquid running down my head and face and all over my clothes. I looked up to see a big fat Italian lady with a mustache pouring the wine from her glass on top of my head. I never saw anyone laugh harder than Jim at that moment.

Chapter 32

Murder, Suicide and Death at the Lord's House

The leaders at Bethel were killing us spiritually, and sometimes they even killed us physically.

Many of the old timers lay in the infirmary, waiting to die of natural causes. Some had served for over fifty years. Many of those old guys never had sex in their whole life. Not once. Just like the Catholic priests, they chose a life of celibacy in order to serve their concept of god. I was told that the Bethel family even had to recite a vow of chastity back in the 1930s and 1940s. Again, that all changed when Knorr showed up married in 1953.

Maybe those old guys didn't care about sex anymore. Just like the old joke.

The ninety-year-old virgin is having his birthday. His best friends get together and say, "We need to get this poor guy a woman before he dies!" They find this knock-out twenty-one-year-old hooker. They tell her what the situation is and that she needs to give their friend super sex, the best ever. She goes to his house and rings the doorbell. The old guy answers the door in his bathrobe and says, "What do you want?"

She opens up her coat, reveling her naked body to the old man, and says, "I'm here for super sex!"

"Okay, before I decide," the old guy says, "what flavor is the soup?"

For many old guys left at Bethel who had past the bloom of youth, the only thing left for them was the soup.

Some of the old timers were really pissed about Knorr changing the game plan.

One of the old guys who gave up the possibility of ever having sex or a family was Wilber Ruth. He was the mail carrier in the factory. He was about eighty-years-old, bald, and five foot five. His biggest thrill was walking around with his shopping cart full of mail and telling the guys what was going to be served for lunch that day. His favorite announcement was, "Liver to make you quiver and ice cream to make you shiver."

Interesting that when they made liver for lunch (about twice a month), one-third of the Bethel family skipped the meal that day. Yet, they always made ice cream to go with the liver. The thought being that they wouldn't have to make as much ice cream.

Lunch on Saturdays was open seating, so you could sit anywhere you wanted. I happened to be sitting at Wilbur Ruth's table with a couple of his old friends. I asked Wilber why he had never married. He said it was too late for him. Once Knorr changed the program and showed up at Bethel married, he said he was way too old to find a wife.

I wonder when Wilbur was lying there in the infirmary dying, if he just laughed it all off, as a big joke. A life without a wife, sex or a real family. Or maybe by that time "it was just soup or sex" and for him, the soup was just fine.

Many died of old age at Bethel but some died younger.

Death came one night to a watchman who fell down the elevator shaft in the Squibb building. He just walked into a black hole that looked like an open elevator. The elevator wasn't on that floor. Goodbye.

Dennis Carlson was murdered while he was cleaning his Kingdom Hall. It seems that Richard Wheelock was conducting a home Bible study with a young Muslim woman. Her Muslim brother who hated all Christians didn't think this was a good idea and was in a rage. He wanted to find Richard and talk to him. He stormed into the Kingdom Hall, looking for Richard, but only found a small group of Bethelites (including Dennis) cleaning the hall. He asked Dennis for Richard's address. Dennis turned around to write the address down on a piece of paper. The guy took out a knife and stabbed Dennis in the back and through his heart. They say Dennis had a look of total surprise on his face. Nobody ever expects to be killed and certainly no one expects to be killed while cleaning a Kingdom Hall.

Many poor Bethelites tried to kill themselves while serving at Bethel. Some succeeded. Richard Wheelock, the pressroom overseer, succeeded. He jumped out of the third-floor window at Brooklyn Bethel. Apparently, Richard was able to kill himself, which is what the young Muslim man had wanted to do to him earlier.

Richard was never quite the same after his wife died. She seemed to be the only one to whom he could relate to. This made sense, because he sure couldn't relate to any of us in the pressroom. He would come over to our press and say, NOTE: Should this be: "Here is your work…get it out." The man of few words would turn and walk away. He was strange and not the type of person you wanted to talk to anyway. On the other hand, wouldn't it be nice if just now and then, like every year or two, a Bethel overseer might ask how you were doing? I talked to a couple of guys in the pressroom, and they told me that Brother Wheelock never once came over to them and asked them how he or his family was doing. Not once in the four years they were there!

Richard seemed like many of the people who had been serving there for a long time: sad and worn out. I'm not trying to pick on Richard. It just seemed the whole atmosphere was one of tortured people overseeing tortured people.

As Bob Dylan once said: "Some of us are prisoners and some of us are guards."

The truth is that not one of my Bethel overseers ever asked me how I was doing in the four years I served at Bethel.

Not Ken Dowling in the laundry or Phil Gluckenbiehl in the bindery or Vern Wisegarver on the elevator or Richard Wheelock in the pressroom.

Do you know why? It's very simple. They just didn't care. Apathy was everywhere. It was unhappy people being led by unhappy people. At Bethel, you could see this attitude had started at the very top of the organization.

Now, I'm sure there were some nice overseers who did give a shit, but I don't know who they were. Even if you worked in a worldly factory, I'm sure someone would come over and see how you were doing once in four years.

But again, they would care if you stayed or not, and Bethel overseers didn't.

Once again, John 13:35. "By their love….." That's just it. It wasn't there.

There was an atmosphere that hung over the place. You could see it in everyone's face. We really didn't want to see it through, and why? Because we were all on a mission from god. Onward, Christian soldiers!

I met James Olson in 1973. He was a sad, shy looking boy with blond hair and blue eyes, and about five-foot-seven-inches tall. He looked about sixteen years old, even though he was nineteen. He was from Kendallville, Indiana. He was cleaning toilets in the factory. Believe it or not, that is considered a good job in the Bethel home or factory because you weren't on the production lines or on one of those damn machines. Plus, no one was on your ass. No overseer to beg to go to the bathroom. You did, however, have to spend your whole day in bathrooms, cleaning the shit out of toilets, all by yourself.

That was the one very big drawback. Even though you were away from all the insanity, it was a very lonely job. There were few people to talk to, and you worked by yourself. It was just you and all those dirty toilets eight hours and forty minutes a day.

I probably saw James more than anyone. He would get on my elevator many times a day to move his cleaning cart and mop bucket from one floor to the next. I didn't have much to say to him. He was a new boy and I had less than six months to go. You just didn't have much to say to the new guys. We were in two different worlds.

James got on my elevator one day with tears in his eyes. "What's up?" I asked. I could tell he didn't want to tell me, but he did anyway. He said that he couldn't take it anymore at Bethel and confessed to me that about a week earlier, he went back home to Indiana. He went AWOL and didn't tell anyone. He told his folks he wanted to come back home for good. His parents had a fit and told him he had to go back and do his duty. He had made a vow, and he had to keep it. He told me he had just left Max Larson's office, and that Max told him he was a disappointment to his family and to the organization.

So, what encouragement did I give this poor kid? Basically nothing. I told him, "Hey, forget it. Just do your time, then go home and enjoy the rest of your life." I basically told him the same thing the guy on the subway told me my first week at Bethel, as I was heading to the Inwood congregation. "Just do your job and keep your mouth shut." Jim, too, was finding out that "They don't give a shit about you here!"

I guess my words weren't enough to keep him going, because I found out he had taken off for home a couple of weeks later. Again, his family made him return to Bethel and once again Max Larson ripped him a new asshole.

The day James returned to New York was October 31, 1973. I saw him that day on the elevator. He looked like a ghost. Little did I know he would soon be one.

"What's happening buddy?" I asked.

"Just got out of Max's office again."

"Really?"

"Yeah."

The whole thing was very strange. It was like he wanted to say something more to me but couldn't. I guess he didn't need one more person to tell him to "just do your job." He had a strange look on his face as he got out of my elevator dragging his cart full of mops and buckets.

I remember that night because it was Halloween. I was working on my car in the garage at the 117 Adams Street building; it was about 9:00 p.m. You could use the garage to work on your cars back then. I was changing the oil in my car when all of a sudden, all hell broke loose. All of the fire alarms went off in building 4. The watchmen ran around, trying to find who had broken into the factory. They looked everywhere, but couldn't find anything. It was very strange. The mystery would be solved a few days later.

On November 2, 1973 about 12:50 p.m., I was on the elevator at building one, taking folks back to work after lunch. We noticed everyone standing on the sky bridges, looking at the back of building four. I joined them and spotted an ambulance. Some men were lifting the stiff dead body of a blond kid from behind the bushes. There he was, surrounded by trash and beer cans. It was nineteen-year-old James Olson! He had been dead for two days. Evidently the alarms going off Friday night was not someone trying to break into Bethel but someone trying to break out.

I was standing next to Norm Brekkie, the ink room overseer, on the sky bridge. Next to Norm was Tom Combs, the job press overseer. Tom Combs said, "He must have done something really bad to have killed himself!" Then Norm said, "I'm glad he jumped off the back of the building and not the front because we really don't need the extra publicity."

Did James get the benefit of the doubt? No, he was dead and judged on that day.

I was around only two of the many Bethel overseers the day they discovered the secret behind building four. Yet, they both had the same cavalier attitude about James' demise. They were just a cross section of the prevailing attitude that lacked empathy and compassion. But most of all the place called Bethel, the House of God, lacked any real brotherly love.

Was there any announcement made about James? Of course not. James had joined the dozens of others who could find only one way to escape the nightmare of Bethel.

Yes, the curtain had been pulled back from the great and powerful Oz one more time.

So, what was the secret behind building four? Just who *did* kill James Olson? Was it the heartless religion? Was it his family? Was it the Bethel Brothers? Was it Max Larson? I'm the only person alive who knows who really killed James Olson that night.

It was all of us!

It was the religion, his family, the Bethel overseers, the Bethel family, and me. None of us gave a shit about this kid, James Olson. As far as I'm concerned, we all pushed him off the building that night.

The real secret that was lying behind building four of the factory complex was this:

An organization of real love would have let this poor kid go home.

Yes, one more time, "By their love you will know them."

Who did they let go home? A couple of years later, they would let Leo Greenlees, the pedophile and Governing Body member, leave Bethel with their blessings and their money, too.

Crazy pills anyone?

Of course, they kept James' body, as they said they would. The papers that we all signed when we had entered Bethel service gave them the permission to do so. He is buried in an unmarked grave in upstate New York. Somewhere close by is Richard Wheelock's grave. I wonder if Richard received a tombstone?

The assistant factory overseer and the toilet bowl cleaner together in eternity. What did they both have in common? They both would rather kill themselves than live one more day at Bethel, the House of God.

They say people who kill themselves really don't want to die. They just can't live one more day in the hell that their lives have become.

Oh, by the way, I just found out that the society told his family that he "accidently fell to his death while he was taking pictures on top of the roof of the factory building one night."

Of course the society knew this wasn't true (I think deep down inside his parents did too) because there was never a camera found or an announcement made about his demise at the morning worship. They swept Jimmy right under the rug, just like they have done with so many other embarrassing situations they have encountered over the years.

I called the Watchtower farm were all the dead Bethelites are buried. I asked for the location of Jim's resting spot. They said they have no idea where he is buried.

The Witnesses love keeping track of how many hours they go door-to-door in their pursuit of new converts, how many books and magazines they place and how many home Bible studies they conduct. Why is there no information on how many thousands of people have joined their organization, like Jimmy Olson, and have decided to leave by way of suicide?

Many years ago, a friend of mine from Bethel sent Max Larson a postcard on October 31, the anniversary of Jimmy's death. The postcard read, "Do you ever think about James Olson? Hey, we all have a resurrection hope don't we…right?"

Chapter 33

Have Another Beer and Forget the Whole Thing

I saw Debbie Stillman when she and her family came through on tour in September 1972. She was standing there in front of the ink room. It was love at first sight. Don't ask me why, it just was.

Our strange Bethel courtship started with me trying to meet Debbie after I saw her on tour. Her brother Mike (the same Mike who was beating the horse-hide glue earlier) worked in the ink room next to my elevator. We were not good friends. He was just a little too "country" for me and too much on the self-righteous side, too.

Anyway, one beautiful Saturday morning in September, I was walking to the factory complex. Mike happened to be walking with me, and he said, "God, I would give anything to get out of this city on a day like today."

I said, "Well, I have a car and no place to go, and you have a place to go and no car."

He wasn't quite sure of me, but next thing I knew, we were on our way to Rhode Island. The car was full with him and his four friends.

Needless to say, it was a great weekend. Debbie, who had just turned nineteen, was happy that her brother finally brought someone home with him who wasn't a complete hillbilly, like her brother's friends.

I think she liked me as much as I liked her. We started to write to each other.

She lived in Newport, Rhode Island, with her mother, Elaine, and her stepfather, Ben Reagan. They had just moved to Rhode Island from Louisiana. One of the reasons for the move was that they wouldn't make Ben an Elder in Louisiana. What a surprise. Ben was a real winner. He looked and acted like Gomer Pyle, only dumber. He would walk around the house and say things like, "You're fat, I'm fat, we're all fat." Or he would say, "I know one thing about Debbie, she is tired." He would say that about thirty times a day. He would pat everyone on the head, like a small child. I'm not sure what that was all about. He was definitely three clams shy of a clambake. He, like so many other Witnesses back then, was a janitor.

They decided to move to "where the need is greater," just like so many other Jehovah's Witnesses did back then. Plus, they were hoping that Ben could finally get promoted to Elder-hood and the ruling class. The move also allowed them to be closer to their son, Mike, who was just one-hundred-and-eighty miles away at Bethel.

At the time, Rhode Island had the worst ratio of Jehovah's Witnesses to normal people in the country. The ratio was one Jehovah's Witness to fourteen-hundred people.

Of course, about a year later, after they moved to Rhode Island, they made Ben this mental giant of an Elder.

The wisdom from this man was amazing. I'll never forget the day I was sitting in the living room with him. He received a phone call from some poor black Sister named Betty Evans who was in his congregation. She had been crying her eyes out because she just got the crap beat out of her by her non-Witness husband.

This is what Ben the Elder said to her: "Well, you must have done something really wrong for him to get so mad. Just have another beer and forget the whole thing."

There you have it. "Just have another beer and forget the whole thing." That could be the answer to a lot of life's problems, but I think she was looking for just a little more guidance. I just sat there. I couldn't believe it. This guy couldn't pour sand out of a boot if the directions were written on the heel, and he was leading the flock of god.

The leaders of the Jehovah's Witnesses told us many times over that the Holy Spirit puts these guys in power. I would have to say that this is one of the biggest lies the Jehovah's Witnesses promote. After my time at Bethel and my fifty years in the organization, I know that is definitely not the case. These guys are not chosen by god. No, they are chosen by the simple fact of whether or not they are liked by the powers-that-be and nothing more. They are promoted to their positions of power the same way corporations and other religions promote their leaders. It's called politics and some serious ass kissing!

Yes, of course, they are put into positions of power by god himself….Really?

There were virtually no college-educated Witnesses back then. There were many Witnesses with little, and in some cases, no education. This didn't stop them from becoming Elders in their local Kingdom Halls. That's right, you could be working on a garbage truck by day and be one of the leaders who ran the whole congregation at night. Ben was the perfect example of this huge organizational flaw.

Debbie's mother, Elaine, was another winner. She was as cold as ice and was a major hypochondriac. I think she was allergic to everything, including air. It was all about her. She would spend hours cooking special food. She never had to do anything she didn't want to do. Her favorite catch phrase: "I'm not feeling too good, so the answer is no." Just like my mother, she played the health card whenever it suited her.

Naturally, she was the one who brought the Jehovah's Witnesses teachings into their family. Just like my crazy hypochondriac mother brought the religion into our family. Is there a coincidence here? I think not.

The crazy ones think this religion is a great idea.

Over the next year and a half, Debbie's parents would do everything in their power to make my life a living hell. I found out later that it wasn't just me; it was anyone who wanted to court their daughter. They had run off her last boyfriend, Tony Silva.

It turned out Elaine was completely paranoid about Debbie becoming pregnant out of wedlock. It seemed to be a family tradition. Her grandmother did it. Elaine did it. Elaine's sister did it. Yes, she came from a long line of fornicators.

Elaine was bound and determined this wouldn't be

Debbie's fate also.

We would be engaged for eleven months, which was the same amount of time that was left on my four-year commitment at Bethel.

We had only two dates in that time period. Our entire courtship consisted mostly of us sitting on a couch in Debbie's living room. We spent hours talking to each other, with one or both of her parents sitting in the next room. It felt like something out of the Victorian period. Still, we managed to sneak in a kiss every now and then.

This was not normal and even over-the-top behavior for the already very strict and sexually repressed practices of the Jehovah's Witnesses.

One of our "dates" was to Allen Andrew's house for dinner. He was the presiding Elder of the Newport congregation. Debbie's parents called Allen's house three times to make sure we were there and not fornicating in the bushes.

What could have been a very pleasant time turned into the courtship from hell. Elaine was a total control freak. We had no money by the time we got married because she wouldn't let Debbie get a full-time job.

When the time came to make plans for our wedding, I told Ben and Elaine that I had some suggestions for the occasion.

Elaine told me, "All you have to do is show up."

I told them, "My parents would like to contribute and get us a band."

Elaine said, "No band. We are planning to spend three hundred dollars and not a penny more."

I said, "So, please can you let my parents contribute? I'm getting married only once in my life. Have you no compassion?" "No! Just show up."

I went to Lyman Swingle for some counsel. He and Ray Franz were really the only two people on the Governing Body who were anywhere near approachable.

Lyman was from Alabama, and he didn't mind cursing now and again. I think that's why I went to him. He seemed "cool" and down to earth and not self-righteous. He might have been a bit of a racist though.

One time, a self-righteous new boy complained to him about what he had heard in the bindery. "Brother Swingle," the kid said, "I heard some Brothers cursing in the bindery!" Swingle didn't bat an eye and said, "Really, just what in the HELL did they say?" I think he liked to shock people.

Another fun story about Lyman Swingle was when he was on the elevator with my roommate and one of the Bethel barbers, Wayne Julliano. Wayne was wearing a black suit with red top stitching (it was the 1970s). Wayne always dressed on the NPG side of things anyway. Lyman looked over at him and said, "Where did you get that suit? Nigger Town?"

I figured Lyman would steer me in the right direction. I told him about Debbie's parents and their power trip. He said, "You're stuck until you get married. She is now in her parent's house and under their total control. After you are married, you can call the shots." "What about the wedding?" I asked.

"Good news there. The bridegroom is in charge of the wedding reception."

"Really?"

"Yes, it's in the bound volumes."

The bound volumes were books the society would make by binding together all the individual Watchtowers magazines that were printed twice a month. This was done every year. If there were any questions concerning the Society policy, one would simply look up the answer in one of the bound volumes. The bound volumes were the true authority. A place that any Witness could get an answer to any question no matter how bizarre it might be.

Sure enough, I looked it up and there it was in black and white. The Society pronounced that the groom was in charge of the reception. So at least our reception wouldn't have to succumb to Elaine's low-budget plan.

I got the bound volume and took it up to Rhode Island to show Ben. I opened it up and read it to Ben. "You see Ben," I said. "It states here that the groom is in charge of the wedding reception." I read it to him word for word.

"So?" He said. I read it to him again.

"No," he said.

"No? What do you mean no. This is information straight from the Society!"

"No!" He said with a confused look on his face. Apparently, he really didn't know if he should follow the guidance from the organization or Elaine's commandments. So just like Adam and my father and all the other pussy-whipped guys on the planet, he chose his woman over his god. Lyman was right. I was screwed until we got married.

Debbie and I decided that after we got married, we would move to the west coast. We were going to move as far away as we could from Debbie's psychotic mother.

One Sunday night, before I made the three-hour drive back to New York, we dropped the bomb on them both. I have to admit, I loved seeing the look on Elaine's face when we told her we would be moving immediately to

California after our wedding. Elaine said to me, "Get out of this house and never come back." So, they kicked me out. I went over to Allen Andrew's house for some counsel on how to deal with my future crazy in-laws. Allen was vague about what to do, because Ben was in the Elder club. However, by this time, I think he and the rest of the Elders at the Newport Kingdom Hall felt they had made a huge mistake by appointing Ben as an Elder. I really don't think god had anything to do with his appointment. Or maybe god just had another beer and forgot about the whole thing.

That is another good thing about becoming an Elder. It's very tough to get invited into their good old boy Elder club, but once you are in, it's next to impossible to be removed.

Since Debbie was of legal age, she threatened her parents with moving out unless I was allowed back into the house.

Even though I was allowed back, things were not the same. I had only three months left before we were married. Since I felt like I had already been through hell by being at Bethel, I knew I could take anything this woman could dish out.

Chapter 34

Starving to Death Outside the Lord's House

Since we planned to move to the Bay Area in Northern California after I left Bethel, I thought the best thing to do was to find out where the Society needed help in that area. This shows how totally delusional I really was at the time. I thought I could still "help" others by moving to an area that had fewer Witnesses. Yeah, right! Just what a congregation needed was another burned-out ex-Bethelite. I went to Merton Campbell. He was in the Service Department. He said, "Well, they don't really need people in California but where we could really use you is in Kansas. Hays, Kansas."

Many say that life is one big circle. I pioneered in Salina, Kansas, which is about 70 miles from Hays, before I went to Bethel. It was way too soon to make that circle back to Kansas. Then I remembered a line from the movie *Doctor Zhivago:* "Happy men never really volunteer for anything."

We didn't move to California. We moved to Narragansett, Rhode Island, with all the swamp Yankees. There were just too many changes happening. I couldn't see making four of the biggest changes in my life within a two-week period 1. Leaving Bethel; 2. Getting married; 3. Moving to California; 4. Getting a job.

Narragansett was about ten miles from Newport. Besides, I felt drained and exhausted after leaving the "spiritual paradise." It would have been just too much to move clear across the country.

There was a toll bridge in Jamestown that cost two bucks. I thought that would help keep her crazy parents away. Funny thing is, after we got married, Debbie's mother never gave us any flack. Since her big fear was Debbie becoming pregnant out of wedlock, she left us alone after we got married.

Most of us went to Bethel thinking we wanted to make it our life-long career. What better place to be right before 1975, when god was coming back to kick some serious ass? The dream of having a long career at Bethel ended for the vast majority of us after just a few months there, when they found out that something was very wrong. Otherwise why would anyone want to leave the spiritual paradise they claimed it to be?

When I went to Bethel in the early 1970s, Bethel leaders were only accepting people who had pioneered for one to two years. By the time I left, they were accepting guys who had never pioneered. Since they were having a hard time attracting people, they even tried a one-year program. They brought in one hundred new boys who had signed up for just a one-year commitment. Guess what? Most of these guys left on or before their one-year mark. There was just a small percentage of people who stayed after their one-year was up.

Now all you had to do was pass the mirror test. If you could fog a mirror, you could be accepted into Bethel service.

In order to leave Bethel when your time is up you must turn in a thirty-day notice.

To this day, I have a dream at night or maybe it's a nightmare. I dream I'm at Bethel, and I'm married, but my family isn't there. I'm working there by myself and people ask me why I haven't turned in my thirty-day notice. I panic and wonder why I'm still at Bethel. I guess a part of me will never be free from the house of god.

Even my email address is newboy499@hotmail.com.

How ironic with just four months before my tour of duty was up at Bethel, I received a job change. I was granted my new-boy wish that I made back in 1970. They put me in the pressroom. This, of course, was a screw up on their part. They would never put someone in the pressroom and train them if they knew you were leaving soon. I was leaving in just four months.

I reported to Richard Wheelock. He asked me what I was doing in his office. I told him I had been assigned to the pressroom. He shook his head. He asked me. "Isn't your four years about up?"

"Yes," I said.

Of course, he then asked me, "Are you staying?"

"No," I said. At that time, we both knew my new job change was a little strange.

I was assigned to the printing press Hoe 10 on what was called Hoe row. Hoe 10 printed the Spanish Awake magazines. My press operator was Craig. The same Craig that years later became the chiropractor they wanted to come back to Bethel to crack backs. Craig had come to Bethel on the exact same day I had come to Bethel only in 1972. The funny thing about Craig was, when I came to Bethel in 1970, he wasn't even a Jehovah's Witness yet.

One day when I was running to my press after lunch, Eugene Alcorn thought it might be funny to trip me. He got down on all fours just as I was running pass him and his press. I did a flip in the air and hit the concrete floor and ended up with a cracked collar bone. I still went to my press and tried to bundle the magazines as they were coming off the press. The pain was unbearable. So, I went to Wheelock's office and told him I had tripped and hurt myself. However, he had heard other reports about what had happened.

I don't know why I covered for Eugene, as he would never have done the same thing for me. As his fight with my roommate Roy had proven earlier.

I don't know the moral of this story. Maybe it's: Don't try to protect people who obviously don't deserve it.

Finally, my time was up; it was March 7, 1974. It was my last day in the pressroom and a couple of the pressroom guys gathered around my press at about 5:00 p.m. and handed me my goodbye card. The tradition of the pressroom and ink room in those days was to give you a handmade card with jokes and some cartoons about you in it.

I got a green card with the title "Casarona's Psychoanalytic Approach to the Art of Printing." Eighteen guys signed it. There weren't a lot of jokes in it. People were careful about what they wrote because the pressroom overseer, Richard Wheelock, would be signing it too. The first guy to sign it was Mark Penn. He wrote:

Cass,

You've always had something to say and sometimes it's even been worth listening to. I know you make it good in your new life and as you do, think about "Hoe row."

Jehovah's Blessings

Mark Penn

There is little fanfare when you leave Bethel. Why should there be? They didn't care about you while you were there, so why would they care about you when you leave? In fact, some thought you were nuts because you didn't want to join their club. Many took it personally and let you know how stupid you were to leave the Lord's House just a few months before the anticipated year of 1975.

The tradition at Bethel was at your last lunch, your table would all chip in on a three-dollar box of ice cream. The waiters would cut it up into ten small pieces, one piece for each person. Sometimes the table would even buy you a farewell card that was signed by the rest of your other table mates.

There is a funny and sad story about my farewell lunch at Bethel and one of the people who was there.

My wife and I ended up at the Lake Oswego Congregation for many years after we moved to Oregon in 1979. Around 1983, I was in Field Service with John Goodwin. He had been at Bethel around the same time as me. So, we were talking about our Bethel experience. I asked John what table he was assigned to when he was there. He said he was on Doctor Dixon's table.

"No way, really?" I said.

"Yep."

"When did you go to Bethel?"

"January of 1974."

"And you were assigned to Dixon's table right off the bat?"

"Yes," he said.

"John, where did you sit?"

"I was the first seat on the left of Dixon."

"You're kidding me. I was the second seat on his left!"

Yes, we had sat right next to each other for three months and didn't even know it. I went home and dug out my going-away card. Sure enough, his name was right there.

That's a good example of how warm and fuzzy the place was.

Anyway, when you leave your table for the last time, everyone smiles and shakes your hand as if to say "we were just kidding." In other words, "all the nasty things we said and did to you really didn't matter."

Other than the two cards, there were no thanks for the four years of life you sliced out for them.

It was just like in the prison movies. The gates open up and close behind you, and you're standing there by yourself.

Even though there is no exit interview, I decided I wanted one. I wanted answers. I wanted more. I wanted someone in a position of power to tell me something, anything that might give me a reason to hope again.

I had done what they told me do. I worked hard and kept my mouth shut for the most part. I had looked behind the curtain at the great and powerful Oz and was truly disappointed. If Jehovah was running this place, there must be more, I thought. Maybe I missed something. I believed in Jehovah and just thought, at the time, that it was the imperfect men who caused all of the many discrepancies I had witnessed. Of course, I was wrong. It was more than that, but I wanted answers.

I decided I would see Bob Wallen. He was Knorr's personal secretary at the time and also the person in charge of all of the missionaries around the world. He had been one of my table heads in the lower dining room years before. He seemed to be a humble person. I really liked Bob and his wife.

On my last day there, I went to Bob's office and asked him, "Bob, what was this all about? I mean there are some things going on here that are just not right!"

He said, "I know what you mean. I look at these poor Brothers in the bindery and I think that there but for the grace of god goes me. I want you to know, I have told the powers-that-be that we need to make a few changes here." He motioned into Knorr's office. "You can help us by going back home and telling them how wonderful it is here!" "What?" I said.

"There is just a year left until 1975, and we really need the help here. So, please go back home and tell them how great it is here. Or if you can't say anything good about the place, please just don't say anything at all."

Yes, tell the people about how wonderful it is here in god's spiritual paradise. But please don't tell people what's behind the curtain.

Bob was just like all the rest of the mindless drones. He had invested his whole life in the dream, the illusion that this had to be god's only true organization on Earth.

My talk with Bob gave me my answer. For the powers-that-be, the end justified the means. Knorr once said, "I can replace any of you with just a twenty-five-cent postage stamp." I know now that he, along with the rest of those men in power, felt the individuals in the organization were expendable. So even if they killed us just like they killed Jimmy Olson, we all have a resurrection hope.

They say the only real power you have in life is a personal boycott. So, I said "No" to the exclusive Bethel club.

The funny thing is, because they were losing so many new boys who decided to leave Bethel after serving just a few months, they changed their program. Just two months before my time was up, they told us that we could now stay there after our four years and bring in a wife. We no longer needed a total of fourteen years of full-time service in order to stay and get married. Yes, I could have stayed and brought Debbie to Bethel with just my four years of full-time service.

I guess that didn't help the poor guys who had to wait the fourteen years before the "light got brighter" once again.

Most of the married couples there didn't seem all that happy. Plus, we could never have children if we stayed. So, for me, it was too little too late. I was still going to leave.

I guess it was time for them to spend another twenty-five cents and find another new boy. Someone to keep his mouth shut and just do his work.

That is why most ex-Bethelites rarely talk about their Bethel experience or the real Bethel, the Bethel that nobody really knows about. Yes, most ex-Bethelites just go home and keep their mouths shut, just like Bob Wallen told me to do. Why is that? Because no one would believe them if they did talk about it. I would have never believed it. How do you describe the color blue to a blind man?

There are millions of Witnesses out there who really don't want to know the truth about the truth!

There is an old quote that says, "When the student is ready, the teacher arrives." In other words, the real truth will find you only when you are ready for it. I, too, wasn't ready for the real truth about the truth and it would take me another twenty-five years to connect the dots that would lead me to freedom.

Thirty days before I met with Bob Wallen, I had turned in my thirty-day notice. Esther Lopez couldn't wait to give me a dig. At one of my last lunches at Doctor Dixon's table, she had her chance.

I was wolfing down my lunch and looked up and caught her eye. Esther smiled and, with a twinkle in her eye, said, "You better eat everything on your plate because you are going to starve to death when you are on the outside."

I didn't say a word, but I thought, I would rather starve to death on the outside of this place, than sit in here with you self-righteous assholes! People really thought that because they were serving at the world headquarters, they would get special treatment when the shit hit the fan during the "Great Tribulation" only a few months away.

Yes, their world did come to an end. There was no "Great Tribulation." However, the world ended for Knorr in 1977. It ended for Larson, Couch, Franz, Henshel, Suiter, Lang, Wheelock and the other Bethel leaders. Just like it had ended for Charles Russell in 1916 and for "Judge" Rutherford in 1943. Their world ended when they all died. Even Esther is gone. But the organization is still there.

Now, forty-five years later, the Witnesses are still telling their children the end of the world is coming any day. They said that, "The generation that saw these things start to occur in 1914 would NEVER pass away (die)." Guess what? They got new light on that famous 1914 miscalculation and had to come up with more new light once again because almost everyone who was alive 1914 is now dead.

However, the organization, just like the Borg in *Star Trek*, is making more mindless drones. Most of this growth is happening in third-world countries where the people aren't as educated. Or maybe they have no Internet. These mindless drones would love to assimilate you too, if they could.

It would still take me another twenty-five years after I left Bethel to figure all of this out. I finally got my new light though. Yes, the little light bulb came on over my head.

I had seen enough of the puzzle way before 2001, but the final piece of the puzzle fell perfectly into place on September 11, 2001. More on that later.

The day I left Bethel, it was pouring rain. I really screwed up. I found out the night before as I was packing things up that I had significantly underestimated how much stuff I had. I had two large suitcases that I could barely shut and a large Army duffel bag, too. I would guess I had over 200 pounds of stuff. My van was in Rhode Island with the engine out of it, so I'd planned to take the bus to Rhode Island.

It was only four big blocks to the subway station. It took me forty-five minutes to get there. The longest forty-five minutes of my life. It felt like the scene in *The Shawshank Redemption* when he crashed out of a sewer pipe in the rain.

I could carry or drag my belongings only about twenty to thirty feet at a time before I would have to stop. I would sit there on top of one of my suitcases, panting for air. I was drenched to the bone and mad as hell. How could I have been so stupid? After a few minutes, I would gather my strength and drag my shit another twenty feet.

As I was sitting on my suitcases in the rain, many people walked by me and gave me strange looks. Most people are not surprised at anything they see in New York. I'm sure I was quite a sight sitting there on top of my suitcases in the rain with everything I owned.

When I arrived at Bethel four years earlier, I had only one-hundred-and-eighty dollars after my cab ride. Now, I was leaving Bethel with about two-hundred dollars. Not bad. I left Bethel with a twenty-dollar profit. Five bucks for every year.

I missed my first bus and had to wait another four hours for the next one to Rhode Island. I was pissed off at everything: Bethel, New York City, the subways and life in general. I had plenty of time to think as I sat there soaked to the bone with all of my earthly possessions.

In the bus station, I made two vows to myself: I would never work for anyone ever again. If I was going to work for a jerk, it might as well be me!

I would never be an Elder or in a position of any oversight in the organization. The biggest thing I learned at Bethel was that power corrupts people and absolute power corrupts absolutely. I would never sit in judgment of one of my follow Brothers or Sisters.

Chapter 35

White, Rye or Pumpernickel?

People would ask me if I was getting married as soon as I left Bethel. I would say, "No, I'm waiting two weeks." Most of the guys who left Bethel got married within a week after leaving the big house! A couple of guys actually got married the same day they left Bethel. Talk about hot to trot.

I was different. I waited two weeks! I had will power. That's not entirely true. There was a circuit assembly the week after I left, so we had to wait an extra week.

We got married on March 30, 1974 in the cold and blowing rain. It was Allen Andrews who gave the wedding talk at the Newport, Rhode Island, Kingdom Hall. My best man was Jack Sutton. Roy Baty, Randy Robertson and Mike Stillman were my groomsmen.

I did just what my future in-laws told me to do. "I just showed up." We had the reception at a Veterans of Foreign Wars hall in Tiverton, Rhode Island, and of course, there was no band. My father-in-law, Ben Reagan, bragged to everyone at the wedding that it only cost him three-hundred bucks for the entire thing. Debbie sewed her own wedding dress. She wore a ripped pair of panty hose. There was no cash for new ones.

It was a strange wedding, indeed. My parents and sister came out from California. My non-Jehovah's Witness

Italian relatives from the Bronx came too. I'm sure my Italian relatives thought this was a hoedown instead of a wedding. When my Italian cousins got married, their receptions would cost thirty to forty thousand dollars—a lot of money back in the 1970s.

Three hundred dollars or not, we had a great time and danced our asses off. Debbie and I were the last ones out of the V.F.W. hall; we just didn't want it to end.

There was only one problem. Jim Pipkorn was supposed to take our wedding pictures. He got lost and finally arrived an hour before the reception ended. Debbie never did forgive him for that. However, now that we are not married anymore, I'm sure she isn't as upset as she once was.

The next day, we went back to Ben and Elaine's house and opened up our wedding presents on the same couch on which we had spent most of our engagement. There seemed to be a sadness in the whole thing – all of the shit Ben and Elaine had put us through and all the things I had experienced at Bethel. It all seemed anticlimactic.

My race to the finish line of getting out of Bethel and into marriage was, of course, the beginning of a new life. New York and Bethel had exacted a high price for this. The cost was my innocence, and I would never be the same again.

We received fifteen-hundred dollars at our wedding. Most of this money came by way of my parents and my Italian non-Jehovah's Witness relatives. This was the most money I had ever seen in my entire life. We were rich – or so we thought. We decided to play and basically did nothing that first month of marriage.

As The Beatles once said, "Oh, that magic feeling nowhere to go."

Do you want to hear something really sick? The only place we went on our honeymoon was, guess where? That's right: New York City! Since her parents would never let her come down to visit me while we were going together, I wanted to show her the city. Now that we had some money, I could show her New York City in style.

At the time, you could rent a room in the Towers Hotel from Bethel. So, we went there for a weekend. I must say, on some crazy level, I liked the idea of having legal sex in a Bethel room.

I also got some kind of sick pleasure from taking her on a tour of the factory. I could show off my new bride to all my horny friends. The guys who still needed to "make their time" before they could leave and get married.

Hey, guys, look what I got! You can get one too someday, if you're lucky!

We had a great time in the city and even went to my grandmother's house in the Bronx. She was happy to see us. We had an amazing Sunday dinner with the rest of my Italian relatives around a big table with lots of people and food. The first course was always the pasta with gravy. There were many courses to follow. Debbie didn't know that there would be more food after the pasta, and she was full after the first course. She told my Grandmother she was full and couldn't eat anymore. I whispered in her ear, "You better eat some more, because if you turn down her food, you are turning down her love!" She kept going but needed some Brioschi when it was all over.

My Italian relatives always made us feel at home. Even though, looking back, I realize we didn't deserve it. I had gone to my grandmother's home maybe half a dozen times in the four years that I had lived in New York.

My grandmother Mary was a hard-working Italian lady who would do anything for her family, including working in a sweat shop for forty years in the garment district in Manhattan.

She scared me to death when I was only five years old. She grabbed me and pulled me close to her and, after kissing me repeatedly, she said, "I love you. I'll kill for you… I die for you!" With the look she had in her eyes, I knew she was serious. Even as a child, I knew what murder was and yet this woman was willing to do the unthinkable for me. I really didn't know what she was trying to tell me back then with those words.

It would take me many years later to finally figure it out. She was telling me about the most powerful love there is on the planet, unconditional love.

My grandmother was willing to give that kind of love to me. I could never give that kind of love to her because she was a Catholic and would probably die a Catholic at Armageddon, which was supposed to happen just a few months later, in 1975. My church, as well as my mother, hated her and all Catholics. The Witnesses believe all religions are run by Satan, but Catholicism is believed to be Satan's favorite. My mother had treated my father's family with contempt because of the religion in which he grew up. I'm sure they felt her disdain and self-righteousness every time she visited over the years. My mother wouldn't even let my father go to his own father's funeral because it was inside a Catholic church. She was afraid that Satan would snap him up the second he walked through the doors.

For many years, my father's family sent us gifts and Christmas cookies, even though they knew we didn't celebrate Christmas. I would be lying if I said as a kid I didn't look forward to those gifts. Of course, there was never any thanks given in return for these undeserved acts of kindness.

They showed us a true family's love, and we were self-righteous jerks.

I did feel a little weird every time I visited her and my Italian relatives because I'm sure they knew what we and my religion really felt about them.

At twenty-four years old, I could operate a freight elevator and knew how to make tacos at Taco Bell. All of my Italian cousins had earned good educations and became doctors, nurses and other business professionals. Now they are all retired with great pensions and retirement programs. I'm seventy years old and still working, with none of those things.

I'm sure my Italian cousins thought that I was in some strange religious cult that believed in shunning higher education. Guess what? They were right!

Back in 2008, after the great real estate collapse, I ended up driving a taxi in Portland, Oregon. I had mentioned my new job to my Italian aunt back in New York. My father was mortified when he found out. This really embarrassed him. "Why would you tell them that?" He wanted to know. "Because it's true," I said. I was done with foolish pride.

Before we left New York City to head back to Rhode Island, we went to Momma Leone's famous Italian restaurant. We spent almost forty dollars there. It was the most money I had ever spent on a meal up until that time. When it was time to pay, I didn't calculate the tip correctly, and I inadvertently shorted the waiter. He followed us outside the restaurant, yelling profanities and telling me and everyone else on the street what a cheap son of a bitch I was.

At the time, I had no idea what he was yelling about. Finally, a few hours later, I figured out why the waiter was so upset. That's me, not very quick on the uptake.

David MacFarlane told me about a time that he, too, had a New York City kind of experience. It took place around noon in a crowed deli. There were many people waiting in line ahead of him. It seemed everyone knew what they wanted by the time they got to the counter, however, David was undecided. Finally, it was his turn to order.

"What do you want?" The heavyset clerk barked.

David, with a confused look on his face, stammered, "A…I … guess…"

The frustrated clerk snapped back, "What do you want, buddy? I don't have all day!" "I… guess…. the roast beef?"

"OK… white, rye or pump?"

"Aaa… I guess I'll try the white rye."

"White, rye, or pump ass hole! Which is it?"

David, fearing for his life, said, "I'll take the pumpernickel!"

After that David used to say, "Just because you're paranoid doesn't mean they won't get you!"

My last story about New York City is kind of like the Momma Leone's story were I inadvertently pissed off another New Yorker. I call this story The Sweater Slap Story.

The first winter in Rhode Island was rough. That summer, I had no problem finding house-painting jobs. However, by the fall, when we got back from the road trip to see Debbie's father, all of the painting work was gone. By that time, Jack and Hedy Sutton had moved to Rhode Island, also. We were doing anything we could to make a buck that first winter.

Jack, Hedy and I decided to make a road trip down to New York City. There was a big swap meet in Queens, and we thought we could make some money selling our wares. Jack would sell some leather goods he was making, and I would sell my collection of Saturday Evening Post magazines.

Things at the swap meet went well and we made a few bucks. By the end of the day, we shut our booth down and decided to walk around to see what other people were selling. There was this one booth that had a swarm of people around it. They were selling clothing at ridiculously low prices. The prices were so cheap my guess is it was probably stolen goods. I found a beautiful white turtleneck sweater that they were selling for only five dollars. I tried it on and then took it off. I gave the man five bucks and threw the sweater over my shoulder and started to walk off. Jack, Hedy and I were about twenty feet from the booth when out of nowhere someone slapped me as hard as they could on the right side of my face. I turned around to see who hit me and this crazy woman was screaming at the top of her lungs. "You son of a bitch, you are going to pay for that!" I was stunned and could say nothing. She grabbed my sweater and was going to hit me again but Hedy said, "He has already paid for it!" A man yelled out, "Stop, stop Susan. She is right! He has already paid for it!" She looked at me with disgust and threw the sweater back at me. "Well, you could see what I thought!" She was still pissed off as she turns and walks back to her booth.

Of course, there was no apology. She didn't even say, "I got new light" on the matter.

That night, New York City wasn't quit done with us. Since it was late, we decided to drive back to Rhode Island the next morning. We were going to spend the night at Jack's in-law's house in Queens.

After a wonderful Polish dinner, we were all watching TV in the living room. As we were watching, I would get up from my seat every fifteen minutes and walk over to the window and look down three stories to check on my van, which was parked across the street from their building. Since my van had Rhode Island plates on it, I knew it was like a sign that said, please rob me!

After I did this a couple of times, Jack said, "Really, Keith? Give it a rest buddy!" I don't remember what I said back to him, but I did check the van one more time. This time when I looked out the window, there was a swarm of teenagers around the van and the side window had been busted out. Our stuff was strewn all over the sidewalk.

We ran down the stairs and by the time we hit the street, they had all scattered. We then gathered up what was left of our stuff. We knew now that we had to head back to Rhode Island. We got some card board for the window and headed home.

It was January and about twenty degrees outside. This turned out to be the second time I would be driving back to New England in the winter with missing windows in my car in less than one year.

Yes, I guess David was right. "Just because you're paranoid doesn't mean they won't get you!"

After getting vandalized, robbed and slapped all within a few hours, I got the message. It would be awhile before I headed back to the Big Apple.

Chapter 36

Jesus Liked Wine at Weddings, not Beer

After Debbie and I moved to Narragansett, we attended the Wakefield, Rhode Island, congregation. The Wakefield congregation was cold as ice. The Swamp Yankees would laugh and say if you move here, it won't be your children but your children's children who will be thought of as true New Englanders. That turned out to be more true than funny. Brother Wolf moved there in 1947 from Alabama after WWII, and thirty years later, the congregation still hadn't warmed up to him.

After four years of being in New York City, I noticed something about the Wakefield congregation. Wakefield, and all of the congregations I attended and, in fact, have ever attended, had one thing in common: They were all miniature Bethels. They were the mirror image of the headquarters. They all had the same class distinctions, power trips, gossip and human imperfections that any group of people in close proximity of each other would have, no better and no worse.

Going to Bethel wasn't a different or unique experience. Bethel was just a concentration of the Jehovah's Witness experience. If you are a Jehovah's Witness long enough, you will experience everything we experienced at Bethel. All Bethel did was condense that experience from thirty years in any Kingdom Hall around the world, down to four or less years.

The Wakefield congregation was no different. Everyone there were way too concerned about what everyone else was doing in and outside the Kingdom Hall.

Here's a funny example of this. An older Sister went to one of the Elders to report a serious matter that she felt the elders needed to know about. She was very concerned about my wife's behavior. Every time I missed a meeting, my wife would sit next to this young, good-looking, single guy named Mike. The Elder had to tell this concerned Sister that since Mike was Debbie's real brother, it was probably okay for this to happen.

It was one of those Kingdom Halls where three families ran the whole show. It was the Conns, Burgesses and Braytons.

At my very first meeting, Buddy Weber came up to greet me. He told me how he had left a very good job in Seattle. He had his own radio talk show and was making big money in Seattle. He was now a janitor, living in Rhode Island where he felt "the need was greater."

I stood there listening, as he gave me the "what I've done for Jehovah story." He wanted to share his "spiritual credentials" with me. How he had given up a good job so he could serve the Lord by cleaning windows in Rhode Island. He did this because he knew the end was coming in 1975, just a few months away…blah, blah, blah.

The Witnesses love to martyr themselves. And even though they say we are all equal, they love positions of authority and power. Deep down inside, they believe that some people are really better and more spiritual than others, and that somehow, they are working their way into what they call the "New System" or the promised paradise that will be coming any day.

When I first got to Bethel, I loved the notoriety of being a Bethelite. But after a while, I hated being introduced as "this is Brother Casarona, he is a Bethelite." Being a Bethelite meant to many Jehovah's Witnesses that you are special and maybe better or more spiritual. But after a while, it meant nothing to me. I wasn't more or less spiritual than anyone else, just as the overseers and elders at Bethel sure are not more or less spiritual than anyone else. Franz confirmed that during his speech on Black Thursday when he stated, "Bethel overseers were not appointed because of their spiritual qualifications."

Buddy Weber continued to talk, telling me how wonderful he and his family were, except for his son Mike Weber. He wasn't pioneering like his other children were. Thus, Mike was a piece of shit. Even though Buddy didn't come right out and say it like that, I got the drift.

I really liked Mike, and he ended up working for me a few years later.

Buddy asked me if I was visiting the Wakefield congregation. I said, "No, we are moving in."

He said not batting an eye, "Well, you have moved to the wrong place because they really don't need any help here."

I thought, I'm not here to help anyone. I just wanted some place to hide and lick my wounds.

We rented a small eight-hundred-square-foot apartment, which was on the top floor of a huge house in Narragansett. The house looked like old New England money. We rented the attic apartment for ninety bucks a month. The apartment was, at one time, used as the servant's quarters. It had an exterior entrance and another entrance that came through the house. There hadn't been any servants in the house since the great stock market crash of the late-1920s. It was nice and just four blocks from the beach.

Maybe it's due to the cold winters, but most New Englanders are a stout group of people with a no-nonsense attitude about life. Our landlords, who lived in the house with us, were the Berrys. They had lived in the area their entire lives. Mr. Berry had fought in World War I. He had no problem pulling his pistol out and chasing dogs around the neighborhood. They were your typical old New England couple. They didn't talk much but instead grunted responses.

Debbie and I really believed they came in to our apartment when we were gone because Mrs. Berry would make comments about the apartment that they couldn't know unless they had been inside it. Or she said, "Are you sure you don't want to barrow the vacuum, dearie?"

Every day at about 4:00 in the afternoon, Mr. and Mrs. Berry would sit at their kitchen table and break out a bottle of Old Fitzgerald and have a couple straight shots each. They were both in their eighties, and I thought how cool that was to have a couple of shots of whiskey with your wife in the afternoon. I could only hope for the same thing sixty years in the future, however, that would never come to pass.

Our honeymoon was fun for about four weeks. The time to rest and recuperate was soon over. Our money was almost gone.

It was time for me to get a job. Debbie, like most of the Jehovah's Witness wives back then, would stay at home and take care of our small apartment. Many in the congregations back then felt that only married couples who were very materialistic would both be working. Since Armageddon was just around the corner, the prevailing attitude was to just make enough money to get by and then spend as much time as possible in Field Service, trying to save people from the coming destruction. It was never said to your face, but back then, if your wife was working when you didn't need the extra money, you would be talked about.

After sitting in hundreds of car groups during Field Service for over fifty years, I have heard it a hundred times. "So, that new couple in our hall are nice. It seems he has a good job making great money. So, why is it she has to work, too? She has no children and could pioneer and spend her time in full-time service to Jehovah! He just bought a new boat. I guess they just don't believe the end is near."

The biggest pastime among Jehovah's Witnesses is comparing themselves to the other Brothers and Sisters in their Kingdom Halls.

Of course, that has changed now. Not the comparing part – that will never go away. What has changed is now both husband and wife can work. Just one of the many things that have changed over the years. New light is wonderful stuff. I think the Society backed off the working thing because more people working means more contributions for them.

Before Bethel, I worked in fast food restaurants, at minimum wage. I had no job skills and no real education.

I did have a letter from Bethel stating that I could work a 1920's freight elevator and operate a letterhead press. Both jobs were skills people hadn't needed in decades. These jobs had no value in the real world.

I had done some G-Jobbing as a house painter at Bethel. So, I went door-to-door, looking for odd jobs and painting work. The first day out, I received some painting work, thus my Pioneer Painting Company began. At the bottom of my business card, it read, "Licensed, Bonded and Insured." I wasn't any of those things. I did drink bonded whiskey. I did have a driver's license and car insurance. I should have called the company, "A Wing and A Prayer Painting Company."

Jack Sutton and his wife Heddy moved to Rhode Island in 1974. Jack and I partnered, and for the next couple of years, we scraped by doing house painting, cleaning carpets and the occasional odd job.

I managed to save enough money to buy the first Trim Line franchise in the state of Rhode Island in 1976. It grew, and in a couple of years, I had three Brothers working for me.

That summer in 1974, we went to the Divine Purpose District Convention where the Society gave us all new light. The Divine Purpose Convention was going to give us new light on how Jehovah wanted us to handle those who had been Jehovah's Witnesses in the past. This new light turned out to be really good news for my new wife Debbie. The Society said that we could now have "limited contact" with dis-fellowshipped persons.

Debbie hadn't seen her real father in about ten years because he had been dis-fellowshipped way back in 1958. Now she thought it might be a good time for a road trip to California to see her long-lost father. Since I was going to be the best man in Roy Baty's wedding in Kansas, we thought we could kill two birds with one stone. In September, we left in my 1966 Ford Econoline van for what would be an eight-thousand-mile road trip. We left Rhode Island with our life savings of one-hundred-and-fifty-dollars and a gas credit card.

Our first stop was Bethel, where we picked up Roy and his belongings. Roy had made his time and, just like me, was going to wait an entire week before he got married. We drove straight through to Kansas with a stop in Missouri to change a water pump.

The week before Roy's wedding, all hell broke loose. Roy wanted to have beer at his wedding reception. No one could remember anyone ever having any alcoholic beverages at a Jehovah's Witness wedding in Salina, Kansas, before. Of course, at the weddings in New York City, the booze flowed like water, even at the Jehovah's Witness weddings.

However, in Kansas, this turned into a huge problem with half the congregation saying they were not going to attend the wedding. The main guy against it was John Norman, the Elder from Abilene—the tight-ass Brother I admired so much before I went to Bethel. John hadn't turned into a pompous ass; he had always been one. I just couldn't see it before I went to New York. Looking back, I think I was a pompous ass before Bethel, too.

John asked me about Bethel. I didn't say much. I think I told him that famous line from the movie *Jeremiah Johnson*: "I've been to a town." He knew that I had changed.

Roy asked me what he should do about the beer problem. I said, "Screw them, Roy. They made you wait four years for this girl. You deserve to have a cold beer at your own wedding, and besides, didn't Jesus drink wine? In fact, wasn't his first miracle turning water into wine at a wedding? You know, Jesus? Our leader?"

Well, I guess someone always has to be the first one to do anything, right? If those uptight Kansas Brothers and

Sisters only knew how much booze the boys back at the headquarters drank, including their leaders, they would shit a brick!

This was the same congregation in which Roy and I pioneered for two years before we went to Bethel. We're talking major tight asses back then. We had one congregation gathering in two years. It was a picnic after working all day, remodeling the Kingdom Hall. Roy and I stood around, eating corn on the cob with all the old ladies; it looked like a Quaker meeting.

A week after the picnic, our congregation overseer Merle Freeman gave us the new light. He looked and talked just like Elmer Fudd. At the end of the service meeting, he read a letter from the Society that warned us about the dangers of organized gatherings, a place where there could be over-drinking and immorality. It seemed the Brothers in Southern California would rent out a whole roller rink once a month for their kids. Some of the Brothers would be drinking and screwing in the parking lot. The Society got wind of it and thus the letter was created. So "Elmer" read this letter to us. After the letter, he said, "So, we won't be doing any more of those!" No more picnics with corn on the cob and old ladies in Salina, Kansas.

Roy bought five cases of Coors beer. It was a great wedding, and yes, most of the tight asses did show up, including John Norman. John enjoyed the beer along with everyone else! In fact, I think he had more than just a couple of beers. In the end, all of the beer was gone.

So, there you have it, the first Jehovah's Witness wedding in Salina, Kansas, to serve beer.

Many of the Brothers like to make a pretense of being righteous, but in the end, most everybody likes a cold beer.

Chapter 37

One More Casualty of the New Light

Debbie loved her real father, Robert Stillman, more than anything, even though he was dis-fellowshipped and lived three thousand miles away. The best times in her young life were with her father and not her mother. What a surprise.

However, if Debbie even said her father's name in front of Elaine, she would get her face slapped. Bob left Debbie's psycho mother back in the 1950s and married another woman. He was, of course, dis-fellowshipped. It was his only way out of his nasty marriage.

Say you are a Jehovah's Witness, and you are in a really bad marriage. There is physical, emotional and maybe even sexual abuse going on. For many years, there was only one way to get out of this kind of hell: Someone had to commit adultery. That's right. Of course, you could get a divorce for any reason. You just couldn't get remarried unless one of you committed adultery. For decades, it has been the Society's only provision that would allow you to get remarried.

There was a time when that was only allowed if you had sex with someone of the opposite sex. How about sex with someone of the same sex? Divorce was NOT allowed. How about sex with farm animals? Divorce was NOT allowed. For many years, sex with someone of "different sex" was the only "scriptural" grounds for divorce and the only way to get out of a totally toxic marriage.

Of course, this sounds crazy!

Kool-Aid, anyone?

This new light came out while I was at Bethel. In the Watchtower, Jan 1, 1972 issue, pp.31-32, a reader asked this question: Do homosexual acts on the part of a married person constitute scriptural grounds for divorce, freeing the innocent mate to remarry?

This new light will blow your mind.

The Societies' answer to the question was this:

"Whether an innocent mate would scripturally be able to remarry after procuring a legal divorce from a mate guilty of homosexual acts must be determined on the basis of what the Bible says (or what our current interpretation is) respecting divorce and remarriage. In homosexual acts, the sex organs are used in an unnatural way, in a way for which they were never purposed. Two persons of the same sex are not complements of each other, as Adam and Eve were. They could never become "one flesh" in order to procreate. It might be added, in the case of human copulation with a beast, two different kinds of flesh are involved. Wrote the apostle Paul: 'Not all flesh is the same flesh, but there is one of mankind, and there is another flesh of cattle, and another flesh of birds, and another of fish.'—1 Cor. 15:39. While both homosexuality and bestiality are disgusting perversions, in this case NEITHER one is the marriage tie broken. It is broken only by acts that make an individual "one flesh" with a person of the opposite sex other than his or her legal marriage mate."

So, there you have it. Your mate could be having sex with farm animals, but that does not break the marriage tie. Yes, a good Christian wife would have to share her marriage bed with a goat, if her husband wanted a threesome.

A few years later, guess what? After thousands of people's lives were destroyed by the societies' toxic new light, the Society changed its tune once again. Now you can get a divorce and remarry if your mate had sex with someone of the same sex or with farm animals.

Yes, the new light kicked in once again and canceled out the old new light. Welcome to the Twilight Zone.

Sadly, many of the people who are dis-fellowshipped for adultery every year are not the abusers in the relationship. They are the victims. The abuser doesn't want to leave god's loving organization by divorcing their spouse. So, what they do is pretty much drive their spouse into adultery. This has happened thousands of times. Is there mercy for the victims of this kind of abuse? No, the rules are clear; so, in the vast majority of cases these victims are dis-fellowshipped and shunned.

After being dis-fellowshipped, these victims get to sit in the back of the Kingdom Hall for months or even years, waiting to be reinstated and accepted back into god's loving fold. The adulterer doesn't have to wear a large scarlet letter "A" on their clothes but, they might as well for how they are treated.

Moving right along. If we look at the story of Bob and crazy Elaine, I'd say Bob made the right move in the question of staying married to Elaine or getting dis-fellowshipped. He dumped a bad marriage and a bad religion all in one move.

A short time after her divorce to Bob, Elaine married Ben, and they moved 1,500 miles away to Ruston, Louisiana. After the move, she made Debbie and her brother write a letter to Bob. The letter said they had no desire to see him ever again. That was their mother's idea, of course, sweet woman that she was. For poor Bob, it probably looked like this was his only future with his Jehovah's Witness children. Fast forward ten years and Bob would be getting a break in 1974, with this wonderful new light.

After Roy's wedding we drove to my parents' house in Southern California. From there we went to San Jose for the long awaited reunion with Debbie's Father.

Debbie was so excited to see her father, who she loved so much. The love I saw between those two was amazing. When they met, it was like a scene out of a movie. Father and daughter united again in love, after all these years. I found him to be a very sweet and kind person, nothing like Debbie's psycho mother.

How strange to be sitting in his living room while Bob and his wife Donna were watching a slide show of our wedding pictures. Bob had this big smile on his face, smoking his pipe. He was seeing his own daughter's wedding for the first time—the wedding he was banished from and wasn't even invited to attend.

I wondered what Donna was thinking. I'm sure she must have thought we were sick and sadistic people. We didn't invite this poor man to his only daughter's wedding. Then we came into their home and showed him the pictures of a wedding from which he was shunned.

I'm sure Donna couldn't wait to join Bob's old religion. The religion that brags about how much love they have for everyone.

We spent a whole week at their house. I'm sure Debbie was looking forward to having a relationship again with her long-lost father. I was looking forward to having a real father-in-law and not Ben the village idiot.

After we left Bob's house, we had been in California for almost a month. We then headed to Idaho to see Gary Kennedy and his wife Ann Marie. Then we headed east again. After two months on the road, we were back in Rhode Island. We were broke and heading into our first New England winter with little to no work.

It was tough. I worked odd jobs with my friend, Jack. We cleaned carpets, painted and even went to the city dump and picked through trash for stuff we could sell at yard sales. We both heated our homes with wood, so we put a small ad in the city paper for FREE tree removal. This would be free fuel for our pot-belly stoves.

We went to one lady's house in a really nice neighborhood on a cold winter's day. She wanted us to cut down this large oak tree that was just a foot away from her carport. She said she had received a bid for more than four hundred dollars to do the job, so she was happy to see us. Normally, we would have never accepted this kind of job. However, since the tree was on a hill and leaning away from the house, Jack and I figured we would take the chance. The tree came down with a crash. It missed the carport but it did destroy two smaller fruit trees and put a big dent in her grass and yard. We started cutting up the tree as fast as we could, throwing the wood in my van. We took the firewood we wanted and left the rest of the limbs and debris. She could see we were getting ready to leave so she came running down the hill in a panic. "Where in the hell are you guys going?"

"We have another job to do, so we got to go."

"You guys did a number on my yard! Just look at these two trees you destroyed and what about all this trash that is still here!"

"We're really sorry about the trees, but since it was free, we don't include yard clean-up, too. By the way, what did you expect for free?"

We did feel really bad about her yard. I guess it is true, you get what you pay for.

In 1975, I scraped enough money together to buy a Trim Line franchise. This was a car-customizing company that was started and owned by Jehovah's Witnesses. My days of picking through the dump and free-tree removal were over.

In 1976, Bob and Donna came to Rhode Island to see us. Debbie and her brother really put the sale on him to come back into "the truth" and the home of the "new light." He just couldn't do it. I think he was afraid. He was afraid that if he screwed up again, the love would be yanked away from him one more time. As it turned out, he would have been right. Plus, Donna hated Jehovah's Witnesses for some odd reason. So how does one choose between his kids or his wife? This hell is experienced by many people in the same circumstances.

We had moved into a small bungalow across the street from Indian Lake. Bob and Donna parked their travel trailer on our property and stayed with us for over a month. We had a great time together during that visit. Bob and Donna left and headed back to California.

We stayed in Rhode Island for four years. I sold my Trim Line distributorship to my friend David McFarlane and his wife Cheryl. We bought another distributorship in Northern Louisiana and Southern Arkansas known as Trim Line of Ark-La.

After the record snow storm in Rhode Island in 1978, we moved to Farmerville, Louisiana. Debbie had been raised in Ruston, and we were ready for a change.

Farmerville had one gas station and one restaurant. The biggest thrill was coming home from work every day and going by the bank and reading the time and temperature.

Farmerville, Louisiana, was thirty miles northeast of Ruston. It was a really small country town.

Debbie had grown up in Ruston and had known many people there. The two people who proved to be like parents to Debbie as she was growing up were JoAnn and Jack Needham, who basically started the Farmerville Congregation. I must say, I loved Jack Needham, too. I wasn't real close to my MIA non-Jehovah's Witness father. So, Jack was the closest thing I had to a real father.

Jack always had a smile on his face. He looked quite dapper with his grey hair and handle-bar mustache. He looked just like a Royal Air Force pilot. Come to find out, he had been in the RAF during the war.

Jack had lots of great stories about the war. He had been shot down over Nazi Germany in 1943. He told me how some German night-fighters shot his Sterling Short Bomber down while they were on a bombing run over Cologne on July 4th. He was the bombardier on that mission. The twenty-millimeter canon shells had put large holes through his bomber. There was no lights or hydraulics, and the plane had lost all forward motion. It was now free falling straight down. Jack couldn't crawl back to the rear of the plane. He found a large hole in the plane from one of the canon shells and preceded to crawl out through the hole. His clothes and parachute were ripped on the jagged metal as he climbed through the hole and out of the plane. He was now falling straight down next to the destroyed bomber at the same rate of speed. There was no way he could deploy his parachute just a few feet away from the burning plane as it fell. He took his leg and pushed as hard as he could again the fuselage of the plane. Slowly he drifted away from the burning bomber. He said as soon as he was about twenty feet from the wing tip, he yanked the rip cord. He said that at the same moment he did this, he saw the tops of the pine trees. It yanked him up but he still hit the ground with a terrible force. He broke both ankles and lost most of his teeth. The burning bomber crashed not too far away. He was captured immediately and spent the rest of the war in a prison camp.

Jack was actually in Stalag 3 during the war. This was the same Stalag, a German prison camp, that was in the movie *The Great Escape*.

Jack was a rebel, and he would receive more flack later on in life because he refused to shave his mustache. I found out later the only reason he had a mustache was to cover up some nasty scares he got from his plane crash in the war. Beards or mustaches weren't allowed in the Society back then if you wanted to be an Elder or a pioneer. Jack broke their rules about that, but they still made him an Elder. He was his own man.

Rules at Bethel that are still in force today include allowing mustaches, but no beards, if you are black. If you are white, mustaches and beards aren't allowed. Period.

Debbie and I bought a little 1920s' bungalow on Bernice Street in Farmerville.

In 1978, Bob came to Louisiana to visit us and our daughter, Kelly, his first grandchild. Because of the new policy changes, Bob was even allowed to go to his own son's wedding in a Kingdom Hall in Louisiana.

Yes, the new light would allow for that sort of kindness now. This new light seemed very reasonable. Back then, I thought, who knows? - Maybe Jehovah is really directing things back at the headquarters.

At his son Mike's wedding, Bob told Elaine what a great job she did in raising their children. It looked like maybe my church could be kind, loving and forgiving at times now.

But all good things come to an end. Just like the policy of sex with farm animals and divorce, god had changed His mind once again about how to deal with those who are dis-fellowshipped.

A few years later, the light got brighter. In 1981, the Society said we were going back to the "old way" or the "old new light," which was not the "new light" they received back in 1974. This new light would, of course, cancel out the "old new light" of dealing with those who are dis-fellowshipped. We were all told we had to go back to the old way of dealing with dis-fellowshipped people by shunning them and treating them like dead people once again. This new light is still enforced to this very day.

One day in 1981, Bob called us up. We were living in Oregon then. Bob said he wanted to come up to Oregon for a visit, to see us and his only grandkids, my children. Poor Bob didn't know about the new light yet.

I said, "Come on up Bob. We would love to see you." Debbie grabbed the phone out of my hand and told him that he wasn't welcome anymore and that he couldn't come up for anymore visits.

Bob was, of course, very upset with the organization's new light. This meant that he would be losing his family once again. For many years, he wasn't allowed to see his own children. Then the Society gave him his family back. And now they had taken his family away from him for good.

Debbie wouldn't talk to him anymore, but she did send her father a subscription to The Watchtower and Awake magazines. So now, at least twice a month, Bob would receive spiritual food in the mail from the people who kept taking his family away from him.

For some odd reason, the magazines couldn't replace the companionship and love he could have received from his family.

I can't talk to you, Dad, but please read our magazines. The magazines will tell you about how much love we have in our organization.

Bob never did visit us again, and we had little-to-no contact with him for many years. I had no idea what was going through Bob's mind that night in 1993. Robert Stillman, with little family left and no possibility of seeing his children and only grandchildren, set on a couch and picked up a .38 special from the coffee table next to him and blew his brains out.

Yes, one more casualty of the Watch Tower Bible and Tract Society and their new light.

To this day, I don't think Debbie or her brother Mike feel any responsibility for his demise. Why would they? My wife didn't make the decision to shun her father; her church did that for her. She was just a good Christian soldier following orders.

However, I do feel responsibility. This is the second time in my life that I just stood back and did nothing. Someone I knew was suffering, to the point that death seemed like their only option. Where was I?

They say a person is as much responsible for the evil he commits as the evil he permits.

The term "blood guilty" comes to mind. However, the Jehovah's Witnesses use this term another way.

Since guilt is such a wonderful tool used by the Jehovah's Witnesses, one of the terms they love to use is "blood guilty." They have actually used this term to guilt their members into doing more and more Field Service. They have told us on numerous occasions at the Kingdom Halls and other major gatherings that a person could be blood guilty for not going out in Field Service activity enough.

The reason is this. Because you didn't go out in Field Service on Saturday, Mr. Sinner never got a chance to hear the Jehovah's Witness's message about the coming destruction of all the bad people. Because Mr. Sinner never heard this message, it means there is a high probability he and his family won't join the religion. Because he didn't join the only true religion, he is still a sinner. Jehovah now has no choice but to kill Mr. Sinner, his wife and their two small children at Armageddon. However, even though Mr. Sinner and his family are killed by god, you are now blood guilty because you never knocked on his door in the first place. Now of course, Jehovah holds YOU accountable for their deaths! So even though Jehovah did all the killing, you are the real reason this happened.

Do you see the logic here? Let's take this one step further. I stopped doing door-to-door work eighteen years ago. Does that mean all those thousands of people with whom I never had the chance to share the message of salvation will now die at Armageddon because I left the organization many years ago?

I guess I'm blood guilty whether I'm in their organization or not. I'm sure they will come up with some more "new light" about all this a few years from now. Doesn't this just sound like some form of insanity?

Anyway, back to Debbie and her dead dad. Debbie wanted to be with her father one more time, or at least part of him. She was nice enough to go to California to help Bob's wife, Chloe, spread his ashes down a canyon wall. I wondered what Chloe thought about Debbie wanting to be with her father and helping with his disposal, now that he was dead, though she didn't want to associate with him while he was living.

To people on the outside of our club/religion, we must look insane!

Here is another crazy pill. Check this out.

At the time of his death, the only thing Bob was doing that wasn't in line with the Society's rules and regulations was smoking. He wasn't living in sin or doing any other type of gross immorality, but because he left the organization back in 1958, thirty-five years earlier, he could no longer have association with his children or grandchildren.

Yet my father, who left the organization back in 1961, was still smoking at the time of Bob's death. I'm sure my father was fornicating, stealing and just about anything else you can think of. Yet he could come up to visit his children and his grandchildren anytime he liked. How could that be? How could he do that? Because he was no longer dis-fellowshipped; he was reinstated back in 1965. However, after he was reinstated, he just dropped out for good, or "faded away" as the Witnesses like to call it nowadays.

Just one of the many loopholes and double standards that they don't want you to know about.

John 13:35 states. "By this all men will know that you are my disciples, if you love one another."

This whole dis-fellowshipping and shunning policy was something that Knorr and Franz dreamt up back in March of 1951. At that time, Knorr gave the Witnesses the new light, which led to hundreds of thousands of people being dis-fellowshipped and thus shunned in the years to come. Dis-fellowshipping didn't even exist in the first seventy-five years of the organization's history. The word itself, dis-fellowship, doesn't even exist in the Bible.

Even though Knorr has been dead for over forty years, his policies continue to kill people and destroy families to this very day.

How many lives has this cruel shunning policy taken? How many families has it destroyed?

The new light is funny stuff. Sometimes it gets brighter, then dark, then bright again. But one thing is true about the new light. It is never, ever wrong!

Right?

I guess Jehovah gets confused at times and just can't decide which way to go.

Or maybe god has nothing to do with the Society's decisions.

What if eight old guys who call themselves the Governing Body back in New York are making this stuff up as they go along? It kind of looks that way.

How could those eight guys and the eight million people they lead be wrong?

I guess the same way ninety million Nazis could be wrong.

It's amazing the things a few guys meeting in a basement in a Pittsburgh, Pennsylvania, church or a beer hall in Munich, Germany, can come up with.

Chapter 38

Norma's Hope or More Dead Grandparents

My mother favored my daughter over my son. She would send a box of presents to the house with nine gifts for my daughter and one for my son. Looking back, she never really liked or trusted the men in her life. I think it started with my great-grandfather, who took advantage of her as a young child.

I really don't think she trusted anyone with a penis. My father, my son and I all felt the distance in her fake smile. But my sister and daughter received warmth and closeness from her.

The last time I saw my mother alive was in 1983, when she stormed out of my house without saying goodbye to my children or me. She had invited herself up to visit my five-year-old daughter, Kelly. It was Grandparents Day at Kelly's school. It also happened to be a circuit assembly weekend. Our house only had one bathroom at the time. Before the assembly, my mother played martyr (as usual) and let everyone use the bathroom ahead of her. Needless to say, she didn't have enough time to get ready. She sat in our car on our ride to the assembly hall, totally pissed off. Her hair looked like the bride of Frankenstein. Once there, she sat with her other friends and not with us. After the meeting, we all went out for pizza with some of our friends. She sat at the far end of the table, telling my friends what a disappointment I was.

When we returned to the house, her friends waited for her as she grabbed her bags and left in a huff.

"Bye, Mom," I said as she stormed out the front door. There was no reply. That was the last I time I ever saw her alive.

Three months later, we got the phone call. She was dead.

She was only fifty-seven and died at her fortieth high school reunion in Kansas. There were only nine people in her graduating class. One guy who lived across the street didn't even bother to go.

Even though she hadn't lived in Kansas in more than forty years, she told everyone years earlier that she wanted to be buried in Kansas. Her wish was granted.

You could say she killed herself. She had a heart valve replaced a few years earlier. After the operation, she was required to take a blood thinner. She stopped taking the medication because she said it made her arthritis flare up. She said herbs would work just as good as any blood thinner. When she was wrong this time, it killed her. A blood clot reached her brain, and she died. You couldn't tell my mother anything.

My Italian father used to tell us kids that when German babies are born, they would open up their heads, take their brains out and replace them with concrete. My mother was one of the most stubborn people I have ever met. That was why she was one of the best Jehovah's Witnesses I ever met. No one was going to confuse her mind with the facts.

Meryl Freeman gave my mom's funeral talk. Like most Jehovah's Witness funeral talks, the speaker spends about five minutes talking about the person who died and about thirty minutes talking about the deceased's "hope." The speaker will talk about how wonderful the Jehovah's Witnesses are and how you should join them, too, if you aren't already one.

Yes, five minutes to describe a person's entire life. The Society never misses an opportunity to plug its beliefs to a captive audience. The speaker even gets to count his speech as service time as if he was going door-to-door.

No wonder so many non-witnesses who attend a Jehovah's Witness funeral walk away shaking their heads in disbelief. I was at a funeral once where the speaker actually talked about the dead person for ten whole minutes but that was very unusual.

Mom was buried at Palacky Cemetery in the middle of nowhere. As my father and sister and I drove to the cemetery, we passed an old abandoned farmhouse that was visible from the grave site. Its roof had caved in. Cows meandered inside and around the farmhouse. Dad told me my mother had been born in that house fifty-seven years earlier. It has been said that life is just a big circle. This circle started and ended just a few hundred yards from each other.

Something strange happened on Sunday, the day after my mother's funeral. There happened to be a family reunion on my mother's mother's (my grandmother) side of the family, the Moggs. I saw my great-grandmother, Anna. She was one-hundred years old. She managed to outlive her daughter, who died almost fifty years earlier in 1934, and her granddaughter (my mother), who was only fifty-seven when she died. Ira, her oldest son, was at the reunion. He was eighty years old at the time. Ira was her second child, and she gave birth to him in 1903 when she was just twenty years old.

In the book *Pioneer Women Voices from the Kansas Frontier,* there is a picture of my great-grandmother, Anna Mogg, sitting in a classroom in Wilson, Kansas, when she was just a young girl.

Of course, she didn't recognize me. I was just one of dozens of great-grandchildren. I told her I was Norma's son. She grabbed my hand and told me how sorry she was for my mother's passing.

I didn't cry at my mother's funeral. Not because I didn't love her. I was sad, confused, numb and maybe even relieved.

She was a hard woman and devoid of emotion. Like the Jehovah's Witnesses, it was either her way or the highway. I know it's tough to have empathy if you weren't raised with empathy. On the other hand, we can all choose the path of love and forgiveness.

She died a very unhappy person. Her unhappiness is what made the Jehovah's Witness's promises so appealing. Pie in the sky when you die.

She had a hard life: sexually abused as a child, poor physical heath, married to a man she really didn't love or respect. And there was plenty of guilt. She, like most Witnesses, felt she could have done more to serve her god and organization.

Like thousands of other lost souls, my mother had looked forward to just one thing: the day Armageddon would show up. That wonderful day in the future, when god would be killing off billions of people, so she and her Jehovah's Witnesses friends could finally be happy in their paradise.

So yes, maybe I was relieved when my Mother died. For her the pain was finally over. However, because of her infecting our family with this religion, her grandchildren and great-grandchildren are still dealing with the problems of this contaminated thought system.

The gift that keeps on giving.

My father told me something very interesting a few years later. He said when he went to Mom's house to clean it out after she was dead, he found all kinds of interesting things. To his surprise he found the records of tens of thousands of dollars my mother had given the society over the many years they had been together. This was, of course, to "further the worldwide work." He had no idea she had been doing this, because she had been in charge of all the family's finances from the beginning of the marriage. He told me how there were many times over the years they were barely scraping by and yet the society always got their check for a hundred dollars every month. My father was furious.

He also told me that there were times when I was at Bethel that he wanted to send me some money to help me out. However my mother vetoed this idea. She had told him I needed to make it on my own, and besides, I was in Jehovah's care and the Brothers there would take care of me and my needs in every way.

It looks like after my mother's contributions and the Brothers paying me only $22 a month, they got an indentured servant and still made a cool 78 bucks a month profit. Not bad.

Chapter 39

The Fun Way to Make More Jehovah's Witnesses

We decided to move out of Farmerville, Louisiana, in 1979. It was just a little too country for us. It only had one gas station and one restaurant. It was a dry county, and it was a sixty-mile round trip to Ruston or Monroe to do anything fun.

Most of the people in the Kingdom Hall had moved to Farmerville to help the struggling congregation. There were only two families who were actually from the area. So, everyone was trying to convince visitors to move there, the reason being that if you could get someone else to move there, you could move out. That way you wouldn't feel guilty for abandon the struggling congregation. We didn't wait to find our replacements. I was weaning myself off of the guilt.

We got on the phone with Debbie's best friend Lynn Garrett, who lived in Oregon. After an hour on the phone we decided to move to Oregon, sight unseen. In fact, we didn't even know it rained there.

When I left Bethel, I made a vow to never work for anyone else, but in Oregon, I got a job as a lumber broker at Sun Tree Lumber Company and then at Western International Forest Products. I worked my way up to division manager. Even though I made great money, I hated the corporate politics. In 1990, I started working for myself again and became a real estate agent.

I figured if I was going to work for a jerk it might as well be me.

My whole life seemed to zoom by in a blur. Weeks turned into months. Months turned into years. Week after week of Witness meetings. Five meetings a week. Thousands of meetings. Endless meetings. Jehovah this and Jehovah that. Hurry, Jehovah is coming, no time to waste.

How did I rationalize everything I had experienced growing up in the Jehovah's Witnesses and what I saw at Bethel? No one wants to believe his or her whole life is a lie. For many years, I couldn't connect the dots. I guess that's not true. I didn't want to connect the dots. If I had, those dots would have pointed me in only one direction: the backside of building four with my friend Jimmy Olson.

To paraphrase Scarlet O'Hara at the end of *Gone with the Wind*, "I can't think about that right now. I know I'll think about that tomorrow. After all, tomorrow is another day!"

If you ever back a Jehovah's Witness into a corner, and they have to admit to the problems and insanity that is going on around them, they will tell you one of two things: "You must have faith" or "Jehovah will take care of all the problems someday." See how easy that was? Now you don't have to think about all those discrepancies and the things that make no sense whatsoever.

In my fifty years as a Jehovah's Witness, there were a few occasions when it happened. When I thought to myself, I'm in a religion just like all the others. It would be on those darkest nights when my thoughts went into the forbidden zone of doubt – the zone the Society said you could never go to.

Once, many years after Bethel, I was with several of my old Bethel buddies, guys who had been Jehovah's Witnesses and Elders for thirty, forty and even fifty years. These guys had seen all kinds of insanity associated with this religion. We sat in my hot tub and gazed up at the stars. And the words came out. The thoughts that I believe almost every Jehovah's Witness has had at least once in his or her lifetime. You might say the words to your closest friend or you might just think them to yourselves.

The words are: "Even if this isn't the truth, it is still a good way of life…. isn't it?" Really?

In the end, this rationalization is how most Jehovah's Witnesses coped with all the discrepancies, flip flops and the amazing new light that made absolutely no sense whatsoever. We rationalized the insanity by thinking that we were living "a good way of life."

On the other hand, doesn't this really mean the end justifies the means?

Usually most, if not all, of our family are Jehovah's Witnesses, plus all of our friends are part of the Society. There is no world but that world, their world. I wasn't ready to leave the only world I had ever known. If I had connected the dots back then, there would have been no place to go. I would have been on the outside looking in.

To lose the only life I had ever known would have put me on the couch looking at the .38 special revolver on the coffee table. Just like my father-in-law had. I stopped thinking about it. I couldn't think about it.

I was back in bindery-line mode. I was just trying to get through one day at a time.

There is a rope that pulls one even tighter into the cement of the Witnesses' organization. It was one of the key reasons why a crazy old man named Charles Russell could turn just a few followers into millions and create an organization worth billions of dollars.

I didn't know it at the time, but the rope of bondage to their organization for me and many others was actually an umbilical cord attached to my two children. We now had two new young ones who we were charged to indoctrinate. As children, they had no choice in the matter. My mother never asked me what I thought of her new religion, and my children did not have that option, either. They could make the decision to leave the religion that felt like "the Borg" from Star Trek years later. Of course, if they left also, it too would cost them everything.

Even if I didn't take a lead in indoctrinating my children, my wife surely would. At the time of their births, I was still a believer, so my path was clear.

Now that I had a family, we had one more meeting each week added to the five meetings we already attended. That meeting was called the Family Home Bible Study. This weekly study was required to mold the children to the will of the organization – to the will of the all-powerful god Jehovah. It was easy to do.

There would be only one world for my children: the world we showed them. Just like me, they were eager to join their new family – the family of millions of Brothers and Sisters all around the world. They soon became the righteous and zealous followers we wanted them to be.

Our children sometimes didn't go willingly into the Jehovah's Witnesses thought system. Just like most Jehovah's Witness parents, we too employed corporal punishment at times. We were told by our leaders that our future young converts needed to be kept in line. It was not unusual and you will see it often—Jehovah's Witness parents in the Kingdom Hall grabbing up their screaming two year olds and taking them outside for an attitude adjustment by way of a spanking. For some odd reason, it wasn't easy to keep a small child sitting in their seats quietly for over two hours.

The Witnesses love to quote the famous phrase, "spare the rod and spoil the child" even though this phrase is not in the Bible. The actual quote was written by Samuel Butler, a 17th century poet, but it is likely inspired from the Bible verse in Proverbs 13:24, "Whoever spares the rod hates their children, but the one who loves their children is careful to discipline them."

This meant that my father would take me out into the parking lot and explain this wonderful Bible passage to me many times growing up as a child. I would, of course, be doing the same thing to my children years later.

The beat/beatings goes on. No pun intended.

There is an interesting true story about a rambunctious five year old the Witnesses love to relay and laugh about. In the middle of the Watchtower study, a young mother annoyed by her child's behavior grabs him and throws him over her shoulder. The child obviously knows what is waiting for him in the parking lot. As they are heading down the aisle and towards the exit he looks back over his mother's shoulder and yells out, "Please pray for me!"

There was one time when my five-foot, sixteen-year-old daughter stood up for herself. She wanted to do something that was not in line with the church's policies. It became a yelling match and I, who no longer could defend my position became enraged and out of control. There was no logic to my defense and she knew it. I guess on some level I knew it too. I got up from my seat and slapped her across her face. I will never forget how she looked sitting there in silence, with tears in her eyes. I had totally crushed the spirit in this young woman. I knew in that moment I had crossed over some line. I truly hated what I had become, an enforcer of the church's unreasonable policies.

Just like it was for me, there would be no school dances, no school sports and no school friends who were not Jehovah's Witnesses. My children, too, would be isolated for their protection and for the protection of the organization.

They both left high school so they could be home-schooled. The Witnesses love to create a vacuum in which they insulate their children. This was one way to keep the children safe and away from the contamination of any worldly influences and desires. The information the children received and their environment were strictly controlled. Many Jehovah's Witness families don't even own a television set. Some even refer to the TV as "the Devil's box."

It their teens, my children were both baptized. We had done our job; they had joined the club and were now locked in. They both pioneered and went to pioneer school, so, just like the vast majority of Witness children back then, there would be no college education for them. Most religions, like governments, like to keep their people ignorant.

We even took them back to New York in 1996 to visit Bethel. My son was seventeen and my daughter was nineteen. In some sick way, I was hoping my son would want to go there too. You know, to make a man out of him like it did me. It seemed like a good idea at the time, since I was still taking my "crazy pills."

I really do believe that kids today are so much smarter than their parents. After my son walked through the old factory and book bindery, he knew it wouldn't be a place for him. He said he couldn't find one smiling face there.

He was right of course, because twenty years later things hadn't changed much.

In fact, it was the wisdom (the ability of spotting bull shit) from my children, just a few years later, that would be instrumental in my departure from the church also.

My daughter likes to relay the story about a lunch she and I enjoyed many years ago. This was a couple years later, after our Bethel trip. I forget what we were talking about. However in the course of the conversation, she got the nerve up to tell me there were many things about the church's policies that made no sense to her and she frankly was having a hard time believing in anymore. She set there waiting for my response. What happened next, was a defining moment for her and for me too. I guess she was waiting for me to regurgitate the church's propaganda and defend the insanity. I could not do this any longer. Instead I set there with what she would describe as a funny, little, weird look on my face. She told me years later that in that moment, not by anything I said but just the look I had on my face, she knew I wasn't buying the program anymore either. For me, I realized that my daughter was coming to the same conclusions I was having. Yes, our days of drinking Kool-Aid together would soon be over.

Anyway back on our Bethel Tour. We went through the new laundry and saw Peter Hollingsworth. He had been at Bethel for twenty-seven years and had worked in the laundry the entire time. I told Bob Rains that they needed to give poor Peter a break and let the guy out of the laundry.

I found Daryl Christianson stuck in the Squibb building, working by himself on a deserted floor. I don't know what he was doing, maybe sorting paperclips or something.

Daryl had only one memory about me that he wanted to relay to my children. I had known Daryl for four years and all he could think about was a time twenty-five-years earlier when my car was acting up. He told my family how I decided to turn the car around and go back to Bethel instead of going to the meeting that Sunday. Yes, because of me and my car troubles, he had missed a Watchtower study. It was probably the only Watchtower study he had ever missed in his thirty years at Bethel.

What a jerk.

Daryl looked and seemed like all the other old, dried-up, company men I had known years earlier.

We sat at Norm Brekke's table for lunch and ate hamburgers. There wasn't much conversation. Dozens of people were chowing down. The dining room was deathly quiet, just like the old days.

I sat there and wondered how many other suicides Norm had known about in his fifty years at the headquarters.

After lunch, I met with my old friend Cerio Aulicino. He had a very prestigious job in the writing department, received a job change to the hand bindery in the factory back in 1973. He went from writing the articles in the *Watch Tower* and *Awake!* to pasting song books together in the hand bindery. Of course, they told him his new job was a "privilege of service." I'll never forget the look on his face when I had to inform him that his "privilege of service" was really "the shaft" instead. He couldn't believe it. He just couldn't believe it was possible after so many years of faithful service.

However, now twenty years later, Cerio informed me, with a smile on his face, that he was back in the writing department and no longer in the hand bindery. The shaft had been removed. He was back on top again.

I didn't know it at the time, but Cerio was the person who was chiefly responsible for turning the Watchtower Bible and Tract Society into an NGO (Non-Governmental Organization) member of… the United Nations!

If you are a not a Jehovah's Witness reading this, you probably couldn't care less about this. But if you are a Jehovah's Witness, this is huge. Why? Because the Jehovah's Witnesses had spent decades condemning the United Nations as the scarlet-colored wild beast in the Book of Revelation. They have always believed this organization is run by the Devil himself.

The Society became a Non-Governmental Organization Associate Member of the UN in 1992. In order to join this organization, they would have to sign and AGREE to the UN charter. This charter clearly states that, as a member, the Society must "support and respect the principles of the charter of the United Nations."

Do you see a problem here? Let's connect some dots. According to the Witnesses, the United Nations is an organization run by Satan himself and will soon be destroyed by god himself. Now they agree to join one of Satan's organizations and respect its charter.

Does this Kool-Aid taste strange?

For nine years, the Society was a member of the United Nations. In 2001, the Society resigned its membership. Why? Did they get some more new light on the matter? It could be, but the real reason was because of the shit storm that their membership created within the organization. Many of the smart Jehovah's Witnesses could see the bullshit and severed all ties with the Society for what they considered to be a hypocritical and dishonest chapter of the religion's history.

Anyway, back to my reunion tour of the Lord's house. Before that day, I hadn't been back to Bethel in twenty-two years. I left the headquarters for the second and last time in my life. I had a strange feeling that nothing had really changed there. It was like walking back in on an Orwellian movie.

From Brooklyn, our tour bus headed north and finally ended up at the Watchtower Farm. I had never been to the Watchtower Farm. Yes, I had been at Bethel for four years and never visited the farm, not even once. I told people it would have been like showing a starving man a steak dinner. I knew if I had seen it back then, it would have made my stay in Brooklyn that much harder. For people who were transferred to the farm from the factory, it was like leaving a concentration camp and being sent to Hawaii.

I tracked down Ester Lopez, the old bat from Dixon's table. She was still alive and was now at the Watchtower Farm. I had her paged. I stood there in the lobby, waiting for her with my family. I had looked forward to this moment the whole day.

She walked into the lobby with a total look of surprise. "It's you! It's you!" She said.

"Yes, it's me." I didn't say anything more as I walked right over to her and grabbed her hand and put it on my stomach and held it there. I had put on a few pounds since I left Bethel.

I held her hand and patted it on my stomach, "You were wrong, Ester. I didn't starve to death!"

She had a confused look on her face and of course she had no idea what I was talking about but I remembered what she had said to me back in March of 1974.

The Great Tribulation that was to happen before Armageddon that she and millions of others had hoped for hadn't come. This, of course, meant I didn't have the opportunity to starve to death as Ester had hoped for.

That was twenty-three years ago back in 1996.

May the old bat rest in peace.

Chapter 40
Don't do that Again, Bubba

If the Elders call you into the back room for a "service talk" or "committee meeting", they will never tell you ahead of time what your possible sin or transgression has been.

Sometimes the offense could be quite trivial, like if a Sister's dress is too short. We sure don't want to be seeing too much of a woman's knees, do we now?

Sometimes the offense could be quite tragic, like child molestation.

The problems of child molesting in this organization are huge right now. Why is it such a big issue currently? Because for years, the Society has tried to sweep this problem under the carpet. If a child had been molested, the local Elders would meet with the accused and decide what actions (if any) should take place. They were under strict orders from the Society never to go to the police or secular authorities. They would handle this problem in the congregation, privately and behind closed doors.

Do you see a problem coming here?

There are thousands of stories over the years that went something like this:

Marylou in Mississippi walks in on her husband Bubba molesting his five-year-old step-daughter Suzie. They are both members of the local Kingdom Hall. Marylou doesn't go to the local police; she goes to the body of Elders as she is instructed.

The Elders form what is called a Judicial Committee. This committee will consist of three Elders in the local Kingdom Hall.

Who are these three Brothers? Remember Ben Regan, my old father-in-law? He could have been there, plus Brother Smith, who works on a garbage truck, and Brother Jones, who is a car salesman. Of these three men, probably the highest level of education they will have achieved is high school. However, remember that is not a requirement to lead the flock. Who knows? Maybe one of these Brothers went to community college for a couple of years. The bottom line is, what credentials do these men have to deal with these kinds of serious matters?

You guessed it. Practically zero.

These three Brothers will have a meeting with Bubba and Marylou. Believe it or not, they might even require little Suzie to be in attendance. Yes, it's not unusual for the young victim to have to be present with the abuser in the meeting.

(A side note: Depending on the state you live in, most authorities require anywhere between 160 to 200 hours of formal education before they can talk and interrogate a victim of sexual abuse.)

These three learned men, Ben the janitor, Brother Smith in waste removal and our car sales friend, will now decide the fate of poor Suzie.

This is going to be a recipe for disaster.

For many years, the Society, in their wisdom, has said there must be at least TWO witnesses to this type of offense. Marylou tells the Elders what she saw. Bubba says he didn't do it. He was just checking the girl's temperature with his fingers. It is one person's word against another and there is no second witness to the offense, except Suzie, who will likely be too traumatized or terrified to tell the truth. Bubba may have threatened her to keep her mouth shut.

Question: How many pedophiles carry out their deeds with an audience standing by?

Guess what happens most of the time? Nothing. Case closed.

Ben tells Marylou to go home: "Have another beer and forget the whole thing."

Bubba goes home with Marylou and slaps her around. They have a couple more beers and decide to move to Alabama.

Bubba, Marylou and Suzie all move to Alabama. They move into a new Kingdom Hall where no one knows them. Bubba gets a fresh start with Suzie and the beat goes on.

Later on, Suzie invites other young girls from their congregation for a sleepover, all under Bubba's watchful eye.

Even if Bubba had been caught by two people (eyewitnesses) and dis-fellowshipped, the authorities would not have been notified!

Most of the time, if the case is dropped, this information will not be sent to their new Kingdom Hall either.

See a problem coming here?

Fast-forward twenty years. Our traumatized Suzie finds out the Brothers had received information on what was happening to her and did nothing about it. She finds out that she was just the first of other children who were molested by Bubba. Suzie takes legal action.

This is one of thousands of examples of how the Societies' policies to protect themselves from bad publicity are now biting them in the ass.

So now, years later, there is a shit storm of legal problems on the Societies' doorsteps because of their policy of protecting themselves and not the young children in their organization. The Society is now paying out millions of dollars in court fines yearly!

They can't sweep this under the rug now, like they did with Leo Greenlees.

Now it's Leo Greenlees times ten thousand!

Thousands of abused children who didn't like the way the Society handled their situation are now taking legal action.

On June 23, 2016, in San Diego, California, Superior Court Judge Richard Strauss grew tired of the Watchtower Society fighting his order to produce the 1997 letter sent to all Elders worldwide. So, he sanctioned the religion with a fine of four-thousand dollars per DAY until the Society complied with that order.

An Elder who left their organization, because of the injustice concerning child abuse, was kind enough to make a copy of this letter public. What did this letter say?

"The March 14, 1997 letter to all Elders contained an instruction that inadvertently admitted they had a big problem: "It may be possible that some who were guilty of child molestation were or are now serving as elders, ministerial servants, or regular or special pioneers. Others may have been guilty of child molestation before they were baptized. The bodies of elders should NOT query individuals. However, the body of elders should discuss this matter and give the Society a report on anyone who is currently serving or who formerly served in a Society appointed position in your congregation who is known to have been guilty of child molestation in the past.

In your report please answer the following questions: How long ago did he commit the sin? What was his age at the time? What was the age of his victim(s)? Was it a one-time occurrence or a practice? If it was a practice, to what extent? How is he viewed in the community and by the authorities? Has he lived down any notoriety in the community? Are members of the congregation aware of what took place? How do they and/or his victim(s) view him? Has he ever been dis-fellowshipped, reproved, counselled, or otherwise dealt with? If he has moved to another congregation, please identify the congregation to which he has moved."

They go on to state: "This information should be sent to the Society along with any other observations that the body of elders has. Please send this to the Society in the "Special Blue" envelope so that the factors involved may be given due consideration; this information is not to be made available to those not involved. This letter is confidential and should NOT be copied but should be kept in the congregation's confidential file. Elders should not discuss this information with others."

So, does the world headquarters know about all the child molesters in their organization? You bet they do.

This corroborates that the Society had knowingly appointed molesters to positions of authority.

Because of this, a California appeals court upheld the order for the religion to pay four-thousand dollars PER DAY in fines until it turned over these documents.

The ruling stems from a case in San Diego where Osbaldo Padron sued the Jehovah's Witnesses for failing to warn congregants that a child abuser was in their midst.

Padron, a former Jehovah's Witness, was sexually abused as a child by an adult member of his congregation named Gonzalo Campos. Campos confessed to sexually abusing seven children.

According to court documents, leaders at the Jehovah's Witness's world headquarters in New York knew that Campos had abused children, yet they continued to promote him to higher positions of responsibility in his congregation and took no action to prevent further abuse.

The non-profit organization Reveal from The Center for Investigative Reporting reviewed multiple cases involving Campos as part of a larger investigation into the Societies' institutional cover-up of child sex abuse in its congregations.

According to internal Watchtower documents, the Jehovah Witness organization instructed congregation leaders to keep child abuse a secret from law enforcement as a matter of policy since at least 1989.

In 2015, Padron sought those documents in court as part of his lawsuit, hoping to show a pattern that extended beyond his own case. The documents also would provide a road map to likely thousands of known or accused child molesters in Jehovah's Witness congregations across the country.

The Watchtower argued repeatedly that fulfilling Padron's request would violate the privacy rights of people named in the documents, confidentiality privileges between

Elders and congregants, and the organization's religious protections under the First Amendment. The court dismissed those arguments. But the Watchtower has refused to fully turn over the documents.

In upholding Strauss's order, the appellate judges called the Watchtower a "recalcitrant litigant who refuses to follow valid orders and merely reiterates losing arguments."

Should the Watchtower again refuse to comply with the court's order, the judges wrote, Strauss would be justified in kicking the Jehovah's Witnesses out of court and ruling in favor of Padron.

"Indeed, we find Watchtower's conduct so egregious that if it continues to defy the March 25, 2016 order, terminating sanctions appear to be warranted and necessary," the judges wrote.

The case was settled out of court for a large amount of money. Fast forward.

The government of Australia has determined that the Watchtower Bible and Tract Society has hidden the activity of no less than one-thousand-and-six pedophiles. That is in just one country alone. How many pedophiles have found a safe haven within their local Kingdom Halls around the world? The number of Jehovah's Witnesses in Australia according to their website is sixty-seven thousand, seven-hundred-and-forty-eight. If you take the number of Jehovah's Witnesses in Australia and divide it by the total number of Jehovah's Witnesses around the world, 8,457,107, and if the ratio is the same that means the Society is hiding the activity of tens of thousands of these pedophiles, worldwide!

I wonder if they prayed to Jehovah on this one. "What should we do god? Should we help the known pedophiles in the organization and pay the millions of dollars in fines and judgements, or should we protect our children and the future children of our church?"

It looks like after they prayed, the Governing Body got the answer they wanted and took a vote on it. They all agreed they would settle out of court for millions, but they would NOT turn over their list of pedophiles!

Of course, it makes sense. What do you think would happen to their organization if this information were made public? It would be the end of the Watchtower Bible and Track Society as we know it. Only the most stupid of their followers would remain loyal.

I heard recently that one of the Governing Body at Bethel received a different answer from god. He told the other leaders there that their policy wasn't right and they were just like the churches of Christendom. He stood up for Jesus and the little children.

I guess the Governing Body decided to give him a job change and reassigned him to The Gather in the bindery (just like Fred Barnes) so he could think things over before he had his heart attack. Kool-Aid, anyone?

Chapter 41

No More Toasting for Me

One day in 2000, Brother Day came up to me and said the Elders would like to have a word with me, after the meeting. So, of course, for the two hours until my meeting/tribunal, my mind was racing. *What did I do? What did I say? Did I put my foot in my mouth once again?*

So, what was my offense?

It turned out that I got into trouble at a wedding for toasting and saying the word "fuck." Both things are frowned upon. I could see why cursing wasn't appropriate. On the other hand, why is there a problem with clinking two glasses together?

What's funny is that the woman who turned me in for saying the word "fuck" was doing just that. She was screwing a guy in the local Kingdom Hall, and they weren't married.

At the time nothing happened to her for doing it, however I got into trouble for just saying the word.

Welcome to the Twilight Zone.

I had to sit in front of three Elders and apologize for my unchristian behavior. Yes, it was the Old Indian Navajo Trick one more time.

There is a trend I've noticed many times over the course of decades in the organization. Many of the people who like to turn in other people are usually the ones who are doing some really nasty things themselves. "See god, how righteous I am! I'm not so bad. I'm trying to help you and your organization, even though I can't keep up with your rules myself."

It seemed the woman who turned me - in came from a family who moved out of Southern California because she had gotten into trouble down there. She and her family needed a fresh start in Oregon. I call this millionaire family the vampires. The family who moved from Southern California were not pedophiles; they were spiritual vampires. They would move from congregation to congregation, sucking the life out of their new friends. Once their old friends saw them in the light of day with their teeth exposed, the friends would be dropped and new blood would be needed.

There is an Old Italian saying, "Never eat where you shit!" This means, of course, never spread shit around the same place you live in. Yes, the vampires had shit in their local Kingdom Hall in California one time too many and it was time to move on.

There are thousands of Witnesses who must move out of their small congregations every year, congregations where everyone knows way too much about each other. Reputations are hard to get rid of, among Jehovah's Witnesses, and they will hold grudges for years.

I knew a guy in Oregon who was an Elder. He ended up having an affair with a married woman. They were both dis-fellowshipped and were out for a couple of years. They both did what was required and showed real repentance and were reinstated. They got married and were in good standing once again. Even though it had been many years since their indiscretion, they were still semi-shunned. No, the Brothers couldn't forget their trespasses, he told me. Moving out of the area was not an option because of his business.

I looked at him and asked, "Did you kill anyone?"

"No!" He said. "Why?"

"Because King David killed someone *and* committed adultery and yet god was able to forgive him."

"Yes, I know, but the Witnesses are not as forgiving as god," he said.

"Yes, I know."

A change of Kingdom Halls can give everyone a fresh start. This works out well, especially for the thousands of pedophiles in the organization. A fresh start with lots of new children.

The father vampire looked just like Dick Dastardly with his dyed hair and mustache with its white roots.

I remember being over at his house, drinking wine that cost only two dollars a bottle from Trader Joes. "You know,

I *have* to drink cheap wine," I said. "Why do you?" I asked. He just smiled. The cheap wine was for company only.

I'm afraid being a multimillionaire is not really a good thing among the Jehovah's Witnesses. They aren't really liked. Most Witnesses are resentful of fellow Witnesses with lots of money – those who have their paradise now, ahead of everyone else.

The most resentful Witnesses are those who have given up good jobs and very successful careers for the sake of "advancing kingdom interest." The Society just loves to write articles about those people in their magazines. It's fun to read about how very famous people and sports stars have given up fame and fortune for the sake of the Lord and the organization. The Society makes these famous people examples to us all. Yes, you too, should give up any ideas of fame and fortune for the sake of your god.

Many Jehovah's Witnesses wear their poverty like a badge of honor, as I have mentioned before. How else do you rationalize a lifetime of limited education and poor career choices?

Why do they hammer this point home? They want their members out in Field Service, recruiting more Jehovah's Witnesses, not working and trying to get rich in this old system of the world. It's a system that will soon be destroyed any day in the Great Tribulation.

This, of course, has backfired because the end of the old system hasn't come. Much to their dismay, their contributions are way down. Since most of the older Witnesses didn't go out and earn a good education and well-paying jobs, the money just isn't there.

This is unlike the Mormons, who are rolling in dough because they have always encouraged higher education and well-paying jobs among their church members.

Another favorite scripture the Witnesses liked to recite is Matthew 6:19-21: "Do not store up for yourselves treasures on earth, where moths and vermin destroy, and where thieves break in and steal. But store up for yourselves treasures in heaven, where moths and vermin do not destroy, and where thieves do not break in and steal. For where your treasure is, there your heart will be also."

The Brothers would hardly ever tell you to your face that you are spending too much time making money. But you would hear comments like, "Nice new car, Brother Jones," or "You seem to be spending a lot of extra time at work," or "We haven't seen you much out in Field Service lately."

However, sometimes they would say it to your face. Back in 1978, Roy Baty and his wife Marylyn moved to Farmerville, Louisiana. I had a Trim-Line business there. We bought a small 1920s' bungalow for nineteen-thousand dollars. My payment was one-hundred-and-ninety-eight dollars a month. I drove a Toyota that was three years old.

I had four Brothers including Roy working for me in my Trim Line business. I was making about sixty-thousand dollars a year. So, of course, I was considered the rich, materialistic Brother in the Kingdom Hall.

One day after the Watchtower study, my wife happened to be wearing a new dress she had just sewn together. The total cost of the dress was maybe ten bucks. Marylyn was talking to Debbie and happened to mention that her husband, Roy (my employee), had put that new dress she wearing on her back.

I was a realtor in Portland, Oregon, for twenty-two years. I showed my Witness millionaire friend and his wife a house that was on the market for more than one-point-four-million dollars. They loved it and asked me what I thought.

I loved the house too. But when they asked me about the drawbacks of owning the house, I had to tell them the truth.

"None of the 'friends' will want to visit you here," I said. "You will be living in a paradise while they are still waiting for theirs."

Of course, they didn't buy the house. They did buy a less ostentatious house so Witnesses would want to come over to their house to drink their cheap wine.

My wife and I took a trip to New Orleans with some other Witness friends. We were gone four days. We, of course, didn't invite Brother and Sister Vampire to go with us.

My two teenage kids decided to throw a party at our house while we were gone. You know, kids will be kids.

Brother Vampire's kids weren't invited to the party because my kids knew they were snitches. The Vampire kids did hear about the party however. So, they told their parents about it. It was time to play Gestapo, so the parents drove over to our house during the party. They were very thorough about checking out the different cars, that way they could figure out who was in attendance.

Another fun story about Brother Vampire. He was having some problems with his roof. I referred a Jehovah's Witness roofer from another Kingdom Hall to him. This young man had just gotten married and had a new baby. The couple were barely scraping by.

I didn't spend a lot of time at Brother Vampire's house, but one afternoon, we were drinking his cheap wine while his roof was being repaired. It was a terrible winter day in Oregon, with thunder and lightning and sheets of rain. The young man was up and down that roof for four hours looking and repairing all of the leaks. Finally, he came in to be paid. He was completely drenched to the bone. Brother Vampire pulled out a wad of money that would choke a horse. He scrolled through dozens of hundred-dollar bills until he got to the twenties. He slipped out a single twenty-dollar bill and handed it to the young Brother. You should have seen the look on this young man's face. He told me years later, that he took the last nine dollars he had to buy caulk to fix this guy's roof. He also said he came very close to telling this guy, "Keep your twenty bucks, you obviously need it more than me." The only reason he didn't was because he needed the twenty dollars for gas to get back home.

One more bloodless body in the middle of the road.

One more side note about the vampire's daughter who turned me in for saying "fuck." My roofer friend told me that she tried to get his wife into bed with her a couple of times.

Just more eating and defecating in the same spot.

By the way, a few years later one of the vampire's sons decided to leave his house and the organization. He ended up being homeless and sleeping in the streets. My daughter and her husband, who were not Jehovah's Witnesses at the time, bought him breakfast one day. Why did they do that? Because it was the kind thing to do. Most people will even feed a starving dog. But the vampire's son reported to my daughter and her husband that his family had cut him off because he didn't want to be a part of the insanity any longer. What if he died out there on those mean city streets? No matter, his parents thought, tough love would bring him back into their loving organization. That is why shunning is one of their favorite forms of punishment.

Just why does this family of self-righteous vampires upset me so much? I guess because that family seems to encapsulate the organization itself. They are always hunting for the smallest infractions in other people; yet they have no problem overlooking major problems in their own immediate family.

Anyway, enough of the vampires and back to my kid's party.

There were four married couples and four single people at the party. Some underage drinking went on. It would be committee meetings for everyone who was present.

I had told my kids if I had been an Elder, I could have helped them. But since I wasn't in the good old boys club, they were screwed.

I saw many times in the organization that if an Elder's kids were involved in some inappropriate behavior, they would cut those kids some serious slack out of consideration for their parents.

Since lying could be grounds for dis-fellowshipping, these committee meetings would usually go something like this:

Imagine the same feeling as the committee meetings in the movie *The Scent of a Woman*, or the Nazi movie *Swing Kids*.

You are all alone in a small room. Sitting in front of you are three elders dressed in business suits. "Tell us, Billy, who all was at the party that night? If you tell the truth about everything, you will go free and nothing will happen to you." Of course, Billy would name the names.

"Tell us about everything that happened at this party. Remember, we have talked to everyone who was there." Billy would now give up his own mother if he had to.

Then this is the best part: "Is there anything else you want to confess to us? Anything that you have done in the past. Things you would like to confess? Remember, we have talked to everyone there including your family and girlfriend, and she has told us some very interesting things." Sieg Heil!

If you know anything about anyone, and it comes to light that you didn't report it to the Elders, you are considered a transgressor in the crime along with the offending person. It's judged that you were involved in some kind of cover-up. This means you could possibly be dis-fellowshipped for not reporting it.

I had a friend named Richard who was caught in the shower masturbating by his wife. She made him go to the elders of the church and turn himself in. Yes, he had to sit in front of three fellow brothers and explain to them why he was jerking off.

The whole organization is encouraged to rat each other out. I've seen children turn in their parents and vice versa.

Just like in Nazi Germany, people have turned in their best friends and family members who they thought were a danger to the organization.

However, I guess this is true with anyone but the pedophiles. I guess in that case, they really don't want to know about it.

I'm afraid I've been a part of this Nazi style of information gathering, too. I, however, could never be involved in the Nazi style of interrogation. The reason being, I promised myself after leaving Bethel that I would never be an Elder and thus never have to sit in judgment of my fellow man or woman.

Bob Nelson, who was a friend of mine, told me how he had been engaging in what the Jehovah's Witnesses like to call "loose conduct" or "pornea" (sexual sins not involving intercourse) with one of my wife's girlfriends. In fact, my wife had studied the Bible with this woman and brought her into the Jehovah's Witness organization.

Of course, this was something I didn't want to hear about. "Bob, why are you telling me this?" He gave me a strange look. I guess he thought he could trust me with this information. I knew if this information got out, and he mentioned he told me about it, that would not be good for either of us.

I had to tell him. "You have to go and turn yourself in now.

Why did you need to tell me this?"

What else could I do but be a good Nazi Jehovah's Witness?

I had no idea if he turned himself in or not and I frankly didn't care. I had covered my ass by telling him to do that. Seig Heil.

A couple of years later, Bob got married but not to Debbie's friend. He and his new wife came over for dinner one night. It was a beautiful summer night. We all had our bathing suits on and were sitting around our in-ground swimming pool. We had all consumed plenty of wine, too. Bob and my wife Debbie went upstairs to take in some dirty dishes. His new wife and I sat by the pool with our feet in the water. She turned to me and said, "I'll suck your dick if you like." I didn't think she was joking. I was totally taken back. My own wife would never consider doing something like that because oral sex is strictly forbidden as a Jehovah's Witness and could be a dis-fellowshipping offence.

There are a lot of "dos and don'ts" even for married couples when it comes to appropriate sexual behavior. That's right, Big Brother is even in your bedroom at all times.

So, of course there has been a lot of very embarrassing moments because of sexual policies/peculiarities. Imagine for a moment you sitting in front of three men/Elders all dressed in business suits in the back room of a Kingdom Hall. Your wife is telling these men, in detail, about how she had to preform fellatio. There will be many questions asked about the details of what happened that night. I really think many Elders get off on this stuff. These are the Elder's favorite type of committee meetings.

Do you think these three brothers/Elders and their wives will be looking at you differently at the next Watchtower study? It might be a good time to move to where the need is greater.

A few years later, my old friend Jim Pells (who was and is an elder) started to visit us frequently. I knew Jim back in my Kansas days when he was a special pioneer there. Jim needed a place to stay while he was visiting my wife's girlfriend. This was the same Jehovah's Witness girlfriend with whom my friend Bob got into trouble years earlier. Jim told me how she and he were in our hot tub late one night. One thing lead to another, and they got a little too friendly. However, after he told me about his erotic adventure, I didn't tell him to go turn himself in like I did with Bob. I didn't care anymore. My information-gathering days were over. I was done working for the Gestapo. I really didn't care what happened in my hot tub or in anybody's hot tub or bedrooms.

Chapter 42

I'm so Glad I don't Believe the Way You Do!

There were thousands of hours of knocking on people's doors to tell them Jehovah was coming. Please join our club. The-world-is-coming-to-an-end club. We-are-saved-and-you-are-screwed club. Please jump on the ark before it's too late. Time is running out! Hurry, there is no time to waste!

There's no time to be happy now. In the "new system" (another term for their paradise Earth), we can be happy.

Don't waste time trying to secure a good education or a good job. Those things will not help you when Armageddon comes.

I knew some Jehovah's Witnesses who never even fixed their teeth. Why should they? The new system will be here any day, and Jehovah will take care of their bad teeth. Those Witnesses are now wearing dentures.

Millions of Witnesses had no savings and no retirement. Why should they save money? Money will be worthless and thrown in the streets when god's day of vengeance is here.

If you are a Jehovah's Witness, the future is the only place happiness can occur. I remember many times being out in Field Service with Witnesses who were telling me about what mansion they would be living in after Armageddon.

Because once god killed off the rich worldly homeowner, they could easily choose any vacant house in the neighborhood they wanted.

Sometimes people at the doors were upset or rude because we knocked on their door trying to sell them our religion. As we walked away from the house, we would laugh and talk about how the birds would be eating the flesh off their bones after Armageddon, just as Bible prophecy had foretold.

"Your carcasses will be food to all birds of the sky and to the beasts of the earth, and there will be no one to frighten them away." – Deuteronomy 28:26

After their bones have been picked clean, their house would be up for grabs.

Yes, in the paradise new Earth, we would all be happy. After Jehovah finally makes his move.

Something strange happened to me while I was in Field Service in the late-1990s. It was a moment that helped me realize how weird and strange my life really was. I was going door-to-door in Tigard, Oregon. I rang the doorbell to a house, like I had done thousands of times before. How many people had I talked to after over forty years of spreading the good news?

This door was very different, or at least the person behind it was. A pleasant looking blonde man came to the door. He was in his late-thirties and had a slight smile on his face. I launched into my three-minute sermon. He just stood there smiling. So, I pulled out an issue of the *Watchtower and Awake!* magazines and showed him some stupid article about rape in Ethiopia. After rambling on for more minutes, I finally asked him what he thought. He paused for a moment, smiled even wider, and said, "I'm so grateful I don't believe like you do."

I stood there, not knowing what to say. Then he said it again. "I'm so glad I don't believe like you do." I had no idea what to say next. He said, "Wait here." He turned away and came back with one of our *Watchtower* magazines in his hand. He also had with him what looked like his twelve-year-old son. He opened the magazine. "This is your magazine, isn't it?" He asked. I nodded yes. He went on. "It says here, and I quote your magazine, 'In view of the end times we are living in, it might be wise to not to have children.' So you see, if I believed the same way you and your religion does, I would have never known the pleasure of my son here." He put his hand on his son's head and smiled at us and said, "Goodbye." I'm sure I had a dumb look on my face; I wanted to say something but had nothing to say. He stepped back and shut his door.

I walked back down his driveway, shaking my head. This man was right. I had spent more than 40 years knocking on doors, trying to find people who were looking for "the Truth." Yet he had shown the truth to me. I'd seen hundreds of things in the organization after almost fifty years that made no sense whatsoever or just didn't seem right, but in that moment, I came to my truth. I knew I was in a religion that had been wrong about a lot of things. If I had followed the suggestion in our magazines, I would have never known the pleasure of my children either. Because of the indoctrination, there were many years where I didn't want to have children at all. I felt the end was coming any day. That was way back in the 1960s. As I continued down the driveway, I thought about all those at Bethel who had given up the possibility of having children and families because they were told the end was coming. They waited and waited, for thirty or forty years. The end still hadn't come. The only thing that ended for those Bethelites was the possibility of ever having a family.

For many years, I thought the people who hadn't believed what we were telling them were nuts. I put myself for once behind the door I was knocking on. I put myself in the shoes of those to whom we had been preaching and came to the realization that we were the ones in the Jim Jones compound getting ready to drink the Kool-Aid, not them. So, now what?

My wife was raised in this thought system from an early age too. She was the perfect Stepford Wife who was taught to never question anything. So, when I tried to talk to her about some of the dozens of inconsistencies I had found over the years, she stared at me like a deer in headlights. This is the same look many Witnesses will give you when they are asked a logical question about their beliefs.

I was having problems with anger because I felt like my life was out of control. Debbie was convinced the anger was my unsolved issues with my dead mother. I knew that wasn't it. I felt like the guy in the movie *THX 1138* when he stopped taking the drugs that made him a drone. I was mad because I stopped taking the crazy pills, or, like in the movie *The Matrix*, you have a choice of the blue pill or the red pill. The blue pill would provide the blissful ignorance of falsehood and enslavement. The red pill would provide awareness and thus freedom from falsehood and enslavement. Each pill would have its problems.

Debbie even recommended that I see a psychiatrist. This was very unusual and something that the Society has always looked down upon for years. It's something Witnesses will avoid at all cost.

The Society tells about the evils of seeking help from outside their organization. "As a rule, for a Christian to go to a worldly psychiatrist is admission of defeat. It amounts to 'going down to Egypt for help'-Isaiah 31:1. Also, more and more psychiatrist are resorting to hypnosis which is a demonic form of worldly wisdom." – *Awake! 1960*

There was information from the Society about the evils of psychiatry: "Often when a Witness of Jehovah goes to a psychiatrist, the psychiatrist will try to persuade him that his troubles are caused by his religion, entirely overlooking the fact that the Christian Witnesses of Jehovah are the best oriented, happiest and most contended group of people on the face of the Earth. They have the least need for psychiatrists." – *Awake! 1954*

Why would the Society not want their mentally distressed followers to see a psychiatrist? Because they are concerned for the welfare and health of their disciples? No, they don't care if you are about ready to blow your brains out. They don't care if what you are doing makes no sense. Or that you can't wrap your head around the fact that your unbelieving children or your non-believing family members are all going to die at Armageddon.

What are they worried about then? They state it very clearly: "The psychiatrist will try to persuade him that his troubles are caused by his religion."

Wow, the Society doesn't even try and hide what it fears, does it?

What if this is true? What if your whack job of a religion is creating the grief and distress in your life?

Chapter 43
So, Doc, You Can See That I'm Screwed

I took Debbie's advice, and in the spring of 2001, I went to a psychiatrist. I had only two sessions with some guy I found in the phone book.

In our first session, he didn't say much as I told him about my bizarre fifty-year journey as a Jehovah's Witness. It took me two hours to tell the story. I don't think he said even a dozen words as I poured my guts out. It was strange, indeed. I had never actually completely verbalized my whole life experience as a Witness to anyone. He sat there with no judgment listening to the same story that I have related in this book.

Even though he had no judgment, I couldn't help but feel he was thinking I was some kind of alien from a different planet. Hearing the words stream from my mouth, I totally realized how strange my life must have sounded to a normal, healthy, non-Witness, someone who wasn't raised with all the fears, guilt, judgments and dogma to which I had been subjected to.

With him not saying a word, and by my own description of the events of my life, I realized for the first time how truly crazy my life had been.

Even though the Society said, "The psychiatrist will try to persuade him that his troubles are caused by his religion," my psychiatrist never did. He never said a word about my totally dysfunctional religion. He didn't have to. I could see it in his eyes. We both knew it. I had been living in the Twilight Zone. For me, it seemed very real. For him, it was like watching a horror story on television.

After I was through telling him everything, I just sat there. Neither of us spoke a word. After a couple of minutes, I finally said, "So Doc, as you can see I'm screwed either way. If I stay in the religion or if I leave it, I'm screwed."

Without any expression on his face he said, "You're right."

That is the only thing he could say. He wasn't going tell me what to do. How could he? In the end, it would have to be my decision. Either decision would have serious repercussions. He was wise enough to know that it had to be my decision and not his to make.

I got in my car and drove away.

I'm sure the good doctor had a great story to share with his wife that night. "So, honey, what do you know about the Jehovah's Witnesses? I've got a story for you. If there is a wackier religion on the planet, I don't know what it would be."

When I got home that night, I was the one who looked like a deer in the headlights when my Jehovah's Witness wife asked me how it went at the psychiatrist office.

"Great honey, you were right. I'm all cured. It was my wacky mother after all."

There are many signs that tell you when your marriage is doomed. I believe lying is No. 1. I don't care how many more years you are together, when the lying starts, your days are numbered.

But I didn't feel I had a choice in telling Debbie the truth that night. I wasn't ready yet for my marriage and my Jehovah's Witness life to end. I didn't know it at the time, but that day was not far off.

For years, I had made the most powerful prayer a person can make. "Please god, send me where I need to go." I was basically asking god to tell me what to do next. No, I didn't throw the baby out with the bath water. I still believed in god. (I consider myself more spiritual now than ever before.)

For years, I thought maybe my place was inside the organization because for sure they wouldn't listen to people who were out of it.

Whether I liked it or not, I had taken the red pill, which would free me from the enslaving control of the Borg-like religion. However, living the "truth of reality" can be harsh and very difficult.

On the other hand, I could see how the blue pill, with its falsehood and security but most of all the blissful ignorance of the illusion, could be attractive to millions of people too.

However, once the red pill is taken, there is no going back. The blissful ignorance of the illusion is gone forever.

Chapter 44

Do You Want to Shake Hands at Least?

On the weekend of July 28, 2001, we decided to have a *Big Chill* party at our house. Many of our old Witness friends were invited. They came from all over the country. Ex-Bethelites and Elders, people Debbie and I had known for over forty years.

It would be the last Jehovah's Witness gathering I would ever attend. It fact, it turned out to be the last time I ever saw most of my Jehovah's Witness friends.

I didn't know it at the time, but it turned out to be my going-away party.

After fifty years, it would soon be time to make the biggest decision of my life. There were a thousand things that could not be ignored. It was all pointing to just one question: Would I continue to take the red pill or switch back to the blue?

The weekend was full of good conversation and plenty of great music and food.

In one of those conversations, I happened to mention to some who were Elders that I thought the church was losing its grip on its young people. I talked about how my children were not buying into the program like our generation had. How many years can you hype the coming of Armageddon? Especially now that the Society had changed its stance on the year 1914. The truth is, the 1914 generation was all but gone.

Of course, my speech was shocking. To come right out and say the Society was having problems was an abomination! It was like telling Hitler the war was lost in 1945. It might be lost, but it was never something to actually say out loud.

No one at the party came to me with their concerns about my speech. But they did go to Debbie. I have no idea what they said to her. I can only imagine. How could I speak against the Fuhrer and the organization!

It's funny but on Friday before the party, Debbie acted very strange. It was like she was a different person. She danced around the living room as if possessed. It's almost like she knew on a soul level that something was coming.

On Monday, I took the last of our friends to the airport. I came home and cleaned up some of the mess of my "going-away" party. That night, I sat in the living room thinking about the weekend and decided to see what Debbie was up to. I walked back to our bedroom and into the master bath. She was lying in our oversized bathtub staring up at the ceiling with a very odd expression on her face.

I sat down next to her. She never even turned her head to look at me. I sat there for a moment and knew that something was happening to her and to me. I felt that maybe there were some issues in her past, before she even met me, with which she had not come to terms.

I don't know why, but I mentioned that maybe she should get some professional help. That seeing a psychiatrist had helped me and maybe this was something that could help her with things that might be troubling her.

She never said a word and never took her gaze off of the ceiling. It was almost like she was in a trance. I sat there for a couple of minutes more, and then I said, "okay" and returned to the living room. I sat there by myself and was there for about ten minutes before she came into the living room wearing a white bathrobe and a towel wrapped around her hair. She had the same odd expression on her face. She walked over to me and without a word, kissed me on my cheek. Then she turned and walked back into the bedroom.

Don't ask me how I knew it, but in that moment, I knew our marriage was over. Our contract was up.

I knew things would never be the same between us. We had crossed over that final line that couples do. I really don't think she knew what was coming on a conscious level. I'm sure neither of us knew that this would be the last night we would ever spend together.

Her kiss on my cheek would be our last kiss. It felt like the kiss from Judas, though she didn't betray me. It was my religion that betrayed me a long time ago. She was just the messenger.

The message was goodbye. You need to go now.

The next morning, she was going camping for a few days with some of her Witness friends from Washington. She was having a hard time trying to maneuver our car with the attached Sea-Doo watercraft out of the driveway.

After I helped her get the car situated, she got in and put the car in drive. Her window was still rolled down. Before she could put her foot on the gas, I said, "After 27 years, don't you want to at least shake hands or something?"

She put the car in park and got out of the car. We held each other for a few seconds with tears in our eyes. Neither of us said a word. There was nothing to say.

She jumped back in the car, put it in drive and was gone. It felt very strange as I watched her drive away. I was sad and confused. I had never felt more alone in my life than at that moment.

A few days later, she called me from a campground in Washington. She told me that she wouldn't be coming home until I straightened out my attitude about the church.

I said, "I can't do it anymore!"

Chapter 45

You Don't Know Me but I'm Your Brother

"I was raised here in this living hell." – *Takin' It To The Streets,* The Doobie Brothers

Though I said I couldn't do it anymore, it's not like I had a plan for the rest of my life. I loved my wife. We had been together for almost thirty years. She was the first and only girl I had ever kissed. It was love at first sight for me. Of course, we had some problems. However, leaving my wife was never an option. It wasn't a perfect marriage, but now it looked like it would soon be over. Why? Because I didn't want to be in the same religion as her? Could we still be together even though we didn't believe in the same god anymore? Thousands of people around the world do it. Jews marry Christians all the time.

I would have stayed with her if she could have lived with someone who didn't believe the same way as she did. That didn't appear to be an option, even though there were plenty of women in the Kingdom Hall who were married to non-believers. Two of Debbie's best friends were in that situation. But that was okay because their husbands never bought into the program and actually became Jehovah's Witnesses by being baptized.

Another one of my wife's girlfriends was dis-fellowshipped because she was married to a crazy guy who believed he was one of the anointed, one of the 144,000. This guy was three clams shy of a full clam bake.

Just like my father-in-law Robert Stillman, the only way out of her bad marriage was for her to commit adultery.

She did, and, of course, she was dis-fellowshipped. She was out and away from the organization for a number of years. During that time, she married this really nice guy named Lenny. She now has a worldly husband. Eventually she was reinstated and became a Jehovah's Witness once again.

Now, everyone one in the Kingdom Hall is trying to put the sale on Lenny to recruit him into the Borg.

For years, Lenny has been invited to all the Witness parties and gatherings. He gets to hang around with all the Witnesses, with no shunning of course. Why? Because he was smart enough never to be baptized.

At one point in time, my wife, Lenny, his wife and some other Jehovah's Witnesses even had their own band together. They went out and played worldly music.

Lenny is a super-intelligent guy, and even though he loves his wife, he really doesn't want to be a Jehovah's Witness, just like me.

I told my wife, "I wanted to be just like Lenny, please. You can still be a Jehovah's Witness. I don't care. I just don't want to be one." She said, "That is not possible."

A crazy thing happened a few nights later. I went to bed with my mind in total chaos. How could I make sense of a life full of contradictions? What were my options now that I had awakened from my ignorance?

I dreamt I actually talked to god Himself, just like the Governing Body says they do. Thank goodness for this dream because god helped me clear up a lot of things.

In the dream, I sat in a waiting room in Heaven. There were a lot of people waiting to talk to god, so they had me take a number. My number was 499. Finally, my number was called and I was ushered into a room. I was a little surprised at the small size of the room. "Hey Jehovah, what's with the small room?"

He looked up from his paperwork and said, "Well, it is written at 1 Corinthians. 8:5, 'For even though there are so-called gods, whether in heaven or on earth, and some people actually worship many gods and many lords.'"

Okay, if that's the case I had to say, "So, since you are not the only god up here, if I ever write a book about you, I'm only going to use the lower case for the letter "g" in god since there seems to be a lot of you gods and lords running around."

God was starting to get upset. "What is it that you want?"

"Are you familiar with my case?"

"Of course I am. I'm a god, and I'm supposed to know everything."

"Okay, so let me get this straight," I said. "Lenny hasn't done shit for you or your organization. I've spent fifty years and thousands of hours knocking on doors, trying to sell this religion for you. I have spent tens of thousands of dollars on gasoline and thousands of dollars on books and magazines. I gave up a college education and chose to be uneducated just for you because I know you like your people to be stupid. I had fifty years of no birthdays or holidays. I worked in your factory on mindless machines for pennies a day so you could sell your books for only twenty-five cents. Please don't forget about the six years of full time service I put in."

I could tell god was perturbed as he asked me, "Yeah, so what's your question?"

"I now realize the same thing that Lenny already knows and this happens to be the same thing billions of other people on this planet already know. So, let me get this straight, now you are telling me I can never have any contact with my wife, friends and family?"

"Yes, that's true."

"So, I get punished and Lenny gets rewarded?"

"Sorry, it's a loophole. You know, catch 22."

"But I was only seventeen when I was baptized."

"Sorry, you should have known."

"I should have known your religion was bat-shit crazy?"

"Yes!"

"I just want to be in the band with Lenny and the rest of the Jehovah's Witnesses!"

"Sorry, you're screwed! Go away! Oh, by the way, if Lenny ever does join and then decides to leave, he'll be screwed also. But I don't think Lenny will ever join, because he can spot bullshit a mile away!" "Jehovah, you're really mean!"

"Yes, I know. Why do you think I have such a hard time getting people to join my crazy religion and why it takes over 13,880 hours of door knocking to find just one new recruit?"

"True. Oh, by the way god, how do you really feel about pedophiles in your organization? Did you really tell your boys not to turn over the files with the names of them to the authorities?"

"What do you think?"

Chapter 46

Eleven out of One-Thousand

I didn't want out of the marriage, just out of the religion. I loved my wife and never even once thought about leaving her. I was in limbo, for sure.

Debbie stayed in Washington with a friend while I remained alone in Portland. The rumors were flying around the Kingdom Hall. Everyone wanted to know what happened. What was said? What was done? Did someone cheat on someone? In our small community of just one-hundred or so people, the gossip flowed hot and heavy. The Brothers and Sisters had a field day with our separation. I was well-liked by some, so many thought Debbie was crazy for leaving me. Of course, those people didn't know about all the doubts I was having about the organization. Debbie knew only some of them.

I was really mixed up and just didn't know what to do. Should I take the blue pill again and crawl back to her and the church and beg for forgiveness? Or should I keep taking the red pill and head into the great unknown? Both options seemed devastating, just like I had told my psychiatrist a few months earlier.

Funny, my father had told me something interesting a couple of years before all this happened. He was sitting in my living room, and after he had finished off his cognac, he made an interesting announcement about his relationship with the Jehovah's Witnesses.

"I believe it," he said. "I just can't live it."

I turned to him and said. "Well, I can live it. I just don't believe it anymore."

My father had confessed to being a POMI. The term POMI used by Jehovah's Witnesses and ex-Jehovah's Witnesses means they are Physically Out (but) Mentally In.

This is where the person is no longer in the organization physically, for whatever reason. They haven't attended meetings in years.

This person was dis-fellowshipped or just faded away. Or maybe they just couldn't live the harsh and demanding day to day life of a Jehovah's Witness. Yet even though they are out from their influence, because of the brainwashing they have experienced, they still believe the Jehovah Witness story is real/true.

On the other hand, at the time my Dad said this, I was a PIMO or Physically In (but) Mental Out.

So of course it turned out we were both wrong. Me for living the lie and him for believing the lie.

This was the first time I heard my father explain why he was MIA (missing in action) from the Witnesses. He had spent many years of his life trying to live it and going through the motions. However, there was no way he could actually live it, whether he believed it or not. I believe my father had done everything under the sun, except maybe commit murder, and that was even a possibility.

Of course, he couldn't live it. His favorite movie was *The Godfather*, and he lived his life as if he was one. My father liked to lie and stretch the truth his whole life. I really think he made this statement to me because he thought it was something I wanted to hear.

However, it was his compliance and not standing up to my mother that got our family in trouble with this religion in the first place. Yes, he was very good at living the lie and doing what my mother wanted.

I've heard it said, a person is as much responsible for the evil he *commits*, as the evil he *permits*.

By his compliance with my mother, my father created a problem that would take the next two generations of our family to get rid of. It was too late for his lame excuses on why he couldn't stand up for what he knew in his heart was wrong.

Alone in Portland those first few days after Debbie left, I got my first epiphany: Unlike my hypocritical father, I not only didn't believe it anymore, I couldn't live it anymore, either. I was now what is called a POMO or Physically Out (and) Mentally Out.

I was now ready for more epiphanies. Sometimes in life, they come all at once and other times, years go by and nothing at all. Events were now set in motion. I couldn't wait to see what was going to happen next.

It's been said that when the student is ready, the teacher appears.

I had an acquaintance named Mark Wiedcamp. He was getting married at The Flying M Ranch on September 2, 2001. I had worked with Mark at Western International Forest Products for a number of years. I say he was an acquaintance because he was a worldly person. As such, he couldn't really be considered a close friend, at least not until now. If I had still been with Debbie at the time he invited me to his wedding, we probably wouldn't have gone. It's not forbidden to go to worldly weddings, but it is highly discouraged and frowned upon. Worldly weddings are just like high-school reunions or any organized gatherings that have non-Jehovah's Witnesses in attendance. The society really doesn't want you to have a lot of contract with nonbelievers.

The decision on whether or not to go to a worldly wedding was what the Jehovah's Witnesses like to call "a matter of conscience." Sometimes, the Society doesn't want to come right out and say what you can't do because it will make them look totally ridiculous. In these cases, they tell you it's a matter of conscience. So technically, you can decide for yourself.

However, there is a catch.

For example, the Society won't come right out and say you can't go to R-rated movies. They will, however, quote you scripture after scripture on the evils of doing just that. Yes, you can make a decision to go to any movie you choose. But if you choose incorrectly, you will be considered spiritually weak and branded as a bad associate. Of course, most of the time this branding is done behind your back.

Welcome to George Orwell's *1984*. Yes, there are those who love absolute control over every action and thought of their people through propaganda, secrecy, constant surveillance, harsh punishment and sometimes shunning. Just like the book *1984* stated:

"War is peace. Freedom is slavery. Ignorance is strength."

I decided to go to Mark's wedding because I knew Big Brother probably wouldn't be there. I'm glad I did go because I had two major epiphanies there that would change my life forever.

Over the years, I had been to many events where there were non-witnesses in attendance. This one proved to be very different. There were at least four-hundred people enjoying the festivities. I only knew one person, and that was the groom.

Most of the wedding guests were from Mark's church. It was a really nice looking group of people. If I hadn't known it, this could have been a Jehovah's Witness wedding. The guests were of all ages. There were families and singles and many married couples with children running and playing.

All those people did have one thing in common: none of them were Jehovah's Witnesses. I'm sure I was the only Witness there. I wandered among them like a ghost.

My first epiphany happened when I was sitting on this small hill taking it all in. I couldn't help but notice a married couple in the buffet line waiting for their food.

The woman was standing behind her husband and she put her hand on his back as if to say, I'm so happy to be here with you.

It hit me like a lightning bolt. I never really experienced that with my wife. I never really felt wanted by her. Long before I started doubting the church and from the very beginning, there was that spark that was missing from our relationship.

Looking back, I don't think I was Debbie's first choice. Maybe I was just a ticket to get away from her crazy mother —the woman who had chased away many boyfriends before me.

Our relationship felt almost like that of brother and sister. Now I realized we never had any real passion in our marriage, even from the very beginning.

How would I know what passion was? She was the first and only girl I really was ever with. The Society told us the purpose of dating was looking for a marriage mate. It was very clear that dating was not for recreation. In some congregations, if you had more than three dates with a girl, you better start thinking about an engagement ring soon.

Because there was no sex before marriage, there were a lot of teenage marriages, and if you weren't married by the time you were twenty-five, there was something wrong with you (unless of course you were at Bethel).

This is a recipe for disaster. Young people with little or no experience getting married because they were hot to trot or just wanted to get out of the house.

Because you were only getting married once and since your first sexual encounter would be most likely on your wedding night, you were really rolling the dice on sexual compatibility.

Bottom line, there is just as much infidelity and divorce in the Jehovah's Witness organization as in any other church, maybe even more with all of that sexual repression going on.

I knew on that last night that Debbie would leave me for good. I knew when she gave me that last kiss on the cheek, with no words spoken between us, that it was the end of our contract together. I knew it at that moment, and on some level I think she knew it also.

I have no regrets about my many years with Debbie. I wish her the very best and hope she finds happiness with her new Jehovah's Witness husband. (You didn't really explain how she was able to remarry. I'm guessing it's just something you don't wish to discuss, which is fine. But if this was an oversight, you could put the details here.)

My second epiphany came when I looked at all these beautiful people at Mark's wedding. I thought, what if what I was taught to believe was true? Then all of these people would be wiped out in the battle called Armageddon that the Witnesses hoped would take place any moment. These wedding guests had chosen a different religion. Or maybe they, like me, didn't choose a religion, they were just born into one. No matter, they were on the other side of the fence and thus they were doomed.

I wouldn't want to hurt anybody and I wouldn't want to hurt these people at the wedding. Yet, I was worshiping a god who could and would do just that.

I couldn't help but think back to the many large district conventions we had attended when there would be ten-thousand or more Jehovah's Witnesses seated in the auditorium. I remember looking out over the vast sea of humanity seated there. A question entered into my mind. What if the people sitting here today represented the entire population of Earth? What percentage would be Jehovah's Witnesses? There were over seven-and-a-half-billion people on the planet and over eight-million Jehovah's Witnesses. That meant, if you did the math, there would be only eleven people in this entire auditorium that would be a Jehovah's Witness. Those were the only ones who would be saved. The other 9,989 would be going away. That's a lot of dead people.

Then I thought to myself, since I was basically born into the Jehovah's Witnesses, what were my odds of surviving Armageddon? There is no guarantee that just because a person is a Jehovah's Witness that he will survive Armageddon. However, my odds were certainly better because I had been born into the faith. On the other hand, what would be my odds of survival if I was born into a non-Witness family in Ittoqqortoormiit, Greenland. One in 9,989. The math wasn't working here. Maybe there was nothing wrong with the math. Maybe, just maybe, it was my Jehovah's Witness reasoning that was all wrong.

So, back at this wedding, I asked myself: what if Jehovah isn't going to kill these four-hundred people at the wedding? What if He isn't going to kill four-thousand people or four-million or even seven-and-a-half-billion people?

My second epiphany was this. I was raised to be a pacifist, yet the god I was made to believe in wasn't. He was an angry and jealous god who would have no problem wiping out the vast majority of the Earth's population.

I remembered the picture in the book *Paradise Lost to Paradise Regained* when I was only nine years old. The picture of the little girl falling into the great abyss at Armageddon with her dog and doll in hand.

At that moment, I knew in my soul that it was all bullshit.

I'm afraid Mark Wiedcamp's marriage didn't last, but I will carry the memories of that insightful day to my grave.

Oh, by the way, I no longer wanted to be in Lenny's band or any other Jehovah's Witness band. There are many people making beautiful music all over this world. Millions of other bands. I just needed to find them.

Chapter 47

Turn on the TV!

Nine days after Mark's wedding, on a Tuesday morning, I got a phone call. "Get up… get up and go turn on your TV!" It was Mike Spacey, my Jehovah's Witness friend from Seattle.

I got out of bed, walked downstairs and did what he said. There it was right on TV, smoke and flames engulfing the Twin Towers.

"This is it!" Mike said over the phone. "This is the beginning of the end!" I sat in amazement, watching this scene of total horror and destruction. Then it happened. One of the towers collapsed. Total pandemonium. People with grey dust and blood streaming down their faces. People running down the streets. People screaming in sheer terror.

Mike kept mumbling about Armageddon coming, as I sat there totally dumbfounded.

Then it hit me. My next bolt of lightning of conscience.

These people, the Jehovah'sWitnesses, were happy about this event. Their promise was coming true. Their Armageddon was coming at long last. This was the beginning of the chain of events that would take them to their paradise, or so they thought.

I watched people dying before my eyes. So, this was supposed to be a preview of coming events. The events I heard about since I was a small child.

Three thousand people died that day. And the Witnesses were waiting for their god to kill another 7,500,000,000 more!

As Mike continued babbling about the end of the world as we know it, and as I watched the death and destruction of thousands of people, I knew the message was coming to me twice in just a matter of a few days.

I knew that this Jehovah, this god of death and destruction, was not the god I would worship anymore. I had embraced nonviolence and had spent my whole life as a pacifist. Yet this god I had worshipped wasn't about peace at all. I had no desire to hurt anybody, and it was painful beyond words to witness the destruction of people at the Twin Towers. Yet, the Jehovah's Witnesses were hoping that this destruction would be the preview of what would soon be taking place on the rest of the planet. This made absolutely no sense to me.

It was the last defining moment of my relationship with the Watchtower Bible and Tract Society of Jehovah's Witnesses. I got off the phone with Mike and knew there was only one thing left to do: the paperwork.

I sent in my letter of disassociation on September 18, 2001, just twelve days before my fifty-second birthday.

Of course, they didn't read my letter to the congregation. They wouldn't want to create doubts with other fence sitters. The announcement was very short.

Keith Casarona has disassociated himself and is no longer a Jehovah's Witness.

This announcement was read on September 19, 2001, my wife's birthday.

The letter I sent to them said this:

To Whom It May Concern I no longer want to be a member of the Watchtower Bible & Tract Society of Pennsylvania.

For years I have felt that this is a fear based organization. Fear and hatred is something that man has created to control other people. It is very disturbing for me to see Jehovah's Witnesses actually happy over the death and destruction that took place last week, believing that their salvation is now close at hand. Jehovah, the god that I'm worshiping is not the kind of god that would bring this kind of destruction to the entire planet. I believe that God's creation is good and that he has the ability to save everyone. Not just one tenth of one percent of the population.

May God bless and keep you all May God bless & keep the world of Mankind!

Very Sincerely Yours,

Keith Casarona

Chapter 48

Shunning and Shotguns

I was the guy on the Ed Sullivan show. The guy that put up dozens of spinning plates at the end of long sticks. He would put up more and more sticks with more and more spinning plates. How was this all going to end? It ended for me like it ended for him. Unable to keep those spinning plates up any longer, I stepped back and watched them all fall.

I didn't have the courage to leave Jehovah's Witnesses for many years. I knew if I could break free, as I told my psychiatrist, the cost would be immense. When it did finally happen, my worst fears were realized. I ended up losing all my friends and most of my family members, including my wife of 27 years. This all happened, plus financial ruin too, since a big chunk of my Real Estate business came by way of my fellow church members. Just two years later, I filed for bankruptcy. A few years after that, I was driving a taxi cab in the streets of downtown Portland. Welcome to their wonderful world called shunning.

When my letter of disassociation was read to the congregation, this was, of course, great news for my wife. All the talk in the congregation about who had caused our split was now over. I had become the evil apostate. She was now the poor victim of the drone gone mad.

If a Jehovah's Witness calls someone an apostate, it's like calling them a devil worshipper. It's the vilest of all connotations. But the simple definition in the dictionary is this: "Someone who has abandoned a religious or political belief or principle."

My children, who were adults at this time, were totally shocked and taken aback by this sudden turn of events. However, they too, had been having doubts about the organization for many years.

I had mentioned how I had been shunned because of what had happened to my parents back in the 1960s. So, guess what? The same thing happened to my children when I left the organization. They were shunned, not by all of their friends, of course, but by enough of them to make them notice. Yes, they too, were judged, not by their own behavior, but by mine. Just like I had been judged by the Witnesses because of what my parents had done. My children were semi-shunned because I no longer wanted to be a Jehovah's Witness.

The beat goes on.

My children had also seen many red flags popping up. They, too, were connecting the dots. The picture that it was showing them was of an organization that was run and controlled by people, not by a god. Because of this, they had pretty much stopped going to meetings.

Of course, their Witness mother pleaded with the Elders to do damage control. The Elders made many visits, hoping to steer my kids back into the flock.

Many Jehovah's Witnesses will tell you, because it's painfully obvious, that the only time the Elders give you extra attention is when you are either coming into their organization or leaving it.

In this case, the Elders' visits were too late. My son sent in his letter of disassociation a few months later. My daughter didn't want to play by their rules and decided to just fade out.

To this day, my ex-wife believes that I'm totally responsible for taking her children out of the organization. This simply is not true. However, I certainly didn't discourage them from leaving either. As adults, it was their decision. It was an easy one to make too, because the children of today are much better at spotting bullshit than my generation.

For that very reason, those in the younger generation in the organization are leaving in droves.

Debbie totally believes to this day that I betrayed her by leaving the Witnesses. But really, who betrayed who? She chose a religion instead of her husband, children and own father because her religion had told her to do so. For her, the only true family she ever had was her church and the people in it. It wasn't us, her physical family.

So who betrayed who?

In all the years since I chose to leave the Witnesses, she has never asked me why. She really doesn't want to know the answer. However, if you were with someone for almost thirty years, wouldn't you want to know why they were leaving the organization you both grew up in?

It would have made no difference to her anyway. Even if I had said I had seen the whole Governing Body having a mass orgy with farm animals and small children. It would have made no difference to her. It would have been the equivalent of her putting her hands over ears and saying, "Blah, blah, blah. Please don't confuse my mind with the facts."

We now have become part of the thousands of families split up over this religion. Children who have been shunned by their parents. Parents who have been shunned by their children. Siblings not talking to each other. Friends of forty years walking past you on the street and not even looking at you. It's like the last daughter in *Fiddler on the Roof* when she married the gentile. "We have no daughter now."

A few months later, I was getting out of my car and walking towards a restaurant. As I did, Tom McGee, who had been at Bethel with me and was a close family friend, was getting out of his car. I had known Tom for over twenty years. We even went on vacations together. As he was walking toward the same restaurant, I waved at him. He took one look at me, turned around, and got back into his car and drove away. He didn't even want to eat in the same restaurant as me.

Let the shunning begin.

My father, as well as my Jehovah's Witness sister, were both living in Southern California in 2012. My own sister, Carol Baez, never even called me to let me know our non-Jehovah's Witness father had died. She buried him and never said a word about it. I wasn't allowed to go to my own father's funeral because she didn't want to see me there.

It's totally surreal.

Of course, many people have asked me over the years what it was like to leave after fifty years in that kind of controlled thought system. My best analogy would be this one:

You're walking down a street in California and someone stops and throws you in a van and drives you to New York City. The van door opens up and they throw you out into the street. They tell you to never contact any of your friends or family. You are dead to them now. Your new life starts in that vacuum.

For many, the new vacuum doesn't work for them.

Just a few months after I left the organization, two other families would be making national news because of their extreme behavior after their expulsion from the church. Both these families had moved to Oregon from different states to escape the devastating effects of shunning from their friends and families.

In December of 2001, Christian Longo decided to kill his wife and young children. Afterward, he said that he was distraught over his expulsion from the Jehovah's Witnesses in 2000. He said, "I sent them to a better place." Why would he say this? The prosecution mentioned that Christian believed that being a dis-fellowshipped JW meant the sins of the parents could be passed down to the children. It also mentioned the JW teaching about dying before Armageddon and having a chance for a resurrection as opposed to dying during the mythical doomsday war. As crazy as it sounds, Christian Longo thought he was doing his wife and kids a favor. He thought he was giving them a chance for everlasting life by killing them now.

Then, just two months later in February of 2002, just a few miles away from where Christian Longo had killed his family, yet another man killed himself, his wife and four children all because of the shunning of the Jehovah's Witnesses.

It seems that once again the religion has loaded the gun, it is a mentally ill person who sees no way out but to pull the trigger.

An article in *The Oregonian* newspaper reported on the event on March 17, 2002:

RELATIVES STRUGGLE TO GRASP KILLINGS

"Faith ruled the lives of Robert and Janet Bryant. A crisis of faith drove them from California to Oregon. Faith in themselves then created a life in Yamhill County most people only dream about.

"Four outgoing and energetic children cared for by a stay-at-home mom. Plans to build a house on a slice of land they owned free and clear. A thriving new business. Bills that were paid — even ahead of schedule.

"Yet sometime after 7:30 p.m. on Feb. 23, Robert Bryant, who was by all accounts a loving husband and father, picked up a 12-gauge shotgun and almost ceremoniously killed his wife, two sons and two daughters. Then he shot and killed himself. Yamhill County sheriff's deputies discovered the bodies in the family's home Thursday.

"Police, neighbors and grieving relatives on Saturday were still sorting out the circumstances that led to one of Oregon's worst mass murders.

"No clear motive has emerged for the murder-suicide, except that it was perhaps, as Janet Bryant's sister suggests, a desperate attempt by Robert Bryant to keep his children away from his parents and other California relatives. The family had become estranged three years ago after a wrenching break with their Jehovah's Witnesses congregation.

"Robert and Janet Bryant were both 37 when they died. Their oldest son, Clayton, was 15; Ethan, 12; Ashley, 9; and the youngest, Alyssa, was 8. Their move to the McMinnville area last summer was supposed to have been a starting over, of sorts.

"Robert Bryant grew up in Shingle Springs, a rural community about 40 miles east of Sacramento, where homes are nestled between horse ranches and dry foothills. His parents, Keith and Arlene Bryant, had raised their three sons and daughter in the Kingdom Hall of Jehovah's Witnesses in El Dorado County.

"Robert met Janet at a private high school affiliated with the church. Married just out of their teens, the couple held weekly Bible classes and prayer meetings in their home.

"Neighbors recalled watching the Bryant children biking up and down the gravel road and Janet Bryant often walking the children to the corner to catch a school bus. The Bryants home-schooled their children for a while but eventually decided to send all but the oldest boy to public school in California.

"Working with his father and brothers, Robert Bryant had a landscaping business and was often seen driving his white pickup truck and hauling lawn-mowing equipment in a green trailer. 'He worked weekdays and weekends, no matter the weather,' a neighbor said.

"'He seemed very loving and very kind and was always patting his children on the head,' said Dana Jones, who lived next door.

"'The Bryant family enjoyed hunting, fishing and camping trips. They regularly attended prayer meetings with Robert Bryant's parents, his two brothers and sister,' said Mark Messier, an elder of the congregation.

"'Robert Bryant was cordial, very unassuming, mild and meek,' Messier said."

"Jehovah's Witnesses, according to their official Web site, believe that the Bible is the inspired, infallible word of God, whose true name is Jehovah. They believe that Jesus is the son of God but not equal to God or part of a trinity. Members are organized in congregations that worship in Kingdom Halls, and they believe that they are living in the last days before God establishes a kingdom on Earth.

"Three years ago Robert Bryant, who had become a church elder, grew disillusioned with what he considered to be hypocrisy among the members. He decided to leave the faith, for which one of the basic tenets is not to question.

"That decision prompted other church elders to hold a hearing leading to Bryant's 'dis-fellowship' from the church and his isolation from his family and friends.

"The practice, called shunning by non-Witnesses, is based on a biblical passage that urges believers not to associate with 'anyone who bears the name of brother if he is guilty of immorality or greed, or is an idolater, reveler, drunkard, or robber — not even to eat with such a one.'"

"'He was expelled for conduct not in harmony with the Bible's principles,' Messier said. 'If they've chosen to be a certain way, you withhold association from them, hoping they realize the error their ways.'

"Janet Bryant was troubled by her husband's expulsion. She was upset when members of the congregation refused to say hello at the supermarket. 'She suffered fatigue and felt physically drained,' said Sharon Roe, her younger sister.

"'She was very torn,' Roe said. 'But she was the kind of person to hold her feelings in and be strong for her children.'

"Though Robert and Janet Bryant were to be avoided, the children's grandparents and aunts and uncles tried to maintain contact with the youngsters. 'Much to Robert Bryant's distress,' Messier said, 'relatives had even sought legal advice on whether the grandparents could require visitation.'

"With most of his landscaping customers being fellow Jehovah's Witnesses, Robert Bryant lost jobs once he was ousted by the church. He filed for bankruptcy in January 2000.

"In March 2001, Bryant's father disassociated himself from the landscaping business, further hampering Bryant's ability to earn a living in California.

"'The way he described it, they were absolutely horrible what they were doing to him,'" said Albert Clary, who lived across the street from Robert and Janet Bryant in Shingle Springs.

"By June, the couple had sold their house, loaded their belongings in the dead of night and moved their family to

Oregon, where Janet Bryant had lived for a time as a girl and where the family had vacationed.

"'They didn't tell their Jehovah's Witnesses relatives where they'd gone,' Roe said.

"Mark Marshall, a McMinnville State Farm insurance agent, said Robert Bryant had told him last summer that he left California because of a church dispute and that his parents were trying to gain custody of the children to keep them in the congregation.

"Marshall said Bryant told him: 'We're coming up here to get away from them.'

"'Everything seemed to be going great for them,' Skoog said.' Why then, eight months into their new life, would Robert Bryant shoot his wife and then his children still tucked in their beds?

"'A man who feels hopeless and isolated, as Robert Bryant might have if family and church ties were severed, is at risk for suicide,' said Dr. James Hancey, an assistant professor of psychiatry at Oregon Health and Science University. 'If he has experienced big changes in his life, including a new job and residence, the stress in his life is magnified, even if he sought the changes,' he said.

"But Hancey said why a man might kill his family before committing suicide is harder to discern. While he was not familiar with the details of Bryant tragedy, Hancey said sometimes such actions are related to distorted religious thoughts but may arise from other factors.

"Roe said she learned of the deaths about 2 a.m. Friday when she was visited by local law enforcement officers and a chaplain.

"Seated in her living room, she listened to a deputy tell her there had been a murder-suicide in Oregon involving Robert Bryant.

"'I heard Robert. I heard Janet. I heard Clayton. I kept thinking, 'It's got to stop. There's got to be someone left.' Then I realized all six of them were gone,' she said Saturday. 'I rationalize in my mind that whatever he did, he must have done it out of love and out of protection for his family,' Roe said. 'In his own mind, he felt he was protecting them, and that's all I could reason out of it.'

"Critics have said the practice of dis-fellowship severs family ties, shatters individuals and may lead to suicide or attempted suicides. The six bodies were taken Saturday to a crematory. Yellow crime scene tape still surrounded the home."

The late Dave Malone, himself an ex-Jehovah's Witness, went to the Bryants' memorial service. These were his observations:

"Jeb and I pulled up we could see the tall microwave antennas sticking up from atop the News trucks that were parked in the back lot of the church. We arrived about fifty minutes early because we anticipated a large turn out and wanted to make sure we had a place to sit. Being an ex JW and having an ingrained uneasiness for churches I felt a little strange walking into this very large church. I turned to Jeb after we entered the doorway and told him this was only the third time since becoming associated with the JW when I was four years old that I had stepped foot into a church. The other two times were also for funerals for the relatives of good friends of mine many years after I left the religion.

"We walked further down the entry way and signed the register book like I had done at the other non JW funerals that I had attended. After we signed our names we turned and started to enter the main worship area. There by the big double wide doors were pictures of the Bryant family. One large photo in the middle that looked to be a few years old judging by the recent school photos of the Bryant children. I looked at the family photo and thought to myself that this did indeed look like a typical JW family. Father, wife and four children. Two boys, two girls and somewhat close in age. This was a perfect group of what most would consider the ideal family.

"As I looked at the happy faces of the children in the photos something snapped and reality instantly clicked in, I realized what I was there for. Those children in those photos were all dead, all four of them along with their mother and father. These beautiful young boys and girls were no longer smiling faces but lifeless corpses.

"For a few moments I couldn't feel anything, I just stared at the photos. I thought of my own kids and how I love to look at photos of them as they grew up and their appearance slowly changed from cute little babies into young men. These photos I was looking at were the last photos of the Bryant's that would ever be taken. I have been to several JW funerals but not one single one of them ever had photos of the person who had died. JW funerals are not about those who have passed but more of an infomercial for the JW religion.

"In the front there were a dozen or so flower arrangements and three or four wreaths. There were two large pieces of paper with several dozen drawings and notes from many of the kids that attended school with the Bryant children. They were all very nice and considering the circumstance fairly up beat and cheerful looking. I looked at a few of them and one of the notes that was drawn in crayon stuck out. It sad a few nice things about one of the Bryant girls and then at the end there was a simple and personal comment. It said, 'and I'm sorry for making fun of you.' Yeah, a tiny lump shot up in my throat.

"I sat down with Jeb and a little smile came to my face. Even though I felt strange being in a church for a memorial service of people I never met, I didn't feel alone at all. Within a few minutes the main worship area began to fill up. There were reporters in the back with both video and photo cameras and they began taking shots of the kids that were coming in. One of the Bryant children's classmates came and had reserved seats up front. As I looked around

I figured there were around sixty to eighty kids scattered around the room. In total and from my best estimation there were over three hundred people who filled up the main area. All from different thoughts and philosophies in life. All there because they cared about people who lived in their small town.

"A card was read that was written by Sharon Roe and addressed to the people of McMinnville. It was very touching and very thankful for what they had done for people they did not even know. I thought to myself, there wasn't one single JW in the room but all these people from different churches and different parts of town came to pay their respect to people out of one simple concept, LOVE for their fellow human.

"Yes, these are the same people we were taught as JW's that were wicked, evil and would soon be destroyed by Jehovah god. These were the people we were taught that did not know the meaning of true love and only were out to satisfy their own selfish desires. These people had nothing to gain by coming to this memorial. They had no one specific religious philosophy to try and sell nor were they there to judge or point fingers. They were there simply to show genuine love for people who once lived in their small town. This little community of McMinnville Oregon showed more love for their neighbor than I have seen shown by all the hundreds of JW's that I had met in my life. I did not hear one accusation or one single comment that sounded condescending or self- righteous. All I heard was words of comfort and questions about why this all happened.

"As I looked around at the flower arrangements one of them caught my eye. It was a wreath of white flowers and a white ribbon that hung below. The wreath had a few words stapled on the ribbon in gold letters. It said, 'Shunned no more.'

"Of course these words were not true at all, because there wasn't one Jehovah's Witness at their funeral. Not even Robert's parents or siblings took the time to come. So, yes they were still being shunned."

The Jehovah's Witnesses could rationalize the shunning of Robert and Janet Bryant but what about their murdered Jehovah's Witness children? What were their sins?

They were of course judged and shunned by their aunts, uncles, grand-parents and all the other Jehovah's Witnesses who boycotted their funeral. I guess they must have considered the children worthy of shunning because of their association with their dead parents. Guilt by way of association—nothing new among the Jehovah's Witnesses.

As I have said before, it makes no difference if you are guilty or not. Anyone living or dead can still experience this unique Jehovah's Witness punishment!

At the end of another article about the Bryants, *The Oregonian* asked what could push people to this kind of insanity.

I decided to call *The Oregonian* and told them I had some information that might help an outsider understand the devastating policy of shunning a little better. So, Wendy Y. Lawton gave me an interview.

My children begged me not to let the interview go into print. "I publicly went into this religion and now it's time to publicly leave it. Besides," I told them, "maybe somehow I can help just one person escape the hell that this religion has created for them or their families."

It must have been a slow news day because this article ended up on the front page of *The Oregonian* on March 21 in 2002.

SHUNNING CALLED DEVASTATING

"Keith Casarona doesn't pretend to know the mind of Robert Bryant. Why anyone wipes out his family with a shotgun on a Saturday night, then points the 12-gauge under his own chin is beyond the comprehension of this soft-spoken Tigard real estate agent.

"Yet Casarona knows – in intimate and anguishing detail – the pain Bryant felt in his final years. Both men split with the Jehovah's Witnesses. Bryant was expelled three years ago in California. Casarona chose to leave a Beaverton congregation last fall.

"The decision gave Casarona peace and fresh possibilities. But the break was devastating. Casarona said he lost his wife of 27 years and friendships that stretched back for decades. About a fourth of his real estate clients vanished.

"'Witnesses are good people, and I bless their path,' the 52-year-old said. 'But when you leave them, you go into a Never Never Land.'

"The killings in McMinnville last month – the worst mass murder in recent Oregon history – cast a spotlight on Jehovah's Witnesses and their practice of 'dis-fellowship.' In a Christian sect that proudly protects members from the corrupting influence of outsiders, expulsion is the harshest form of discipline.

"There is no official motive for the slayings. Police think Bryant was under emotional strain when he shot his wife, four children and himself. That stress, investigators said, included fallout from his shunning.

"Now anti-Witness Websites are abuzz with accusations. Who in their right mind would ever want to stay in this horrible, horrible, hateful religion? one posting reads. Witnesses, too, are talking. But they're saying the church is the scapegoat for an unfathomable act.

"Leonard Golaboff, a 46-year-old Elder in Oregon City, notes that there is no proof that Bryant's ouster from a congregation outside of Sacramento was directly responsible for the murders and suicide. 'Like all expelled members,' Golaboff said, 'Bryant could have changed his ways and come back.'

"'This is all just a tragedy, a travesty, a shock,' Golaboff said. 'What was going on in this man's mind? I am sure there is a lot that we don't know.'

"What worries Goloboff and other Witnesses is a link between the trigger of Bryant's shotgun and a 132-year-old faith that deplores violence and cherishes family.

"Jehovah's Witnesses are a made-in-America church that boasts 6 million international members. They believe in Armageddon: The world will end, the wicked will die, and God will create a paradise on Earth for the righteous. The name refers to members' watchful return of Jehovah, or God.

"The Bible is their bedrock. Witnesses live their lives in strict accordance to its teachings and follow a rigid moral code. Stealing, drinking, smoking, premarital sex – all are forbidden.

"According to another Bible interpretation, members also must keep separate from a world invisibly controlled by Satan.

"They're not supposed to vote, join the military or celebrate holidays aside from the commemoration of Christ's death each spring. Close ties with nonmembers, or the 'worldly,' are discouraged. The reason is reflected in a standard Witness saying: 'Bad associations spoil useful habits.'

"Protecting the congregation's purity is the point of disfellowship. Members are kicked out before they can harm, or continue to harm, others with conduct or beliefs that contradict the Bible.

"Sherwood Elder Tom Davis said there is a second purpose: Putting a member back on the proper moral path. Davis said dis-fellowship – or even the threat of it – often forces people to make positive changes in their lives.

"'This helps someone realize that they've made a mistake and need to change their ways,' Davis said. 'And we're not talking about little stuff. This discipline comes from violating the stated laws of God.'

"According to Elders, experts and church materials, here is how dis-fellowship works: To get kicked out, baptized members must display a pattern of 'serious un-Christian conduct,' such as molestation, adultery, drinking or lying. Promoting teachings that conflict with the Bible also qualifies.

"It isn't clear what Robert Bryant's offense was. Neighbors and friends in California said he began to question Bible teachings and found the Shingle Springs, Calif., congregation too controlling. An Elder has declined to discuss specifics, saying Bryant had 'turned away' from the faith.

"Elders said they try to avoid shunning through Bible counseling. And, if repenting members convince leaders they've changed, they can stay. If they don't, Elders call a private, judicial-style meeting and expel them.

"The shunned still can attend religious services, officials said, and conduct business with members. But Witnesses are instructed not to socialize with someone who is disfellowshipped.

"John Crossley, a professor and director of the school of religion at the University of Southern California, said a similar tradition of excommunication is shared by Catholics, Mormons and the Amish. But the practice is fading.

"'It is almost impossible to hold up moral doctrine and force people to conform to it anymore,' Crossley said. 'It is especially difficult to continue a practice that is as severe as dis-fellowship.'

"Witnesses point to lives transformed by shunning. People kick drugs, stop gambling and mend marriages. But critics attack the practice as cruel and destructive.

"While families aren't required to split up due to disfellowship, critics and even a few church members said that is often the practical result. Computer sites devoted to attacking Jehovah's Witnesses are loaded with stories of divorce and custody battles and estranged siblings – as well as depression, drug abuse, bankruptcy and suicide.

"Daniel Duron used to be among the angry. After he left the church in 1984 over a disagreement over blood transfusions, the Hillsboro roofer's world turned upside down. Elders came to his door and told him his two boys were 'fatherless.' His wife and friends and extended family became strangers. Duron was so shaken he planned to kill himself. The gun store, however, was closed.

"Soon Duron started fighting. He divorced and won joint custody of his sons. He picketed a local Kingdom Hall. He joined a support group for ex-Witnesses, where he met his second wife. Looking back, the former Elder said the biggest impact of his shunning was the sudden loss of certainty.

"'Everything you believed in is gone with this tight-knit church family,' Duron said. 'The way you look at science, spirituality, the after-life – it's all different. Eventually, that can be very positive. But it's also scary. I wouldn't wish the experience on anyone.'"

I love this line from the article: "To get kicked out, baptized members must display a pattern of 'serious un-Christian conduct,' such as MOLESTATION, adultery, drinking or lying."

Really? Molestation?

I had informed *The Oregonian* to get Tom Davis to explain the Witnesses' side of the story. Thus, the article reported, "Davis said dis-fellowship – or even the threat of it – often FORCES people to make positive changes in their lives."

Yes, if we can, we will FORCE you back to god's loving organization. So much for free will. It is conform or die.

Just two days later on March 23, 2002, after this article in *The Oregonian* was printed, *News-Register,* a local newspaper, published this column by its editor:

THE TALE OF TWO FREEDOMS

"Do you believe in God?

"Do you believe the Bible provides explicit instructions for how to spend your life on Earth? Will you follow the edicts of men who interpret those instructions, even as their interpretations change over time and conflict with basic human values?

"If commanded, will you remain silent about your doubts?

"Can you accept, without question, any proclamation, any theological theory decreed by your church, and withhold your friendship and loyalty from members who don't show total allegiance? If demanded, will you reject, rebuff and shun all contact with your mother or father, your son or daughter, your best friend in life, no matter how sick or distressed that loved one may be?

"Welcome to the world of Robert Bryant, a world in which a perceived mental illness and his known religious conflicts came crashing together to produce a terrible crime against humanity. Welcome to the world of Jehovah's Witnesses, a religion that many consider a cult. But before you judge the members of Jehovah's Witnesses, remember that judgment is the weapon this religion uses to control the minds and souls of its followers. Before you judge Robert Bryant, remember that his mind and his soul were shaped, then cast aside by the religion that dominated his life. His unthinkable response was to leave this world, and take his family with him. Perhaps, as spoken this week by his surviving sister-in-law, Robert Bryant's purpose for being on this earth was to deliver the message that comes from this tragedy. That message, said Sharon Roe, is that you have no right to judge men in the way that the Jehovah's Witnesses judged Robert Bryant, in the way that this religion and others have judged and damaged so many people throughout history. She wants to believe that something of value and consequence can come from this act that stunned our community, our state, our nation.

"I want to believe that, too.

"I know that our Constitution gives the Jehovah's Witnesses, and others, the right to judge men in any way that they choose, and that our forefathers died to protect that right. But we have another important right, that of free speech.

"We have the right to speak out when a religion produces astonishing levels of psychological abuse. We have the right to say that it's wrong, dead wrong, and to ask for a change.

"I join Sharon Roe in exercising that right."

Chapter 49

God Kills Another Baby

Since I had been in a religion that focused on death and the end of the world as we knew it, it was now time to focus on life.

The wonderful line from *Shawshank Redemption* says it so well: "Get busy living or get busy dying!"

I had spent my entire life in a religion that focused on a war that was coming any day –the ultimate war between god and man.

It was a time to rethink everything.

It was just like my analogy. I had gotten out of the van in New York City and was walking around in a daze. I found a new freedom though. I walked down the street and looked at all of the people walking past me. Something had changed. I looked more closely now. Many of the people had smiling faces. Had they changed? No, I had changed. I now saw the world completely differently. It wasn't a world controlled by Satan and his demons. It was just a stage with many different players on it. A world full of endless possibilities.

Even though I did contemplate it many times, I wasn't going the same way as Jim Olson, Robert Stillman, Robert Bryant and thousands of others who left The Watchtower Bible and Tract Society by way of suicide. These people who found there was no existence outside the made up world of Jehovah's Witnesses. They had found death to be their only real option from the hell that their lives had become.

Though I'm sure the Society would have loved it if I had taken myself out, especially after my interview in *The Oregonian*, that wasn't going to happen.

I love the last line in the movie *Papillion*: "I'm still here you bastards!"

One of the many reasons I'm still here is the fact that I had found some new friends, years before I had lost all my Jehovah's Witness friends. My new friends are Gary Zukav, Neale Walsch, Marianne Williamson, Deepak Chopra, Wayne Dyer, Caroline Myss and Eckhart Tolle. These authors and speakers were able to help me leave the mind-controlled environment I had been dealing with for over fifty years.

These new friends helped me make a transition into the real world. The world where there doesn't have to be "us" or "them." It seems the planet has been suffering from this illusion for a long time.

These new friends have showed me the meaning of something called "unconditional love." This is what I would call the purist of all loves. This is a love a mother gives her child. Does a baby get this kind of love from its mother because of its performance? Of course not. The mother gives that child unconditional love no matter what. Are we not all god's children?

Most the religions on the planet believe in "conditional" love. Their love is based on your performance and what you can do for them and their god. Unconditional love is just that, unconditional.

I'm not here trying to sell a new thought system. I don't need people to think the same way as me anymore. I went from door to door for decades, trying to peddle my thought system to others. That is not going to happen again.

We should be here to help and support each other.

For many years, I hosted the ex-Jehovah's Witness meet up group in Portland, Oregon. I heard a lot of sad stories about what people had lost trying to get away from the Jehovah's Witnesses. There were entire families that were wiped out, not usually by shotguns, but by the devastation of shunning and the lack of real love.

One night, a gentleman showed up to one of the meet ups I was hosting. He had a very interesting story to relate.

Bob had been happily married for many years. He and his wife and children weren't Jehovah's Witnesses. In fact, he, like his wife and children, knew nothing about them. That, of course, didn't matter. The Jehovah's Witnesses would soon make his life a living Hell. Why? Because his wife ended up having an affair at work with a married Jehovah's Witness Elder.

She ended up divorcing Bob and started studying with the Jehovah's Witnesses. The Elder divorced his wife and married Bob's ex-wife. Because the adulterous Elder was well-liked in his Kingdom Hall, he was reinstated in just a few months. Bob's ex-wife and her new husband now have custody of Bob's two daughters, who were twelve and fourteen years old at the time she left Bob. The children, of course, started studying with Jehovah's Witnesses also and after their indoctrination were baptized. Now they are one big happy Jehovah's Witness family.

Bob now has a real problem and is now at the meetup group looking for advice. He tells all of us that now when his Jehovah's Witness children visit him, they tell him how he too will be killed by Jehovah their god in the coming war of Armageddon unless he joins their program.

So, now Bob is asking all of us what he should say to his two daughters when they visit him with their message of doom.

Oh, by the way, for some odd reason Bob doesn't want to be a Jehovah's Witness. I guess because he feels, in essence, the actions of Jehovah's Witnesses not only tore his family apart but now the Society is brainwashing his children to be mindless drones also. Go figure.

There was another interesting story from someone who wasn't a Jehovah's Witness but still had their life completely destroyed by them.

During the time I was hosting the ex-Jehovah's Witness meet up group, I got a very sad and interesting phone call from a woman one afternoon.

Beth called me to ask if there was anything she could do to stop her husband from being re-baptized in the Jehovah's Witness church this coming Saturday. It was just a few days away. I said, "Probably not. Why?"

She told me how years ago, she had fallen in love with a man who was raised as a Jehovah's Witness. He had been out of the organization for many years. They had many happy years together and were now married and expecting their first child. She had a daughter from a previous marriage. She told me how everything was wonderful, until his parents started pressuring him to rejoin the Jehovah's Witnesses. Her husband started going back to their meetings.

She also told me how his parents had hated her from the beginning of their marriage because she was a worldly person. His parents even went so far as to encourage him to leave her – even though she was pregnant – so he could eventually find a good Jehovah's Witness girl. Beth told me his parents told her husband that there would be no repercussions for this action because he was already dis-fellowshipped and you can't be dis-fellowshipped when you are already dis-fellowshipped. Since her husband still loved Beth, he declined his parent's invitation to ditch his worldly wife and decided to stay with her.

Beth was desperate and wanted to know what she could do to stop him from rejoining this group of nasty people, who were trying to break up their marriage.

I told her it was probably too late, since he was being baptized in just a few days. This was something that had to be in the making for many months, if not years. I felt I had to tell her what she could expect now that he was going back into the organization. It wasn't going to be easy for her because she had no desire to become a Jehovah's Witness.

I listed possible problems and difficulties she might have to endure with a husband who was rejoining his old church. Little did I know then that she would soon be going through something ten times worse than I could have ever imagined.

Soon, Beth and her husband would be in Jehovah's Witness Hell. If she ever had any desire to join this church, it would soon be gone forever, after what would happen next.

Beth called me a few months later, crying; I could barely understand her. I really didn't know what she needed or wanted. Maybe she needed a shoulder to cry on. I told her we could meet for a cup of coffee. I had no words for what she would reveal to me.

We met a few hours later at a busy restaurant. I wish you could have seen the look of bewilderment on this poor woman's face. With tears in her eyes, she sat there. She told me about what had transpired over the last few months since we first talked on the phone.

She said her husband was baptized as he promised. Being re-baptized, he became a zealot once again in his old faith. He didn't seem to be as interested in her now that he had rejoined his old family and friends. He was now spending less and less time with her, his pregnant wife.

Finally, the baby came. However, there were major complications at birth. It was life or death for the child unless the baby received a blood transfusion. Beth was, of course, in favor of this life-saving option. Her husband was definitely opposed to it.

There were many heated arguments about this. The Elders and his parents got involved. His family informed her husband that he could not waver. There was no way he could give in on this matter. It was more than just a matter of life and death; it was a matter of faith and service to god and obeying His rules about no blood transfusions.

Beth and her family fought her husband to the bitter end. She said he hated her and her stance against him and his faith. This drove a wedge between them even further.

There was no time left and a decision had to be made. For whatever reason, he hung his head in shame and told the doctors to go ahead and give the child a blood transfusion. The Elders found out that he gave the order for the blood transfusion and were furious. They told him there would be grave repercussions because of his decision.

Two days later, the child died.

The Elders actually told her husband they were not surprised about the child's death. In a sense, they implied this was a punishment directly from god Himself. This was because he had actually disobeyed god's commandments on the issue of blood.

Her husband told the Elders he was wrong and blamed his worldly wife for the pressure she had put on him. He begged for Jehovah's and the Elders for forgiveness.

There was nothing I could say to comfort Beth after that story.

Are they still together? I would doubt it.

If you are a Jehovah's Witness reading this, there are two things I would wonder. First, did god kill the baby because it received a blood transfusion to drive home His point to the disobedient husband? No? Even though the Elders implied that?

Second, Beth will obviously never become a Jehovah's Witness. Can you really blame her?

If there is a Jehovah, how could He judge her everlasting life in eternity by not being a Jehovah's Witness when His people encouraged her husband to leave her? Plus, their god supposedly killed her child because her husband disobeyed Him.

To Beth, the Jehovah's Witnesses are total whack jobs.

Yes, my friends, once more, "By their love you will know them."

Even though I have been out of the organization for many years, the strange and bizarre stories that swirl around the Jehovah's Witnesses never seem to stop.

Up until this point, I haven't even brought up the issue of blood transfusions. There are thousands of stories about people dying because of the Societies' policy against blood transfusions.

Take a wild guess who dreamt up the idea about no blood transfusions for Jehovah's Witnesses in the first place?

Charles Russell, the founder of the church? No! Even though blood transfusions were implemented as early as 1914.

Judge Rutherford, the alcoholic and second president? No!

The third president N.H. Knorr? Yes and no, because the fourth President Fred Franz came up the idea back in 1944 (before he became president) but Knorr approved of the concept.

God didn't want to talk to the first two presidents about the blood issue. In 1944, thirty years after blood transfusions were initiated, god finally decided to give President Knorr, by way of Fred Franz, new light on the matter of the use of blood. Since everything produced by the writing department had to be approved by Knorr, here is the wisdom as explained in *The Watchtower*.

"The blood in any person is in reality the person himself... poisons due to personal living, eating and drinking habits...The poisons that produce the impulse to commit suicide, murder, or steal are in the blood. Moral insanity, sexual perversions, repression, inferiority complexes, petty crimes—these often follow in the wake of blood transfusion." – *Watchtower*, September 1, 1961 p.564

There you have it. God has spoken by way of his earthly representatives.

When you stop taking the blue pill, and you take a step back, you can see the insanity quite clearly. However, the insanity is not from you receiving a blood transfusion, as they would have you believe. The insanity comes from you eating their contaminated "spiritual food," which is mixed in with the blue pills.

The Society did mention that a blood transfusion could cause "sexual perversions."

Of course, a person must now wonder if Leo Greenlees, the pervert and Governing Body member, ever had a blood transfusion. This would, of course, explain his perverse behavior.

Chapter 50

The Old Hound Dog Finally Moves

I had been a Jehovah's Witness for over fifty years. People have asked me what it was like to leave that kind of thought system after so long.

My favorite story about emerging into the real world was my first Christmas in 2001. A friend of mine, Gregory Bartels, owns the Christmas Tree Company. I had known Gregory for many years before leaving the Witnesses. Because I was a Witness, he really could only be an acquaintance to me. Now we could become real friends.

He told me he wanted to give me my first Christmas tree free, since I'd been the Christmas Grinch for so long. He told me to go to any of his many tree lots and pick out a nice tree for myself.

I did just that. I told the lot attendant about the free tree from the owner.

The attendant seemed surprised. "So, you're the guy. The guy who never had a Christmas!"

I shrugged. "Yes, I guess so."

"Okay, tell me what's that's like, having a Christmas for the first time ever?"

"Well," I said, "it's kind of like a Jewish guy eating a pork sandwich for the first time. It tastes really good, but it just feels weird."

The other question I get is, "Why did it take you so long to figure it out and finally leave that religion?"

I don't know the answer to that. I was just stupid, I guess. I'm sure not bragging about how long it took. "Hey look at me, fifty years and I finally figured it out." I'm not proud of my stupidity.

My children have told me that they wished I had left years earlier, so they could have enjoyed more normal lives as teenagers. Like me, they too, had missed out on all the school dances, sports and other activities, and of course a good college education that has been denied to many of the children in their organization.

On the other hand, I have told them if I had left when they were just small children and not adults, they definitely would have been in their mother's care for many years. Thus, they most likely would have turned out to be good Nazi Jehovah's Witnesses instead. In that case, like so many other families, my children would have had nothing to do with me ever again. I guess we'll never know what could have happened.

I do know one thing, timing is everything in life.

There are thousands of bad marriages and relationships in the world. People and their religions could be considered a relationship, too. People and religions that are together for all the wrong reasons and have been together way too long. Why? Who knows?

Many of us have suggested to these people that they should get out of their bad situations, whether it's a relationship or a religion. These words many times fall on deaf ears. We all know it's not going to happen until that person has had enough. Then, and only then, will he or she be free to leave.

There is a funny old story about how people can live with different amounts of pain in their lives.

About a hundred years ago, a man walks into a small general store in Alabama. As he walked around the store, he couldn't help but notice a pot-belly stove with a fat old hound dog laying on the wooden floor next to it. Every few minutes, the old hound would let out a mournful howl. This went on for quite a while. Finally, the man went to the store owner and asked what was going on with his dog. "Oh, nothing… the dog is laying on a nail that is sticking out of the floor." The man looked confused and said, "Well…. why doesn't he just move?" "I guess it isn't hurting him bad enough yet!"

You can only howl about things for so long before it's time to move. It was time for this old dog to move on.

It has been said that most people will pick the pain they know as opposed to the pain they don't know. I did this for many years.

It is very much like an addiction. It's like going to your favorite restaurant for a meal. You have this amazing meal with great service. The bill comes and it's one-hundred-and-seventy-five dollars. Well, it was nice, wasn't it? Yes, of course. Next week you are back again and enjoy another great meal. The bill comes and this time it's two-hundred-and-seventy-five dollars. Wow, but it was nice, of course. You go back again and the bill comes to four-hundred-and-seventy-five dollars. This is too much, no matter how great the food and service. Even though you are getting what you want, the price is just too high. The "love drug" you were paying for in your religion or relationship is costing you way too much.

My final bill came on September 11, 2001. I decided my "restaurant" had been overcharging me for over fifty years for bad "spiritual food" and terrible service.

I guess I just didn't want to pay the bill anymore. No more of the Jehovah's Witnesses for me.

Each person knows in his or her heart when that last straw is loaded onto the camel's back. When that happens, it will be tough leaving the pack because there is so much comfort with the rest of the pack and with taking your blue pill.

The crazy thing is, I never searched the Internet for anything related to Jehovah's Witnesses before I left the organization. I did not seek information about them either way, for or against them.

However, after I left the "Borg," I got on the Internet and checked out my old religion. Wow! No wonder the Society preaches against too much Internet research. Much of the information found in this book can be verified online.

The Witnesses will tell you that you should investigate all religions before you join theirs. They also tell you that you need to thoroughly examine their faith before you join it. These two statements are not true. If you did investigate them, you would run like hell in the opposite direction.

Below are some of the fun facts I have discovered about the history of Jehovah's Witnesses that they never bothered to mention when I was in their organization. These would have given me reasons to leave the Jehovah's Witnesses way before I did.

Some of the things the church leaders never talked about are how many predictions they made about the so-called end of the world – the many predictions that never came to be.

I didn't know it at time, and most Jehovah's Witnesses don't know, that Charles Russell (1852-1916), the founder, believed that Christ had secretly arrived in the year 1874 and that he would establish the kingdom of god on Earth in October 1914. Russell based this prophecy on his studies of the Bible and the Great Pyramid. Page 201 of the *Proclaimers* book acknowledges, "For some 35 years, Pastor Russell thought that the Great Pyramid of Giza was God's stone witness, corroborating Biblical time periods."

What is not stated is that Russell was one of the world's greatest advocates of pyramidology, a spiritist religion. His writings, diagrams and charts about pyramids are virtually the same as those that appear in any book on pyramidology. These books are usually located in the occult section of any library or bookstore. Even J. F. Rutherford stated that it was Satan who put it into Russell's mind to figure out god's purposes by studying the Pyramid of Giza, that the pyramid is "Satan's Bible, and not God's stone witness." *The Watch Tower* of November 15, 1928, page 344.

Russell was buried in Pittsburgh, Pennsylvania, when he died. But first, he was embalmed. Then he was placed in a grave marked with a huge tombstone in the form of a pyramid that, curiously, has emblems of the Masonic Lodge engraved upon it. And, as shown in his articles on the zodiac, Russell also believed in astrology and the horoscope. And for nearly half of his presidency, Rutherford believed in the same. Pyramid worship led Rutherford to believe that millions living in 1920 would never die and that Abraham, Isaac and Jacob would return in 1925 and live at Beth-Sarim in San Diego, California. .

Not the Bible, but Russell's belief in pyramidology is the basis for his date-setting. He said the last days began in 1799, Christ's presence began in 1874, the heavenly resurrection began in 1878, the heavenly calling ended in 1881, and the end of the world and the resurrection of the anointed on earth would take place in 1914. All of his prophecies failed, yet the Society still holds onto the 1914 date but with a different application. The Society claims this date is established by Bible chronology that started with the destruction of Jerusalem in 607 BC. However, not even one reputable scholar agrees with the Society that Jerusalem was destroyed that year.

A key component to the calculation was derived from the book of Daniel, Chapter 4. The book refers to "seven times." Russell interpreted each "time" as equal to three-hundred-and-sixty days, giving a total of two-thousand, five-hundred and twenty days. He further interpreted this as representing exactly two-thousand, five-hundred and twenty years, measured from the starting date of 607 BC. This resulted in the year 1914 being the target date for the Millennium mentioned in Revelation. Russell's belief became a key teaching of his Bible students, later known as the Jehovah's Witnesses. Since late in the 19th century, Russell had taught that the "battle of the Great Day of God Almighty" or Armageddon would happen in that year.

Russell said: "And, with the end of A.D. 1914, what God calls Babylon, and what men call Christendom, will have passed away, as is already shown from prophecy." *Studies In The Scriptures*, Vol. III, (1897) "we consider it an established truth that the final end of the kingdoms of this world, and the full establishment of the Kingdom of God, will be accomplished by the end of A.D. 1914" (1889).

"In the coming 26 years, all present governments will be overthrown and dissolved." – Studies in the Scriptures, Vol. II, (1889)

In the years leading up to 1914, many people joined Russell's movement and it expanded rapidly. However, as the year 1914 came and went without the visible appearance of Christ, the Society regarded the start of World War I as confirmation that the process leading to Christ's return had started. They decided that 1914 was the year that Jesus *invisibly* began his rule from heaven.

In November 1914, immediately after Russell's prophecy had failed, he wrote that the period of transition could run a "good many years."

The Watchtower magazine suggested that the destruction would happen "...shortly after 1914 with the utter destruction" of other Christian denominations and the inauguration of Christ's millennial reign. They first predicted that this would happen in 1915. Drawing a parallel with the destruction of Jerusalem by the Roman Army in 70 CE, the authors of the 1915 Edition of *The Time Is at Hand* wrote:

"The Gentile Times prove that the present governments must all be overthrown about the close of A.D. 1915; and Parallelism above shows that this period corresponds exactly with the year A.D. 70, which witnessed the completion of the downfall of the Jewish polity."

After Russell's death in 1916, members of the Society rewrote large portions of his *Studies in the Scriptures* to reflect the new belief that the year 1914 was merely the beginning of the end of Gentile times.

Because of Russell's death and Judge Rutherford's less-than-friendly takeover of the organization, many schisms soon developed. Over three-quarters of the Bible students that were there in 1916 left the organization by 1925.

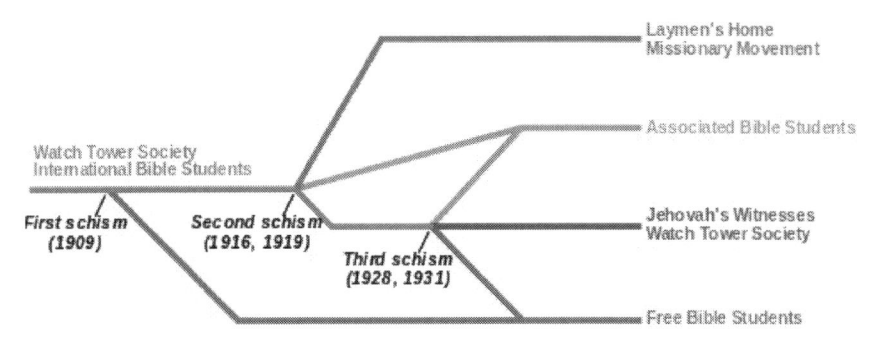

The chart is from Wikipedia

So, not only is there more than 20,000 different Christian sects in the world, there are over four different sects that were created just from the Watch Tower Society International Bible Students that Russel created. Which of all these would god choose to be his only true church?

The Bible students later delayed the millennium/Armageddon to 1918. The 1917 publication *The Finished Mystery* stated:

"In the year 1918, when God destroys the churches wholesale and the church members by millions, it shall be that any that escape shall come to the works of Pastor Russell to learn the meaning of the downfall of Christianity."

That year also passed uneventfully, except for the end of World War I.

The Society then introduced the concept that Christ would establish his millennial kingdom on Earth "before the generation who saw the events of 1914 passes away." With many humans achieving a life span of over 90 years, this could place the War of Armageddon at any time between 1914 and the early 21st century.

The next estimate of the end of things was some time in 1925.

In 1918, J.E. Rutherford, the Society's second president and author of *Millions Now Living Will Never Die* wrote:

"There will be a resurrection of Abraham, Isaac, Jacob, and other faithful ones of old, we may expect 1925 to witness the return of these faithful men of Israel from the condition of death, being resurrected and fully restored to perfect humanity and made the visible, legal representatives of the new order of things on earth. Therefore, we may confidently expect that 1925 will mark the return of Abraham, Isaac, Jacob and the faithful prophets of old, particularly those named by the Apostle in Hebrews 11, to the condition of human perfection." In 1922, Rutherford wrote:

"Fulfilled prophecy shows beyond a doubt that (Christ) did appear in 1874. Fulfilled prophecy is otherwise designated the physical facts; and these facts are indisputable.... We understand that the jubilee type began to count in 1575 B.C.; and the 3,500 year period embracing the type must end in 1925....It follows, then, that the year 1925 will mark the beginning of the restoration of all things lost by Adam's disobedience."

In 1923, a *Watchtower* article predicted: "Our thought is, that 1925 is definitely settled by the scriptures."

As the year approached, the Society appeared to back-peddle once again. The *Watchtower* magazine predicted in mid-1924:

"The year 1925 is a date definitely and clearly marked in the Scriptures, even more clearly than that of 1914; but it would be presumptuous on the part of any faithful follower of the Lord to assume just what the Lord is going to do during that year."

At the beginning of 1925, a *Watchtower* article commented: "With great expectations Christians have looked forward to this year. Many have confidently expected that all members of the body of Christ will be changed to heavenly glory during this year. This may be accomplished. It may not be...Christians should not be so deeply concerned about what may transpire this year."

Just like 1914, the year 1925 came and went to the dismay of the church leaders. Then they regarded the year 1975 as a promising date for the end of the world. This date was based on their original belief that it was the 6,000th anniversary of the creation of Adam and Eve in the Garden of Eden in 4026 BC. The church leaders believed, along with many other conservative Protestant denominations, that the world would exist for exactly one-thousand years for each day of the creation week. Their *Watchtower* or *Awake!* magazines taught that:

"According to reliable Bible chronology Adam was created in the year 4026 BC, likely in the autumn of the year, at the end of the sixth day of creation. Are we to assume from this study that the battle of Armageddon will be all over by the autumn of 1975, and the long-looked-for thousand-year reign of Christ will begin by then? Possibly, but we wait to see how closely the seventh thousand-year period of man's existence coincides with the Sabbath like thousand year reign of Christ...Our chronology, however, which is reasonably accurate (but admittedly not infallible), at the best only points to the autumn of 1975 as the end of 6,000 years of man's existence on earth."

This prophecy was put forward in their publications, notably the *Watchtower* and *Awake!* at their assemblies. The close proximity of the end times encouraged the membership to increase their proselytizing efforts.

Membership rose significantly in the years leading up to 1975. Some members sold their possessions and cashed in their insurance policies, along with other severe life-altering actions in anticipation of the Millennium's/Armageddon arrival.

As you can see, the powers-that-be have mentioned and given dates for the end of the world as we know it many times over the decades. The year 1914 was hyped for years and 1975 was pushed more than ever.

Over the years, three different presidents of the Watchtower Bible and Tract Society have all given dates for the fulfillment of their Bible prophecies concerning the Armageddon. There was 1874, 1878, 1914, 1915, 1918, 1925 and of course 1975.

Now the organization has ditched all these dates except 1914. About 1914, they have stated over and over for decades that the people living in 1914 would see the fulfillment of their prophecies as stated below.

"The countdown that has proceeded for some six millenniums now nears its zero hour. So close is it that people who were alive in 1914, and who are now well along in years, will not all pass off the scene before the thrilling events marking the vindication of Jehovah's sovereignty come to pass." *Survival into a New Earth* (1984) p.184

"The early members of this group are now in their 60's or 70's or older. Jehovah did not allow the ingathering of this group to begin too soon. The "great crowd," including many of the earliest members thereof, will survive into the "new earth."" *Survival into a New Earth* (1984) p.185

"Prophetic information in the Bible about our day details the following: ...The survival of at least some of the generation that saw the beginning of "the conclusion of the system of things." *True Peace and Security* (1986) p.70

Guess what? This was changed too. The light got brighter once again. They finally threw out their 1914-generation teaching with the October 15 and November 1, 1995 issues of *The Watchtower*. The article explains that a generation could extend for multiple lifetimes. Many Witnesses saw this as indication that the Governing Body had lost faith, no longer confident that Armageddon was close at hand.

In 2010, god changed His mind once again to say that Armageddon would be within two overlapping lifetimes. This had little effect in turning around the declining growth rates, being an unconvincing interpretation with no immediate end-time date.

So, for the last one-hundred-and-forty years, every date the leaders have mentioned has proven to be of no consequence. However, the leaders are the first ones to mention that god Himself operates their organization by way of the Holy Spirit.

This can lead to only one of two conclusions: 1. Maybe god is very confused and has a hard time getting predictions or dates right. 2. They are just one of thousands of religions that think god is running their organizations.

All this information about the early years of the religion was never mentioned while I was growing up. Why? Because my parents didn't know about it. The people who encouraged them to become Jehovah's Witnesses didn't know about it either, and my guess is the people who helped them didn't know either.

Most of Jehovah's Witnesses are ignorant about these important facts and the history of their church. They have done little or no searching into the real history of their organization. They know little about the misguided founders and leaders of their organization.

If you walk through their museum about the history of their church at the world headquarters, for some odd reason none of the above information is mention there.

When I went back to Bethel in 1996, more than one person told me that "things" had changed back there and "things" are now different and much better than before. Maybe so, however the basis of the religion hasn't changed. The foundation of the church that was put in place by its first four deranged presidents is still there and many of their unscriptural and cruel policies are still in place today.

But if you do study the first four presidents of their organization, the four men that created the foundation of this church, you will discover the following:

Self-proclaimed Pastor Russell, the founder of this religion, believed in things that would get him dis-fellowshipped if he was alive today: Anti-organizational teachings, celebration of birthdays, Christmas and holidays, tolerance of military involvement, not draining blood from food, considering himself to be the "faithful and discreet slave," selling "Miracle Wheat," dabbling in the occult, and signing his own books. Russell was a delusional person who, after studying the pyramids, believed the end of the world would take place in 1914. He was a total whack job.

The alcoholic and self-proclaimed "Judge" Rutherford, after his hostile takeover of the organization (where almost a third of the members left), also gave the date of 1925 for the end of the world. He too would be dis-fellowshipped for immoral activity. He changed the name of the organization to Jehovah's Witnesses. He eliminated all of Russell's "pagan" influences, like pyramidology and numerology. He told his followers that Abraham, Isaac, Jacob and Moses would appear at their conventions soon. However, he didn't want these dead Bible characters at Bethel. He said he'd put them all up three-thousand miles away in San Diego, California, in his own mansion. Just so no one would get suspicious about the house, Rutherford put their names on the deed to the house. For some odd reason, they never showed up. He slammed all other churches, and broadcasted hate messages against the Catholic Church and League of United Nations. He made Prohibition the enemy, and even courted Hitler's favor. An alcoholic, egomaniac, womanizing whack job, for sure.

Then there is the egomaniac and homophobic Knorr, who instituted no blood transfusions, as well as the policies for dis-fellowshipping and shunning. He believed and taught that the world would end in 1975. With Knorr, everything was satanic. Smoking was banned in 1973, but it was still okay to be an alcoholic Elder. The Watchtower organization became big business; with Knorr in charge, the Society bought millions of dollars in property. Profit margins on publications rose as high as five-hundred percent, which "only covers the cost of printing." He believed sodomites will/won't/will/won't be resurrected.

Organs were considered to be like blood, thus no organ transplants, along with no blood transfusions. You can't/can divorce your husband if he's gay or has sex with farm animals. On the other hand, oral sex will get you dis-fellowshipped. Yes, lots more new and changing light from another egomaniac whack job.

The fourth president and self-proclaimed Bible scholar, Fred Franz, was the architect of the false date of 1975. His claims that he was a scholar of "Hebrew, Syriac, and Latin" were lies. How could he be a scholar in Hebrew and Syriac when they were not even offered at the University of Cincinnati where he attended? Franz only took fifteen hours of Latin, which would hardly qualify anyone as a scholar. He was never asked to attend the Rhodes University as he had claimed. Under his rule, pedophiles and homosexuals infiltrated the Governing Body and were allowed to leave without being dis-fellowshipped. This makes him a hypocrite, whack job and a liar.

It's easy to see how the very basis of the church that was put into place by its first four presidents, its foundation is rotten to the core.

Maybe things look different at Bethel, the world headquarters, now. Hundreds of people every day take a tour of the beautiful buildings at Warwick, New York that is set next to a serene lake. They can take a tour of their museum where they share some, but not all, of the true history of their organization. They show you what they want to show you. However, you will need to look on the internet to find the curtain with the great and powerful OZ hidden behind it.

The funny thing is, Witnesses tell their prospective converts that they should study up on all the other religions before they join theirs. However, if you want to study up on their religion, you are going to hit a brick wall. You can look at other religions, but just not theirs. Why is that? If you go to their website JW.org, to research any of their older publications where they promoted these false dates, guess what? You can't. They have taken down almost all of their publications before the 1980s. A hundred years of Jehovah's Witness history is not available for you to look at.

Why is that? Probably because they don't want you to discover all the contradictions, false prophecies and many other stupid things they have said over the decades.

Of course, you might find out that maybe they are just like most of the other religions out there. They are hoping no one will really look too hard into their clouded past.

I have no judgment here for the people in this book. They are the blind, just leading the blind.

However, what about the organization that was created over a 150 years ago? This organization that has mutated and changed into what is now called the Jehovah's Witnesses. This religion that even Charles Russell wouldn't even be able recognize if he was alive today. This new Borg-like organization that has perpetuated this kind of insanity and continues to create people and their delusional attitudes is blood guilty!

It's not just all the babies that died because of a lack of blood transfusions. It's not just all the people who have taken their own lives because of guilt and shame or losing their families. It's all the emotional pain and suffering that this organization has caused from the insanity of their belief system. It's beyond comprehension.

The sins of the Watchtower Bible & Tract Society has climbed to the heavens themselves.

There is only one purpose of this book. It is the same purpose I had when I went to *The Oregonian* in March of 2002. If I can help just one person eliminate the pain and suffering this organization has created for tens of thousands of people on the planet then it was worth it.

I don't believe in religions and governments with their organized, controlled, thought systems, the "us versus them" mentality they love to sell us. Most of these organizations have been created by men for the sake of control over other men.

I do believe in god. I just don't believe in the type of gods most religions have created. They say god made man in his image, but in truth, man has created god in his image. The church leaders have created gods like themselves: mean, hateful, jealous and vengeful. This sounds more like how an adolescent man might behave and not an all-powerful spiritual being.

I do consider myself a spiritual person. I consider everyone a spiritual person. Yes, everyone is on a spiritual path, whether it looks like it or not – even the misguided people in this book.

I believe that maybe one of the wisest persons to ever live was right when he said, "Reality is merely an illusion, albeit a very persistent one." This was, of course, said by Albert Einstein.

Maybe this statement says it all. Life boiled down to just one sentence.

The Buddhists believe the same thing. What if they all are right? What if our life is just one big illusion?

What if our life is no more real than a movie made in Hollywood?

What if there is reincarnation? What if we choose our story before we even incarnate?

What if we are the writer, director and main star in one of the craziest stories ever told? The story of our life. What if the only real hell is believing that our story is real?

If you think this could be a possibility, I suggest you read my first novel, *Your Crazy Life*. Maybe it's a lot simpler than we ever thought.

This planet is changing and evolving. With the age of information, religions are losing their control over people.

The old mindsets are not working any more. A new Earth is coming…. It's just not the one the Jehovah's Witnesses are hoping for.

It's never too late for change.

"Any action is better than no action, especially if you have been stuck in an unhappy situation for a long time. If it is a mistake, at least you learn something, in which case it's no longer a mistake. If you remain stuck, you learn nothing."
–Eckhart Tolle, *The Power of Now*.

Namaste, my friends.

Enjoy the wonderful journey that is your life.

Keith Casarona

Made in the USA
Coppell, TX
24 June 2021